PELICAN BOOKS

POLITICS AND THE SOVIET UNION

Dr Mary McAuley is Senior Lecturer in Government at the University of Essex; she is also author of *Labour Disputes in Soviet Russia, 1957–1965*.

Mary McAuley

Politics and the
Soviet Union

Penguin Books

Penguin Books Ltd, Harmondsworth, Middlesex, England
Viking Penguin Inc., 40 West 23rd Street, New York, New York 10010, U.S.A.
Penguin Books Australia Ltd, Ringwood, Victoria, Australia
Penguin Books Canada Ltd, 2801 John Street, Markham, Ontario, Canada L3R 1B4
Penguin Books (N.Z.) Ltd, 182–190 Wairau Road, Auckland 10, New Zealand

First published 1977
Reprinted 1977, 1979, 1981, 1982, 1984, 1985

Made and printed in Great Britain by
Hazell Watson & Viney Limited,
Member of the BPCC Group,
Aylesbury, Bucks
Set in Monotype Times

Contents

6   Contents

Part Two
Political Change

Part Three
The Contemporary Political System

Preface

This is a book which has grown out of my teaching Soviet politics to university students over a number of years. As such, all those who have listened and argued have contributed to it and to them, students at York, Princeton, and Essex, I owe a debt. It is as difficult to acknowledge individually the contribution of all the authors whom I have read and who, sometimes decisively, sometimes more subtly, have influenced my way of thinking. In the bibliography, which has to be selective, I hope at least I have acknowledged every author from whose work I draw directly.

It is a more straightforward matter to acknowledge my debt to those who gave time to read the manuscript and made detailed comments and correction: Archie Brown, Leslie Holmes, Kenneth Macdonald and David Shapiro. To them in particular I am grateful, but I do not forget all the colleagues who have helped with information or criticism, nor June Palmer and Barbara Hinds who did most of the typing and retyping. Any errors which remain and the ideas themselves are of course my responsibility.

A rather different word of thanks is due to Dr Peter Chapman and Mr Donald Morrison, whose skilled care and attention, so generously given at the time I was writing the manuscript, helped me to persevere. It is much more satisfying to produce a baby than a book, but this time, thanks to them and the National Health Service, I managed to produce both. And last I should like to acknowledge the forbearance of my husband and other children who suffered during this dual labour.

December 1975.

Introduction

In 1917 the Russian empire was ruled by an autocratic despot, political rights and civil liberties long won in the west were unknown. Within a year two revolutions had taken place: the first attempt at some kind of constitutional government had collapsed, and Russia or the new Soviet republic had a government, the first of its kind in the world, committed to introducing socialism. There was civil war, a 'dictatorship of the proletariat', fierce conflict both within the ruling party and between it and its adversaries; then, after some respite, a 'revolution from above' carried out by the now well-established party with a new leader, Stalin, and a party machine – a revolution which, accompanied by famine and bloodshed, ended private farming and began to transform the country into an industrial giant. By the mid-thirties economy and society had become a huge, State-owned, centrally run concern. All this in itself provides more than enough for analysis, but by the late thirties the Soviet Union, ruled by a dictator, offers an example and a terrifying one of a society in the grip of a mass terror which claimed the lives of perhaps ten million of its citizens. The war followed, a war whose impact on the population was far greater than anything experienced by Britain or the US in terms of death, suffering and deprivation. With Stalin's death in 1953, his type of personal, peculiar dictatorship ended. At the same time a very different kind of society had come into being; a largely literate society, one still sharply marked by the contrast between town and country but with approximately half its population now urbanized, and a new educated professional elite. The Soviet Union had become an industrial and military power second only to the United States. In the twenty years since Stalin's death the political leadership has tried to evolve a different system of government: one which retains the one-party system and its own authority within it yet without Stalin's use of terror; a system that is intended to encourage economic growth, butter as well as guns, and to promote loyalty and enthusiasm. Thus the contemporary period is characterized by the attempt to dismantle a dictatorship of some of its elements; to find a system of government that will provide centralized control and an impetus for social change in an increasingly industrialized society.

One of the problems facing the author of an introductory book on Soviet politics is how to tackle so huge a subject. Russian and Soviet[1] experience is so rich in what it offers to anyone interested in politics that it is impossible to encompass even the major questions it flings up within a single book. It is hard to think of a topic in the realm of politics that is absent. If we adopt a static, institutional approach with the intent of examining the organization of the State at a given point in time, we find a number of contrasts: Tsarist absolutism, a fluid and shifting structure of power at the time of the revolution, a new one-party regime struggling to change existing relationships, a dictatorship coupled with mass terror, then an established one-party regime trying to find new methods of rule. At the very least we have an opportunity of looking at a number of different and contrasting sets of political institutions. But with what purpose in mind? It is sometimes said that politics is concerned with who gets what, when and how. On one level this is a useful statement because it does suggest that politics is to do with relationships of power or influence within society (between people, groups, classes, decision-makers versus others) and the impact that these relationships have upon the distribution of goods and services. Thus one set of questions that arises from a study of the different types of political institutions that have existed in Russia and then the Soviet Union relates to the effect these have had upon who gets what. To what extent, for example, did the collapse of the old Tsarist power structure and its replacement by a dictatorship of the proletariat affect the distribution of society's goods and the relative rights, opportunities and freedom of the different social classes or groups? How was this distribution affected by Stalin's dictatorship and how does it differ today from earlier periods? On a wider level we are asking about the relationship between a certain type of political structure and the kinds of social lives enjoyed (or not as the case may be) by its citizens. In saying this we are led into comparing Soviet political structures with those of other societies in order to find answers. In the USSR today, for example, there is one party which provides the leadership and guidance of a State-owned economy, untrammelled by an electoral system which could remove the leadership from power. What effect, we want to know, does this have upon policy-making or the type of policy produced, upon the relationship between those who make decisions and those at the receiving end. Does this kind of political organization of society mean that there are significant differences between the policy-making process, the policies themselves or the relation between rulers and ruled in the USSR and contemporary western societies where parliamentary democracy exists in a mixed economy and, if so, what are these differences?

But there are other kinds of questions that come to mind, when looking at Soviet politics, which are not so easily subsumed under the title of 'who gets what' or, at least, do not flow so obviously from it. Comparisons of a different kind beg the reader's attention. It is difficult, for example, to look at the revolutionary period without thinking of revolutions in other societies and at other times – the French revolution, and later the Chinese and Cuban – because we want to know both why revolutions (the collapse of the existing power structure and the existing social structure that supported it) occur and why they do not; whether there are particular obstacles to the realization of the revolutionaries' aims that seem to recur regardless of the context in which the revolution has taken place. Do revolutions tend to devour their own children and, if so, why? Or, to take a quite different subject, what are the circumstances that make the introduction of mass terror and then its continued existence possible? How can we explain the periods of large-scale persecution that have existed, those periods when fanaticism and fear combined to produce almost unthinkable acts of cruelty, be they Tudor England or Spain, Nazi Germany or Stalin's Purges?

Then there is the question of political change which inevitably must enter into any attempt to explain how and why certain

phenomena occur. Again the very rapid and marked changes that
have characterized the Soviet period bring this – perhaps the most
interesting and difficult of all questions – forward as a challenge.
How do political structures, configurations of power, arise and
change? In 1917 the Bolsheviks came to power committed to
building socialism – a society without private ownership in which
all as equals should participate in decision-making, in providing
for the material well-being and free creative development of each
individual. Twenty years later Stalin ruled a society where private
ownership had been abolished but the other aims had become a
hollow mockery. How did this happen? How did the attempt to
create the most 'democratic' of all societies turn into its ghastly
opposite? Explanations differ widely depending upon the author's
view of the relationship between political structures and the social
and economic environment, of the role of ideas in history (and
the nature of those ideas), and the importance of individuals.

Perhaps the only subject on which the Soviet experience has
little to offer is the study of multi-party systems in a constitutional democracy with the concomitant analysis of different electoral systems and voting behaviour. Yet such studies, if they are
to be more than a set of empirical observations on the behaviour
of different political parties, voting patterns and the results produced by one electoral system compared with those of another,
if they are to make any suggestions for change or discuss the
desirability of one rather than another – if, in other words, they
are to give some point to the analysis – then they must ask what
it is electoral systems *ought* to achieve and this inevitably leads
into wider questions of democratic theory. Once one says this,
Soviet claims and practice become relevant. Soviet democracy,
the new leaders of 1917 argued, was to be qualitatively different
from democracy in a capitalist society and they took pains to
argue how and why. It is worth looking at the charges they laid
against 'bourgeois' democracy, the alternative concept they proposed and the mechanisms by which they hoped to realize it in
order to compare this with the claims and ideals of their western
counterparts of the time. But both in the Soviet Union and in the
west the concept of 'democracy' – what it is and how it might or
should work – has changed since the early twenties. It is instruc-

tive to compare the kinds of arguments put forward today. After all both sides claim that theirs is the democratic system and expend considerable energy in defending their system against the other.

Often the argument gets no further than the claim that certain features of the particular society (e.g. competing parties, periodic elections, freedom of speech in the one case, public ownership and a ruling party with representatives from all classes in the other) are what constitute 'democracy'. And indeed if couched in these terms it can get no further. But at times other themes are introduced – those of freedom, equality of opportunity or political equality, interests – themes which have engaged both political theorists and activists for hundreds of years and which require thinking about if we wish to understand why men have attempted to create certain types of political arrangements or, indeed, if we wish to improve upon existing ones ourselves.

In 1917 with the October revolution the Bolshevik leaders threw down a challenge to the supporters of capitalism and parliamentary democracy. They called upon the working class in the west to overthrow their rulers; they questioned the 'reformist' tactics adopted by the major socialist parties in Europe, and, within Russia itself, they moved against the supporters of the old order. Hence it is not surprising that the Bolshevik experiment in Russia became of vital concern to those of very different political persuasions, both inside and outside the Soviet Union. No one could remain neutral when writing about Soviet politics and this has remained true ever since, although the nature of the challenge and the attitudes of those involved have changed. After the civil war, sections of the labour movement in the west maintained their interest, but the Soviet experiment was largely ignored by the rulers of Europe. Russia was too weak to present a military threat and the situation at home was under control. But by the thirties, against a background of depression and mounting unemployment in the west, and then the threat of Fascism, opinions changed and, of course, during the allied effort in the war became as favourable as they have ever been. But after the war the Soviet Union posed a new threat: now as one of the two world powers, with military strength surpassed only by the US. The Communist world suddenly leapt in size and strength: not only in Eastern Europe, but also in China, a Communist government came to power and America found itself actively opposed in the Korean war by the Soviet Union. This was the cold-war period when McCarthyism spread its tentacles in the United States and the 'Red Menace' was everywhere. Support for the Soviet Union shrank to the Communist parties who held fast to their convictions that Stalin's Russia was still the promised land. Opinion was sharply polarized. By the late fifties the situation was beginning to change, within both America and the Soviet Union, and in the world at large. This called for a new re-assessment of the Soviet Union in the west and brought a re-awakening of interest in Soviet affairs.

At present attitudes towards the Soviet Union are perhaps more ambivalent than at any time previously. While it still remains true that the Soviet system commands the undying devotion or hostility of some, this total 'for or against' commitment no longer dominates. Western governments (notably that of the US) while still apprehensive of Soviet military might are anxious to find common ground with the Soviet leadership in order to keep down arms expenditure, limit the possibility of nuclear war, and conclude beneficial trade agreements. The Sino–Soviet split and the emergence of Japan as an economic power has opened up new possibilities for international alignments. In turn the Sino–Soviet split has influenced attitudes in the Third World, be they those of military regimes who look to the US for support, new socialist regimes in Cuba or Vietnam, or the governments of India or the Arab world. On the one hand 'uncommitted governments' (a term dating from the mid-fifties) can seek aid from different sources, and even socialist regimes have more scope for manoeuvre; on the other, the gulf between rich and poor which places both the USA and the USSR together in the 'rich' camp provides a new alignment which cuts across the 'capitalist' versus 'socialist' division. While to some the distinction between 'imperialist' powers and 'socialist' powers (or the 'free world' versus the communists) still appears as the most important, to others – and not only those in the Third World – both the Soviet Union and the USA are seen as imperialist, repressive regimes.

This is an oversimplified picture and we, unfortunately, shall only be able to sketch in a few more details in the chapters that follow. But, for anyone interested in the history of ideas, the changes in popular, official, or academic attitudes towards the USSR in conjunction with political and social developments at home and abroad make an unusually interesting subject.

In Parts I and II we try to do two things: to give the reader an understanding of the major changes in the political order from the beginning of the century until Stalin's death and to focus attention on some of the key political issues and problems involved. If we are to understand the present, some acquaintance with the past is essential. This is one of the reasons for starting with the past. Certain aspects – the relationship of the central authority to the different nationalities, foreign relations – have had to be ignored for reasons of space. We have concentrated on those which (in our opinion) have been most crucial in influencing future events, and which raise some of the most interesting political issues. Just as the history has had to be cut so has the choice of issues and, given their complexity, we can do little more than offer a brief introduction to them in the hope that the reader will pursue them further elsewhere.

In Part I we contrast different conceptions of what is a desirable social and political system, introduce the debate over 'democracy', and show the way in which one attempt to introduce a new social and political order was influenced by circumstances. In Part II we are more directly concerned with political change and the kinds of explanation that are offered for it: the reasons that lie behind changing patterns of authority and control. We then introduce the question of the analysis of a particular system of power – Stalinism – and show how approaches differ.

With this as background (both historically and conceptually), contemporary political relationships are described and analysed in Part III. The fairly detailed analysis of the present political system is intended to show how power is distributed, how policy is made and implemented in the Soviet Union. Simultaneously we introduce the reader to the kind of work currently undertaken by those who study politics. Thus throughout we are stressing the relationship between methods of analysis (or, in simpler language, the preoccupations and approach of those studying something) and the subject of study itself.

The aim of the book is to raise questions rather than to answer them. Footnotes and source references have been kept to a minimum so as not to overburden the text. The chapter-by-chapter bibliography is intended to serve two purposes: to direct the reader to the major sources used for a chapter and to give him a selection of further reading, reading that will demonstrate how controversial and exciting a subject Soviet politics is.

Part One
Rival Political Orders

1 Autocracy

Tsarism and its Ruling Class

'The Emperor of all the Russias is an autocratic and unlimited monarch. God himself commands that his supreme power be obeyed, out of conscience as well as fear.'[1] This was the Tsarist credo of Nicholas II. He was appointed by God to rule over the lands inherited from his father – not only Russia, but also the Ukraine, part of Poland, Finland, Georgia, and lands to the south and east; it was his duty before God to preserve the empire, to pass it on to his son, and to preserve his divine right of unlimited authority. This entailed, necessarily, the suppression of any attempts by national groups to gain autonomy, or of demands for participation in government. Anyone who questioned his authority was necessarily wrong. Coercion was justified by God. The officers and church dignitaries, the executors of physical and moral sanctions, were essential elements of the Tsarist system. It was natural for the Tsar to send congratulatory telegrams to regiments which had excelled themselves in suppressing strikes by industrial workers. And there was nothing odd in the Tsar's dismissal of ministers on the prompting of a monk, Rasputin, who claimed to be in direct touch with the Almighty.

In 1905 the Tsarist system of rule was threatened by mass disaffection, not only on the part of workers and peasants who were striking or rioting, but also from professional groups who were clamouring for representation and reform. Faced with a situation which the troops could not control, the Tsar made concessions. A Duma, or representative assembly, was granted, and a Council of Ministers. Once the disturbances died down and the threat faded, the concessions were gradually withdrawn. The Duma franchise was restricted, the Duma itself could not legislate on the more important matters of state, notably the budget, and it was dissolved at the Tsar's wish. The Council of Ministers was not a corporate body but rather a collection of individual ministers, appointed and dismissed as the Tsar saw fit. In acting in this way, the Tsar could hardly be accused of inconsistency or dishonesty. As a ruler whose power derived from God, it was clearly his duty to oppose any attempts to curb his authority, and concessions, made in a difficult situation, were necessarily a political move to enable him afterwards to regain his rightful position.

The Tsar's views on his role and the proper way to order society seem anachronistic in twentieth-century Europe. What we should remember is that the belief in the divine right of kings had disappeared in the rest of Europe because of the attacks upon the monarchy by new powerful groups in society. The Tsar's counterparts, the autocratic monarchs of France and England, had not willingly renounced their right to rule as God's representatives on earth but had been forced, in order to retain some of their rights, to forgo others. The Tsars, in Russia, had never been subject to this kind of successful pressure and, consequently, had never had to rethink their views and justify their existence on other grounds.

The landed aristocracy, who in many parts of Europe had formed an important part of the opposition to the monarch's rights, never played such a role in Russia. They never became a powerful, secure group with an independent source of wealth, a group which felt safe enough to attack Tsarism. Instead they looked to the Tsar to preserve and support them. One important reason for this was the institution of serfdom and the system of property relationships. The basis of the aristocracy's wealth was the land and the peasants or serfs who went with it. Peasants could be bought and sold like any other piece of property. They lived on the landlord's estate and either worked without payment on his land or paid him a tax in kind from the produce of the tiny strips of land awarded to them by the landlord. In return he was meant to see that in bad years they did not starve. Farming, under such a system, was backward and inefficient. Part of the arrangement was that the peasant provided his labour and his tools, and these were usually primitive implements. Instead of changing to a more productive form of agriculture, one which would have involved driving labour off the land and making use of new mechanical inventions, the Russian landlord continued to squeeze his income from an unproductive, captive labour force. The only way in which he could increase his income, since labour productivity could not rise under such primitive methods, was by squeezing his peasants even harder which, in turn, made them even less willing or interested in increasing the fruits of their labour. But even this was difficult – the estates were simply not producing enough to satisfy the aristocracy's desire for grand country houses, a house in Moscow or St Petersburg, the expensive proper education of their families and the keeping up of appearances. Instead of prospering they were running into debt. By 1861 the aristocracy had resorted to borrowing heavily from the State, which in turn meant further borrowing to meet the interest charges. As well as mortgaging their lands, they mortgaged their serfs – approximately two thirds of private landlords' serfs had been mortgaged by 1861.

In that year, for a number of reasons a not unimportant one of which was the desire to help the indebted aristocracy, serfdom was abolished. We shall look at the Edict on Emancipation as it affected the peasants in a later section, but for the landlord it meant that the State 'paid' him for that part of his land which he chose to sell to his serfs, and that he no longer could command the labour and lives of the peasants. In law he became an employer rather than a master. In theory the landowner could now develop his estate, and introduce new techniques. In practice the Russian aristocracy did little of this. They had neither the ready capital, nor the enthusiasm, and the labour that they did employ was still the peasant, reluctant to try new methods and anxious to be employed, for very low wages, given his poverty. Primitive labour was still the cheapest commodity for the landlord. Throughout the period from 1861 to 1914 the aristocracy continued its previous existence, selling land to make ends meet and borrowing from the State, in order to keep up appearances.

The Tsar supported the aristocracy, bailed them out when necessary, provided them with titles, jobs and sinecures, because he needed the loyalty and support of this privileged group. They in turn needed the continuation of the Tsarist system if they were to retain their privileged position. The position of the Russian aristocracy contrasts very strongly with that, for example, of their English counterparts. By the eighteenth century the English aristocracy had successfully limited the power of the crown, were enclosing the land and making it profitable, and beginning to show an interest in commerce and industry. By intermarriage and their own efforts the landed aristocracy forged ties with the new class of entrepreneurs until, by the end of the nineteenth century, the ruling class in Britain was a marriage of land and commerce. This kind of strength enabled the new 'aristocracy' to produce 'conservative' doctrines (of which social reform and widening the suffrage were a part), doctrines which stressed the importance of property, gradual change, law and order, and the Church. Burke and Disraeli were the major spokesmen of this supremely confident, powerful class in society – a class which could afford to make concessions in order to retain its power, and one which could produce a coherent and strong case for its dominant position in society. By contrast, in Russia, the aristocracy neither developed its land nor participated in commerce and industry; it never challenged the crown, never established an independent base of power for itself, and consequently never evolved an independent justification of its existence. When a Russian 'right' did emerge at the turn of the century as some kind of a political grouping, it had none of the strength of its West European counterparts, neither in personnel nor convictions. Some members of the aristocracy, a few industrialists, officers, and merchants. Their creed was little more than an affirmation of Tsar and church, nationalism and anti-semitism, and violent disapproval of socialism and agitators. Conservative ministers, such as Witte and Stolypin, who attempted to provide securer foundations for Tsar and aristocracy, had none of the power of their European equivalents. They depended for their influence upon the Tsar not upon the backing of powerful groups in society, and thus were compelled to defend the very system of government which was hindering the emergence of an independent and prosperous ruling class.

In Russia it was the State, not individual entrepreneurs, which played the major role in developing industrial production. Following her defeat in the Crimean War it became clear that, if Russia was to retain her position as one of the great powers of Europe, she must manufacture the modern weapons of war, and build a transport system.

During the period 1880 to 1914, apart from a few years of depression at the turn of the century, industrial production grew at an average rate of 8 per cent per annum. The government invested in railways and heavy industry – coal, pig-iron, and metallurgy. Foreign capital was encouraged, and a high tariff wall prevented cheaper foreign goods from competing with the new home products.

If we compare the pattern of industrial production in Russia in 1914 with its older-established European competitors, the following differences are the most striking. First, Russian industry was to a much greater extent either State owned or financed, and a third of all industry was foreign owned. Secondly, some branches of industry were highly developed, others hardly existed. The railway network was good, roads very poor. Thirdly, industry was dominated by large companies and large plants. The average size of industrial concern was larger than in Europe. As a newcomer to industrial development, Russian industry could employ the latest technical inventions and equipment imported from abroad. It had some of the most modern plants in Europe but its labour force was still largely drawn from the countryside and relatively unskilled. The stratum of managerial and technical specialists was relatively very small, many of them trained abroad or themselves foreigners.

The capitalist class proper – industrialists and bankers – was thus very small. They were not sufficiently powerful to threaten the monarchy and indeed there was no real reason why they should. The State's sponsoring of industry, the tariff policy, and its willing repression of discontent among industrial workers aided expansion and high profits. The industrialists did not need to challenge the landed aristocracy's privileged position in the Councils of the Empire because they provided no threat to industry's interests. The landed aristocracy in turn, although beginning to show signs of interest in the profits to be made from investment, stood as a separate group who primarily sought additional income in government service: ministerial jobs, governorships, and of course in the armed services.

The Intelligentsia

Between the Romanov dynasty, the aristocracy, and the industrial magnates on the one hand, and the vast mass of peasants and workers on the other, lay a small commercial and 'white-collar' stratum. These were the merchants, shop-keepers, civil servants, teachers, doctors, and lawyers. A rather different social group, although one which drew many of its members from the professions, was what was known as the intelligentsia. It is difficult to define an 'intelligent', but roughly the term applied to those with an education, who followed intellectual pursuits or showed some kind of critical awareness or interest in social problems. Members of the aristocracy could therefore be members of the intelligentsia, as could working-class students. It was from this educated group, frustrated by despotic Tsarist rule and the backwardness of the country, that political ideas of reform or revolution emerged; it was this group that provided many of the leaders of revolutionary groups.

But it would be wrong to see the intelligentsia as predominantly revolutionary. At the turn of the century a liberal movement began to emerge and this probably had the sympathy and support of most of the intelligentsia. The demands were for a representative assembly, a ministerial council responsible to the assembly, control over taxation, legal reform, greater freedom for the press and of assembly. These demands were strongly influenced by the example of constitutional government in Western Europe. Russia, it was argued, could and should follow the example of Western Europe; this would cure her social ills and ensure social justice. When, in 1905, the Tsar temporarily granted some of the demands, the political wing of the liberal movement split into two: the Octobrists who took their stand on the reforms announced by the Tsar (this far and no further) and the Cadets (or Constitutional Democrats) who accepted what was given but pressed for more.

Thus at this time the political groupings reflected the unique pattern of Russian society: a reactionary 'right' in favour of autocratic monarchy, something which had practically disappeared from the European scene; no strong 'progressive' party of the right; a weak professional liberal group, similar in ideas if not in strength to its contemporary European equivalents; and, in addition, the revolutionary groups who proposed extreme, radical solutions. These had their counterparts in the revolutionary movements which came and went throughout European history – the Levellers, peasant movements, Chartists, anarchists, and early socialists – but by the later part of the nineteenth century, Social Democracy, which could only flourish under the relatively favourable conditions of parliamentary democracy and freedom of association, had emerged in Europe as the most powerful force for radical change and absorbed much of the revolutionary aspiration of earlier periods. In Russia this was not possible: Social Democracy, a labour movement with unions and parliamentary representation, could not emerge as an important force in a largely peasant society under despotic rule. Consequently it is not surprising that the solutions proposed by revolutionary members of the intelligentsia were different from those which held sway in the west.

The Peasantry

Understandably it was the peasants who preoccupied the thoughts of those interested in revolution or anxious to prevent it. If one compares Russia at the turn of the century with the other European great powers, the most striking difference is the relative size of its peasantry. It accounted for over 80 per cent of the population, more than 100 million people. This huge social class, 'the dark people' as they were called, occupied the thoughts of Tsarist ministers, of revolutionaries, of Tolstoy and Marx. Many would have agreed with Witte, a Tsarist minister, when he said: 'The condition of the peasantry is the fundamental cause of those morbid social phenomena which are always present in the life of our country.'[2]

Before the Emancipation of Serfdom in 1861 most of the

peasants belonged to the landlord, whether he was a private individual or the State. The Edict of Emancipation itself was extremely complicated, but its main provisions can be simplified as follows. The peasants were granted some of the landlord's land but they had to pay him for it. Since they did not have the money, they borrowed from the State who paid the landlord. The peasants then had to repay the State over a number of years, both the original loan and the interest on it. The land did not go to the individual peasant but to the commune or peasant community on the estate. This collective body then divided up the land, in one of two ways: either individual peasant households received a house and plot, and a number of scattered strips which became theirs; or each household received its house and plot, and a number of strips which were theirs to work until the commune decided to re-distribute them in a different way. Some strips were better than others and therefore it seemed fairer to re-distribute them from time to time. It was usually the commune, not the individual peasant, who was responsible for the redemption payments, the repayment of the loans to the State, and for other taxes.

The system introduced under Emancipation produced neither of the results most desired by the Tsarist government. The aristocracy failed to become a prosperous, efficient landowning class, and the peasants remained, as before, poor, dissatisfied, and ready to resort to violence to try and improve their lot. The existence of the strip system meant that, as before, the peasant spent his time trudging from one of his strips to another; he had no great incentive to care for his land, particularly if it was going to be handed over to someone else in the near future; the only way to work the strips was for everyone with adjoining ones to work to a common cycle, and usually this was the age-old three year rotation system. None of this made for profitable farming, and the peasants fell steadily behind with the redemption payments. The peasant could not leave the land while he still owed money for it, and by the turn of the century the debt was often larger than the market price. All this time the peasant population was growing. There were more mouths to feed and, with more families, the size of the average family's allotment was shrinking.

Besides redemption payments, the peasant had taxes to pay, for example a poll tax, and any basic commodities he wished to buy – matches, sugar, vodka, kerosene – were subject to tax. He was being taxed at every turn at a time when the price of grain, which was the main source of his income, remained low. The State, committed by now to promoting heavy industrial development, needed funds to finance it. One way of getting funds, and an important one, was to extract them from the peasantry, either by taxation or by buying grain cheap, exporting it, and using the proceeds to buy capital equipment from abroad. But one consequence of this policy was that it kept the peasants permanently poor and thus restricted the size of the market for goods within the country. The peasants were too poor to buy goods; therefore there was no incentive for industry to expand and provide consumer goods for them. The incentive for industry had to come from outside, from State action, which in turn depressed consumer demand even further. The peasant has one answer in such a situation: produce less, just enough to cover immediate needs.

By the turn of the century, and particularly after 1905 against the background of famine and peasant uprisings, the authorities began to rethink their policy towards the peasants. The poll tax was abolished and redemption payments cancelled, but these were simply measures taken to alleviate immediate distress and could not, by themselves, serve as any long-term solution. The peasants considered that the land was theirs, by right. In the words of peasant spokesmen at a Congress in 1905: 'Land is not the product of human hands. It was created by the Holy Spirit and therefore should not be bought and sold. No one really bought it in the beginning for money; somebody knew how to take it away from the peasants ... it is not necessary to pay compensation to anyone ... With millions of voices we insistently declare the sacredness of our right to the land. If persuasion does not help, then, friends, ploughmen, get up, awake ... for the moment we shall lay our ploughs aside and take up the club.'[3] And this was what they did. The authorities' answer, once the risings had been suppressed, was to try to destroy this kind of attitude by turning the peasantry into proprietors who would defend property rights. It was argued that the importance granted to the commune by the Edict of Emancipation, and the repartition system, had encouraged dangerous socialist ideas. If only the peasant had been able to consolidate his holdings, to become an individual proprietor, he would have a stake in the present system of property relations, would recognize the importance of legal rights, and oppose anarchist attempts to seize lands and distribute them among all. A class of peasant farmers, who owned their lands and farmed them profitably, would, it was argued, be supporters of the present regime and oppose attempts by their less fortunate or less successful brothers to destroy private property. Stolypin, the Tsarist minister most responsible for the new policy, expressed the matter thus: 'The government has placed its wager, not on the needy and drunken, but on the sturdy and strong – on the sturdy individual proprietor who is called upon to play a part in the reconstruction of our Tsardom on strong monarchical foundations.'[4]

In 1906 and 1910 laws were passed which encouraged and in some cases compelled peasants to consolidate their strips, to put an end to the repartition system, and to become hereditary owners. It became much easier to leave the commune. At the same time a Land Bank provided loans to those wishing to buy land and provided a channel through which peasants could buy and sell land. Throughout the period, up until 1914, both the State and the aristocracy were selling lands to the peasants.

It is very difficult to assess the results of these new policies. One of the problems, and it is one to bear in mind when thinking of almost any aspect of Russian or Soviet society or politics, is that in a country of its size with sharply differentiated regions there were considerable variations in different parts of the country. In addition the information that is available does not provide black and white answers. It does seem though that, if anything, the policies were having some effect in producing a class of richer peasants at one end of the scale and a growing number of poorer, landless peasants at the other. In other words differentiation among the peasantry did increase slightly during the period. It is even more difficult to say anything about changes in peasant attitudes. Probably all that can be said is that the

Stolypin reforms did, by attacking the commune, begin to shake up established patterns of country life.

Revolutionary Alternatives

The peasant potential for revolution was clear to all. But what was not certain was what kind of a revolution the peasants could or would achieve. What was it after all that the peasants wanted? The abolition of private property in land, or ownership of small farms? The evidence could be interpreted either way. In the 1870s a group of the intelligentsia, many of them young, argued that the peasant commune could provide the basis for a society of equality and cooperation; the peasant could save Russia from capitalism; all that was needed was the peasantry to revolt, throw out the landowners, the Tsar and his police, for a socialist republic to come into being. The concept of 'socialist' was not tightly defined: it included ideas of the abolition of private property (but no clear agreement on how the common property was to be administered), of brotherhood and equality. To this extent the ideas were similar to – indeed they were clearly influenced by – the early socialist ideas current in Europe. The Narodniki, as this group was called, went out to the peasant villages to preach the message, to live with the people, but were received with suspicion and hostility. This populist trend in revolutionary thinking re-emerged with the foundation of the Socialist Revolutionary party in 1899. Although claiming as its aim the unification of the peasantry, proletariat, and intelligentsia in a revolutionary working class, the main target of the party was the peasantry. The SRs favoured strengthening the commune, and opposed the Stolypin policy of creating individual peasant proprietors. They argued that the collectivist nature of much of Russian agriculture and the dominant role that agriculture played in the economy as a whole provided a socialist base for society. Russia, they argued, unlike Western Europe, has only a very small industrial sector; capitalism still lies far in the future and, as our situation is different, there is no reason why we should follow the same path of development. We have a socialist base which is being slowly eroded by the spread of private industry and by the Stolypin reforms; it is our duty to act now, to bring a socialist society into existence now; the longer we wait, the more difficult it will become. Once we have our socialist republic, then industry will be able to develop on a non-capitalist basis with workers' communities managing industry.

By the 1880s Marx's works on the development of capitalism in Western Europe had reached small groups of intellectuals in Russia. Marx had argued that only after capitalism had become fully developed, had reached a stage where the capitalist form of production was actually hindering further development of the productive resources of society, would the socialist revolution occur. This point, he argued, had already been reached in Western Europe. Impressed by Marx's analysis of history and contemporary social developments, yet troubled by the difficulty of applying his analysis to Russian society, some of his supporters wrote to Marx and Engels for their views of possible future developments in Russia. (Marx himself was interested in Russia and had set himself the task of learning the language in order to be able to study the subject properly.) His and Engels's answer, both to SR claims and to Russian Marxists, ran as follows: there is nothing in the Russian commune that justifies calling it a superior socialist form of ownership (communal ownership of land pre-dates private ownership, and relics of this primitive type of land tenure can be found in Europe); but neither is there any 'law' which means that Russia must travel the West European path of development; if capitalism does develop in Russia, then it will destroy the commune, but if a revolution occurs in Russia which overthrows Tsarism and, at the same time, sparks off a proletarian revolution in the west, then 'the prevailing form of communal ownership of land in Russia may form a starting-point for a communist course of development.'[5] For Marx it was the extent to which capitalism was disrupting older relationships that mattered.

The Russian Marxists who at the end of the 1890s had formed the RSDLP (or Russian Social Democratic Labour party) argued that the commune was doomed; although capitalism in Russia was still underdeveloped in comparison with Western Europe, it was growing fast; a class of industrial workers did exist. Where the Social Democrats differed from the SRs was in the importance they attached to the industrial development taking place in Russia, in their scepticism of peasant socialism, and in their belief that a socialist revolution could not be a purely Russian phenomenon but must necessarily be bound up with the forthcoming socialist revolution in the west.

The industrial labour force on which the SDs focused their attention, was very small compared with the peasantry. Figures vary but, by 1914, it was something of the order of three to four million compared with over 100 million peasants. It had grown very rapidly over the past three decades and still had strong ties with the land. It was relatively unskilled and concentrated in a few large centres. Compared with the industrial workers of Western Europe, the Russian worker was poorly paid, lived in worse conditions (often barracks), and had no legal organization to fight for his rights. In the aftermath of the 1905 unrest, trade unions were allowed to exist, then suppressed. Strikes were put down by force.

Despite the repression, the industrial labour force was anything but passive. Strikes and protests were part of the industrial scene, although their intensity varied from one period to the next, as did the demands. At times economic demands came to the fore, at others, for example in 1905, political and economic demands were voiced together. Even a short-lived general strike was organized in 1905. After 1912 the strike figures rose again and during the first part of 1914 half the industrial labour force were on strike.

Compared with the peasants, industrial workers had the great advantage of being concentrated in large plants in large centres. But it was extremely difficult to agitate, spread information, and organize meetings with secret-police surveillance and informers in the plants. Barrack life did bring the workers together but presumably the informers were present there too. The economic foundations of Tsarism might be weak, but its coercive apparatus was very strong.

Russian Marxists, in their efforts to decide what the appropriate programme of action should be, were faced with a dilemma. The more successful capitalism became and the greater the importance of private property in the countryside, the more difficult it was going to be to overthrow. At the turn of the century the Russian bourgeoisie was relatively weak: the revolutionaries were not faced with a strong, consolidated ruling class nor with reformist trade unions willing to work within parliamentary democracy. Thus, while welcoming the spread of capitalism because, in one sense, it hastened the likelihood of a socialist revolution, they had to recognize that, in Russian conditions, capitalism merely increased the number and strength of their enemies. Socialists in Western Europe were not faced with this problem: the enemy was already there, firmly entrenched, and the task was simply to overthrow it. Not surprisingly, in trying to grapple with the problem, the Russian Marxists had to find new answers, and, again not surprisingly, conflicting solutions were advanced.

Bolsheviks and Mensheviks

One group, 'the economists', argued that the appropriate strategy was to work towards a bourgeois republic: to support the workers in their economic demands, to join with liberals in pressing for constitutional reform, trade-union rights, and freedom of the press. Once this had been achieved – a proper framework for capitalist society with its bourgeois rights and liberties – then it would be time to work inside the labour movement to achieve socialism.

The main body of the Social Democrats refused to accept this on the following grounds: the workers were already making radical political demands of a socialist kind; it was betrayal to ignore these and to work with the liberals; the socialist programme should be kept distinct. It was as part of this debate that Lenin wrote his pamphlet *What is to be done?* in 1902, in which he argued for a tight, organized party of committed members to spread socialist ideas among the workers, and stressed the danger for socialism if the party restricted activity to supporting claims for better wages and shorter hours. Unless socialists provided a coherent socialist programme, he argued, and encouraged the revolutionary potential of the working class, their revolutionary tendencies could become submerged in 'trade-union consciousness', in beliefs that liberal solutions would end the inequities of the capitalist system. We need a revolutionary organization, he argued, because under Tsarist conditions it is impossible to organize a mass party; a small committed party can provide the spark which will ignite the workers, and together we shall overturn the whole of Russia; if we abandon our duty to the workers, then they will not rise as a united socialist force.

Lenin's views were accepted by the other leaders of the party but when, in the following year of 1903, a Congress was held and Lenin proposed certain organizational forms to make this strategy effective, differences arose and the party split once more, into what consequently became two major factions, each claiming for itself the title of RSDLP.

Lenin suggested that party membership should be limited to active revolutionaries, and that tight control by the leading organs in making decisions, announcing policy through the party press, and seeing that party members acted accordingly, was essential. His opponents argued that to vest such authority in the central organs could lead to a divorce between them and the membership, and a lack of inner-party democracy; they also argued against such a strict concept of party membership on the grounds that all kinds of revolutionary groups were springing up which should be brought under the party's wing, and that potential supporters, who might through joining the party gradually become more active, would under Lenin's scheme be lost to it.

It is hard to see why differences of this kind should have resulted in a split which produced two separate parties: the Bolsheviks, under Lenin, and the Mensheviks. In order to understand both the split and the two parties which had emerged by 1917, we must remember the environment in which they operated. The party leaders spent most of their lives in prison, exile, or abroad. They were engaged in a frustrating, and often depressing, struggle to make ends meet, avoid the Tsarist police, smuggle in illegal newspapers, and study Russian developments. They saw painful attempts to build up revolutionary groups destroyed by one informer, the repeated suppression of hopeful beginnings by the Tsarist police. No wonder the respectable leaders of the socialist parties in Europe found it difficult to take seriously the

Russian emigres, endlessly plotting and squabbling at the cafe tables of the European capitals. In such an atmosphere personal rivalries and antipathies between different leading figures became sharper and more bitter, and differences of opinion over minor matters hardened into points of principle. We are not suggesting that Martov's criticism of Lenin's rules on organization did not raise an important issue – how, in any democratic organizations, is the membership to retain control over the leadership without so weakening the leadership that none exists? – but we must look to the circumstances in which the debate was conducted to understand the refusal to compromise, and the bitterness with which each side defended its position.

Some western commentators since the revolution have suggested that the reason the Bolshevik party of the twenties and thirties became a highly centralized organization, with limited membership and strict control from above, was the faithful adherence to Lenin's views of 1903. Soviet commentators too, although from a rather different standpoint, suggest that Lenin's early concept of party organization provided a set of rules which ensured Bolshevik success in 1917 and afterwards. Such a curiously deterministic interpretation of history is difficult to accept. Despite the apparent differences between the leaders of the two groups in 1903, the two parties which emerged were not really very different. Both were conspiratorial, the criteria for membership were not clearly defined nor applied consistently in practice, central control of the branches' activities was not feasible in Tsarist conditions. Indeed right up until and after 1917 some local committees included both 'Bolsheviks' and 'Mensheviks' who were not at all clear what it was that had caused the wrangles at the top. Both parties, where one could distinguish them, remained small, and in 1905 and 1917 when the parties achieved a legal existence the Bolsheviks were willing to admit anyone who wished to join. The idea of committed revolutionaries was not meant to apply to circumstances where mass recruitment became feasible.

Perhaps more important, it is impossible to relate Bolshevik and Menshevik policy in 1917 to the attitudes of the two sides in 1903. In 1903 it was Lenin who was emphasizing the importance of a committed party spreading socialist ideas among the workers who, if left to themselves, could lose their incipient socialist demands in liberal trade unionism; it was the Mensheviks who believed the workers were already firmly committed to socialism. In 1917 the workers showed that the Mensheviks had been right, and Lenin wrong. They did not need the Bolshevik party to prompt them to action, they acted. And it was because Lenin, as leader of the Bolsheviks, realized this and adopted their demands, that the Bolsheviks rode to power on their shoulders. The Mensheviks had adopted the position they had opposed in 1902, that of the 'economists', and were pushed to one side. But this is to run ahead. Let us now look at what happened between February and October 1917.

2 Revolution

In January 1917 the Russian empire was ruled by an autocratic monarch, flanked by the nobility, church, army, and bureaucracy. A year later a Bolshevik government, committed to the introduction of socialism and a classless society, held power. The Tsar was in prison, the nobility in exile or fled to the south; the peasants had taken the land. The officers were left without an army; civil servants sat at home and churches were ransacked. The Cossacks, the most loyal of Tsarist troops, were on the side of the workers who, organized into trade unions or committees, had in some cases taken over the factories. In the space of one year the old order, the whole fabric of social and political relationships, was destroyed. The old ruling class collapsed, its established institutions fell like a house of cards. Everything connected with the old order came under question – religion, property, discipline, social class, culture, and art. Here then we have a social and political transformation of an unprecedented kind. How was it that such a change took place? This is a question that has absorbed historians and provoked many answers. All we can do here is to give one answer, one that focuses on the reasons for the *Bolsheviks* coming to power.

The February Revolution

In 1914, at the outbreak of war, Russia joined with France and Britain against Germany and Austro-Hungary. The socialist parties of Germany, Britain, and France, which together with other socialist movements in Europe had formed the Socialist International and pledged themselves to peace, supported their respective governments – which meant the end of the International. Lenin, in exile abroad, denounced the war as an imperialist war, but inside Russia support for the government came initially from all sections of the community and political parties. During the following three years the effort of waging the war strained the Tsarist system to breaking point. On 23 February 1917[1] a bread queue in St Petersburg (renamed Petrograd to give it less of a German flavour) turned into a demonstration and the troops fired on the demonstrators. The Tsarina reported to her husband that there was nothing to worry about; all that was needed was a firm hand to deal with such trouble-makers. The Duma sent yet another delegation to the Tsar imploring him to form a new government. Meanwhile on the streets of Petrograd larger demonstrations of workers and professional people formed each day and, on 27 February, the troops refused to fire and joined the demonstrators. The Tsar's response was to dissolve the Duma. Leading members of that body were in despair. As Rodzyanko, one of those who had been most active in imploring the Tsar to act as a responsible monarch, put it: 'I do not want to revolt. I am no rebel, I have made no revolution and do not intend to make one ... I am no revolutionary. I will not rise up against the supreme power. I do not want to. But there is no government any longer. Everything falls to me ... All the phones are ringing. Everybody asks me what to do. What shall I do? Shall I step aside? Wash my hands in innocence? Leave Russia without a government? After all, it is *Russia*! Have we not a duty to our country?'[2] Some of the members decided it was their duty to disobey the Tsar. They formed themselves into a Provisional Government and, after unsuccessful attempts to persuade the Tsar to abdicate in favour of his brother or son, pronounced themselves to be the new government of Russia. That was the end of Tsarism. People rejoiced in the streets. The troops mingled with the crowds while the secret police and Tsarist informers hid themselves and traces of their former activity. 'Power fell into the streets' in Trotsky's words.

Not surprisingly the February revolution was welcomed in the west. Woodrow Wilson came out strongly in favour. The allied governments welcomed the new regime because now, it was believed, with sensible progressive conservatives at the helm who would stand by their commitments to the allies, the Russian war

effort would receive new life. Liberal public opinion was strongly
in favour: the Tsar, that bastion of autocracy, had been overthrown by the Russian people who, democratic at heart, had won
their freedom and would now follow their more advanced neighbours along the natural path to parliamentary democracy; now
that they had something to fight for, the Russians would wage
a successful war against the Germans. As for the socialists of
Western Europe, they saw the February revolution as the beginning of a bourgeois revolution, of a bourgeois regime under
which the socialist movement would have a chance to grow; its
leaders could of course count on the support, advice and encouragement of their more mature and experienced western
brothers.

Lenin's Contribution

In February 1917 it was thought by no one that within a year the
Bolsheviks would be in power. When in June, at a Congress,
Lenin (in answer to a rhetorical question) called from the back
of the hall that the Bolsheviks were prepared to take power, the
response was laughter. Yet by October everyone in the capital
at least was debating not whether the Bolsheviks would take over
but when they would. This change came about for two reasons:
first, the social conflict released in Russia as a result of the fall
of Tsarism led to an increasing polarization within society and a
radicalization of workers' and soldiers' demands; second, the
Bolshevik party, led by Lenin, was prepared to accommodate
itself to this, to move to the left in order to keep up with the
masses, and hence act as the spokesman for their demands.

When the army abandoned the Tsar, the aristocracy was revealed in all its weakness and there was no forceful up-and-
coming new class to take over. It was a society with a vacant
throne and no obvious contenders. The conflicts between peasant
and landlord, worker and employer, soldier and officer, the different nationalities and their Russian rulers, town and country
began to emerge now that the old authority structures had collapsed. During the period until October, three issues dominated
the rest. These were the war, property relations, and who or what

was to be the authority in society. Initially there was very little understanding that these would create problems: Tsarism had gone, now justice and a new more democratic system would cure the social ills. During the following months writers again and again referred to the spirit of February, when all were united, and bewailed its evaporation; if only it could be brought back, as surely it could with a little good-will. The trouble was that all that united people in the early days was gladness at seeing the end of Tsarism. As soon as the question 'what now?' arose, there was a clash of interests, of irreconcilable demands, over what the new society should look like and what the policy of the government should be.

Lenin was one of the few who saw, from the beginning, that the overthrow of Tsarism had only released problems, not solved them. In April, on his return from abroad, he called for the transfer of power from the Provisional Government to the Soviets (the workers' and soldiers' councils), and an end to the war. Initially he found himself in a minority of one, even within the Bolshevik party which only gradually came round to adopting such a radical and, at the time, unpopular programme. Where Lenin's role was crucial was, first, in his correct estimation of the inability of the existing political arrangements to cope with the social conflict and in his having sufficient authority within the party to persuade it to accept his analysis and programme; and secondly, in October, without his insistent support it is doubtful that the vacillating party leadership would have gone along with those elements in the working class which were determined to bring the Provisional Government down. In other words we are arguing that the Bolsheviks did not come to power because they were better organized, because they were modelled on Lenin's *What is to be done?*, because of some revolutionary theory and strategy worked out over the years, but rather because the situation was one which favoured a radical solution and Lenin both realized this and had the strength to carry the party with him. It was not a committed band of professional revolutionaries who brought radical consciousness to the masses; on the contrary, the revolutionaries nearly got left behind by the industrial workers and soldiers. But then Lenin was no longer arguing in these 'pre-revolutionary' terms – because he recognized that the situation was now very different. The party was thrown open and membership leapt from perhaps 20,000 to 200,000 between February and October.

Dual Power

On his return in April, Lenin characterized the situation as one of dual power. What did he mean by this? On the one hand there was the Provisional Government, composed of leading members of the Duma, both Octobrists and Cadets. Prince Lvov, one of the landed aristocracy, was premier; others came from the aristocracy, the professional middle class, or owned industrial concerns. They called themselves 'provisional' because they had no proper legal claim to be the government: they were merely acting as caretakers until proper elections could be held in which the people would decide what kind of a constitution Russia should adopt. Plans were made for drawing up electoral lists prior to holding an election to a Constituent Assembly where such decisions would be made. In the meantime the Provisional Government saw its role as one of running the country in general and, in particular, of waging a war. Freedom of speech and association were announced, the Tsarist prisons opened. New ministers were appointed, the generals swore allegiance to the Provisional Government. Thus here in name was the government of Russia.

But in Petrograd a second organ of power, the Petrograd Soviet existed. During the disturbances of 1905, Soviets, or councils of workers' deputies, had sprung up in some of the industrial centres. The most important of these had been the Petrograd Soviet, in which Trotsky had played a major part, and which had virtually run the affairs of the city until Tsarist order had been restored. When Tsarism collapsed in February 1917, those who had taken part in the 1905 Soviet reassembled, factories and regiments sent elected deputies, and an Executive Committee consisting largely of those who had participated in 1905 was hastily formed. The Executive Committee, dominated by SRs and Mensheviks, issued proclamations calling upon the people to form Soviets, to defend the revolution. They announced that they would not participate in the Provisional Government, but would watch over its activities and they themselves passed decisions on, for example, discipline in the army or reached agreement with employers on the length of the working day. Here then was a body which not only claimed the right to act as watchdog over the government but which issued orders and had the support of the soldiers.

The War

The first serious clash between the Petrograd Soviet and Provisional Government came over the handling of the war. The new slogan, a revolutionary defensive war, sounded fine but the slogan could and did hide quite different meanings. For the generals and the Provisional Government it meant carrying on as before, observing commitments to the allies and defeating the Germans. The best defence, after all, may be to attack. The Soviet understood the slogan to mean that revolutionary Russia was no longer interested in annexing territory, claiming indemnities or other 'Tsarist' aims but that she would fight to defend her territory from aggressors. When, in May, Milyukov the Foreign Minister published a note to the allies which stated the government's intention of continuing the war as before, the Soviet objected, demonstrations took place, and Milyukov was forced to resign.

In the army itself every shade of opinion was represented. Some soldiers fraternized with the Germans, some deserted, others were in favour of an offensive. Discipline had largely broken down. The Soviet, in its famous Order no. 1, had abolished flogging as a form of punishment, and authorized the creation of soldiers' committees to participate in decision-making. Officers were in constant danger of being lynched, fearful of taking even simple decisions, and the generals were in despair.

The Provisional Government, with some new more liberal members, made vain attempts to suggest a peace conference to the allies. It then fell back on the policy of continuing the war in order to bring about peace and, as part of this, a decision was taken on a June offensive to drive the Germans back. Kerensky, the extremely popular Minister of War, toured the front, speaking to the troops with great if short-lived effect. Initially the offensive went well but it quickly became a disastrous rout. The front was pushed back and the soldiers began to desert in their thousands. A new government was formed with Kerensky as Prime Minister, but by now some of the generals had lost patience with a government that demanded military successes while refusing to repeal the Order no. 1 which had, in their eyes, reduced the army to an undisciplined rabble.

Country and Town

The desertions from the army by the peasant recruits were linked with the question of land. Following the February revolution the peasants at home simply began to take the land, to rise in their bands against the landlords. The Provisional Government argued that such a difficult and complex question as the proper distribution and ownership of the land could not be decided by them, a provisional body, but must wait until a proper government had been formed, once the Constituent Assembly had met. But the peasants refused to wait. Authority in the countryside had broken down and each successful seizure of land prompted others. News of what was happening at home in the villages encouraged peasant soldiers to get home as quickly as possible to share in the spoils. Chaos in the countryside increased throughout the summer months and this in turn affected the supply of food for the towns. The February revolution had been sparked off by demands for bread; naively it had been thought that with a new government the problem would be solved. Instead it became worse.

In industry the situation was little better. Following the February revolution trade unions were formed and they, often together with the Soviet, began to bargain with employers over wages, hours, and conditions of work. Arbitration procedures for settling conflicts were drawn up both by unions and by the Soviet. As might be expected, the conflict between employers and workers, so long suppressed and now let out into the open, became particularly sharp. Employers refused demands which, they argued, were impossible to meet; the workers struck and production came to a standstill. In the factories militant workers' committees began to voice demands not merely for higher wages and better conditions of work but for participation in decision-making, expropriation of the owners, and workers' control. Throughout the summer, as discussion and bargaining between employers and unions failed to produce the desired results, these factory committees, particularly in Petrograd, gained increasing support from the workers who now saw their salvation in more radical solutions. This attitude in the workplace necessarily affected attitudes towards authority in other spheres. If the attempt to reach solutions under a system of bargaining between employers and unions had failed, the attempt to resolve social problems under a governmental system of a Provisional Government (where the bourgeoisie was still strongly represented) bargaining with the Soviet (or workers' and soldiers' representatives) was equally suspect. If workers' control was the answer in industry, then surely the supreme authority in the land must be the Soviet? Hence the factory committees' demands for workers' control became linked with demands for an end to the Provisional Government and all power to the Soviets.

Right and Left

The Bolshevik leadership inside Russia had, together with the Mensheviks, hailed the February revolution as the bourgeois revolution; it would take time, they argued, for the socialist movement to develop. Lenin, however, on his return had argued, as had Trotsky earlier, that in Russian conditions the bourgeois revolution could be transformed into a socialist one. The rest of Europe was ripe for socialist revolution; if Russia could provide the spark, or 'snap the capitalist chain at its weakest link' (i.e. Russia), then the rest of Europe would rise; socialism could be achieved, even in backward Russia, if she had the help of the strong arms of the European proletariat. Lenin won over the Bolshevik party to his point of view and, with the return of Trotsky to Russia in May and his subsequent entry into the Bolshevik ranks, gained eloquent support for his case.

Bolshevik representation on the Executive Committee of the

Petrograd Soviet was negligible at this time, largely because the Bolsheviks had played little part in the original 1905 Soviet. And the views of the party on Soviet power and an immediate end to the war seemed almost ridiculous to the Menshevik and SR leadership, and not only the leadership. The First Congress of Soviets with delegates from different parts of the empire, held in June, was still dominated by the moderate left. The SRs had 285 delegates, the Mensheviks 248 and the Bolsheviks 105. But the mood in the capital was swinging further to the left. In mid-June a Congress of Factory Committee delegates produced a Bolshevik majority and on 3 July a demonstration originally sponsored by the Bolsheviks quickly developed into a massing of angry crowds who demanded an end to the Provisional Government, an end to the war, and all power to the Soviets. The Petrograd Soviet itself was surrounded by sailors and workers who called upon the members to take power when it was offered to them. For two days authority in the capital broke down. Then the demonstrations petered out, and blame was laid upon the Bolsheviks. Trotsky and others were arrested, Lenin and Zinoviev went into hiding.

The relationship between the Provisional Government and the Soviet had changed over the months. Following the resignation of Milyukov (the Foreign Minister) in May, overtures had been made to the Soviet to provide some ministers in a new government. After much debate, some agreed to serve. Then, following the failure of the June offensive, a new government was formed by Kerensky which contained more SR and Menshevik leaders, while the extreme right opted out. The government became more representative but even less able to produce a policy that would satisfy the different social and political groups in the country. And, by joining the Provisional Government, some of the leaders of the left had unwillingly, and unwittingly, identified themselves with its failure. Kerensky made desperate attempts to hold right and left together. In August a conference was held in Moscow, at which representatives of the right (the Cadets, Octobrists) sat one side of the hall, and those of the left (the different socialist parties) the other. Leading delegates sat on the stage and, in the middle, Kerensky spoke for hours on end as though his oratory could reconcile the two sides. More ominous than the acrimony between the participants was the arrival of General Kornilov (one of the most popular army generals), given a triumphal welcome by his supporters, and the success of the excluded Bolsheviks in calling for a one-day strike in Moscow. Whereas in February neither a military dictatorship nor Bolshevik rule would have gained more than a minimum of support or been seen as even a remote probability, by August these had become the real alternatives. From then on, while the politicians talked, met at one Council or Convention after another, the extreme right and extreme left sought and gained increasing support.

It was the right, led by General Kornilov, which struck first in a motley coalition of generals, industrialists, and members of the old aristocracy. Kornilov marched on Petrograd to restore order and install a strong government. Kerensky, in near hysteria, called upon the people to defend the revolution; weapons were distributed to the workers who formed themselves into a Red Guard and kept the weapons afterwards. Kornilov's troops abandoned him, and the attempt failed. The leading Bolsheviks were released from jail and by September the Petrograd Soviet had a Bolshevik majority, Moscow and Minsk shortly followed suit. Local elections of the time showed an increase in votes for the right (the Cadets) and for the left (the Bolsheviks). The SR party split into a left wing and a right. The Baltic fleet went Bolshevik.

The October Revolution

By the beginning of October the Petrograd Soviet was calling for an end to the Provisional Government, for peace, and all power to the Soviets. Lenin, still in hiding, was sending furious letters to the Central Committee of the party, demanding that the opportunity should not be allowed to slip; power should be taken now before the right regrouped its forces and imposed a Kornilovite dictatorship. The right was still weak, recovering from its earlier failure, and everyone seemed to be waiting for the Bolsheviks to act. The Second Congress of Soviets was due to meet in Petrograd on 25 October: something surely must happen by then. It was at this point, against the background of wavering on the part of some leading party members, Zinoviev's and Kamenev's open opposition in the pages of the press, and an irresolute decision by the Central Committee to act, that Trotsky engineered Bolshevik victory.

A Military Revolutionary Committee was formed, under the auspices of the Petrograd Soviet, to defend the revolution against attack by the Provisional Government. Kerensky, growing desperate, at last decided to act and ordered certain battleships known to support the Bolsheviks and certain regiments to be prepared to move away from the capital. The MRC countermanded the order, and the Aurora cruiser sailed up the Neva to take its position opposite the Winter Palace where the Provisional Government met. The next day Kerensky sent troops to shut the Bolshevik printing press. This was pretext enough for Trotsky to act: the Provisional Government was attacking the revolution. Troops loyal to the Bolsheviks re-opened the press, and the Military Revolutionary Committee gave orders to save the city. Throughout that night and the following day troops occupied the key posts of the city and surrounded the Winter Palace. Late that night, after little opposition, the Palace was taken and the members of the Provisional Government, except for Kerensky who had fled in search of loyal troops, arrested. Simultaneously the Second Congress of Soviets opened. Lenin left the flat on the northern outskirts of the city where he had been hiding and made his way, still in disguise, to Bolshevik headquarters and thence to the Congress.

The Congress, with perhaps two thirds of the delegates in support of the Bolsheviks, declared that power had passed to the Soviets and accepted a new government, the Council of People's Commissars, composed of Bolsheviks and left SRs, with Lenin as chairman. The opposition (Mensheviks and right SRs) walked out. While the Congress passed decrees on peace (an immediate end to hostilities) and the abolition of private ownership of land, news of the revolution was spreading to other parts of the country. There was fighting in Moscow before the Soviet eventually managed to take control, Kerensky marched with some troops to the outskirts of Petrograd but found his supporters less and less willing to fight. Finally, disguised as a sailor, he fled. Within the city there was opposition both from the civil servants who refused to serve under the new government and from some of the trade unions who demanded a government more representative of all the socialist parties. The railway workers, who were Mensheviks, in particular were hostile to a Bolshevik-dominated Council of People's Commissars. Some attempts were made to reach a compromise, but the Bolshevik leadership was not prepared to agree to demands that Lenin and Trotsky be excluded from a government nor to bargain away the fruits of victory. Not only were the civil servants refusing to cooperate, the middle classes hostile, and some of the labour movement prepared to oppose the Bolsheviks by strikes, but generals and officers were only too anxious to march against the Bolsheviks as soon as they could put together an army, which would be backed by the aristocratic and business world. The Bolsheviks drew their support from the working class, from the rank-and-file soldiers, and from the peasants who now had government support for their seizure of the land. Would these groups remain united in support of the Bolsheviks? Could they, the poor and uneducated, run the country even if they could withstand the attacks of the skilled and prosperous, and what if the Germans did not agree to peace?

3 Socialism and Democracy

The Response from the West

During the summer the allies' representatives in Petrograd and their governments at home had become increasingly disillusioned with the Kerensky government which was failing to hold either the army or the country together. Briefly Kornilov had seemed the man to save the situation but he too had failed them. Thus the October revolution came as no surprise to the military attaches in Russia and was not unwelcome – as a temporary extremist government which must surely be overthrown and replaced by a government more conservative, pro-war, and stronger than Kerensky's. But back in the European capitals the news, when it came, was greeted with dismay and as time went on this attitude hardened. First and foremost it was the Bolshevik demands for peace and then their insistence that they at least would sign a separate peace with Germany which antagonized the allied governments. The Bolshevik refusal to abide by commitments of the previous Russian governments, their publication of the embarrassing secret treaties, and their renunciation of responsibility for the foreign debts of the Tsarist government or for foreign capital invested in private industry – all made them a thoroughly undesirable government and one which the allies refused to recognize. Furthermore their appeals to the working class of Europe to throw off their rulers and the propaganda directed towards those under colonial rule were not only offensive but, the allied governments feared, positively dangerous at a time when discontent at home and war-weariness were expressing themselves in militant industrial action, and when calls for independence were beginning to be heard from the colonies.

To liberals and many labour leaders too, Bolshevism appeared as an extremist tyranny. The February revolution had been welcomed as a democratic revolution against the most despotic rule in Europe, and as important, if not more so, had been the conviction that now the Russian army would become a more positive ally against the Germans. But this take-over by a handful of 'German agents'[1] who confiscated property, burnt churches, 'nationalized women and children', and relied upon direct action by rank-and-file workers' groups as a way of rule was clearly not 'democratic' and hardly 'socialist'. To the big socialist parties in Europe, the Bolsheviks were wild extremists and dangerous. At a time when labour's policy of cooperation in the war effort had brought only misery, hunger – a *worsening* of their position – to the working class, Bolshevik success in achieving power, their denunciation of the war, and call for action could only cast even more doubt on the correctness of such a policy.

Over the next few years it seemed to many that Europe was trembling on the brink of Bolshevism. The Soviet in Hungary under Bela Kun, the short-lived Bavarian Soviet, and later the temporarily successful Red Army counter-offensive against Poland, the unemployment and discontent at home which, it was thought, must provide a fertile breeding ground for Bolshevik ideas – these made the Red Menace seem very real. But, and perhaps it is surprising, there was little active support for Bolshevik ideas or actions in the labour movement of the time and this was not only a result of the bad press. Even in Germany it was only a minority that came out in support. In Britain sympathy for the Bolsheviks was strongly related to the question of conscription. With allied intervention against the Bolsheviks in the civil war (1918–20), the fear that the war would be prolonged or a new war started was enough to rally working-class and labour opinion behind the Bolsheviks – but primarily as a government which should be left to manage its own affairs rather than because of its intrinsic merits as a socialist government. In the distant United States there was even less support. There were exceptions to this – individuals and groups who advocated the imitation of the Bolshevik 'Soviets' and direct action by workers and soldiers – but for most of war-weary Europe and America Bolshevik rule was seen as something strange and alien which must surely soon collapse.

This attitude persisted into the twenties. With the failure of the Whites (that is, the opponents of the Bolsheviks) in the civil war, the allied governments' hopes faded and they retired from the Russian scene to face their own troubles at home. The new Soviet republic was still an unnatural monster but one best left alone to come to its senses. It was so weak after seven years of war that, with the people starving and industry in ruins, it could pose no military threat. The ideas put forward by the leadership were dangerous but it was hoped or believed that their very unrealism would lead to chaos and then a return to normal behaviour. In addition the twenties, particularly in America, were a prosperous time for business, a vindication of capitalism's strength and efficiency, a time which could prompt the happy and self-confident comment that 'Russia was the biggest business failure in history'.[2] The labour movement, which experienced the other aspects of capitalism, split into those who as time went on supported the new Soviet government, saw Russia as the promised land, would brook no criticisms of Bolshevik policy, and found themselves tied more and more closely to Moscow,[3] and those who felt sympathy but refused to support the Moscow line. This split in the labour movement which gradually hardened into hostility had tragic results for the labour movement as a whole and, in Germany in particular, disastrous social and political consequences in that it was to be one of the factors which enabled Hitler to rise to power.

For those who studied politics and even sometimes had a hand in it, the Soviet experiment was of little interest. For the academics of the time politics meant constitutions, the legal framework, checks and balances between the legislature, the executive, and the judiciary. They devoted themselves to devising a framework for the new League of Nations or a constitution for the Weimar republic which would ensure Germany's future as a democracy. What was happening in Russia was an aberration of no value or interest to those who thought of constitutional democracy as the 'natural' form of government. Before we look at what it was the Bolsheviks were attempting to do and the problems they came up against, a brief outline of what the parliamentary democrat understood by 'democracy' will help us to see where and how the two differed. For it remains true that, despite the poor reporting, the ignorance of what was going on in Russia and what the Bolsheviks were attempting to do, the response from the west, both from those who supported Bolshevism and those who opposed it, was right in its recognition of Bolshevism as a radical alternative to capitalist democracy. Bolshevism *did* threaten the allied governments and propertied classes of Europe, it was not imbued with liberal or moderate labour ideals and attitudes, and it *was* an attempt to provide an alternative type of society to that existing in the west.

Parliamentary Democracy

When supporters of parliamentary democracy talked in the twenties of democracy, they meant a number of things: an elected legislature with power to curb the executive, civil liberties, freedom of the press and speech. Although the way in which these aspects of democracy were interpreted by the conservative was different from that of the liberal or in turn the labour spokesman, there was sufficient common ground between them for us to be able to talk of the concept of parliamentary democracy. Ideas on who should be represented had and did still differ: universal suffrage was only introduced in Britain *after* the First World War (when women received the vote) and only then against the opposition of some who considered themselves democrats. The original demand 'no taxation without representation' and subsequent extolling of the virtues of representative government had, after all, been based less on the conviction that all men were equal and therefore all had a right to vote, than on the conviction that, without some kind of a representative body to curb the monarch, there was no guarantee that the ruler would act in anybody's interests except his own. Representation was necessary in order to defend one's own interests. The conservative, who identified the interests of society with those of the propertied classes, was certainly in favour of representative government – as a system which returned the 'proper' people who then ruled on behalf of rich and poor. The liberals in the nineteenth century had begun to argue (somewhat uneasily) that, if representation was a necessary safeguard of one's interests, it was necessary that all should enjoy this safeguard. And, not surprisingly, the labour movement, taking up this argument and bolstering it with demands for equal rights, had made universal suffrage an important part of its programme. With 'one man, one vote' the working class would make up the majority of the electorate and should be able to elect a government which would act in their interests. In both Germany and Britain the labour movement – seeing this possibility – had channelled its energies into achieving this end, into working within a parliamentary framework to improve the lot of the working class through legislation.

Civil liberties, free speech, sturdy individualism and freedom – these were the other cardinal elements in the democratic picture. Again here, initially, an attack had been made upon the powers of the king and government and the use of their powers to stifle opposition and criticism. By the nineteenth century, liberty had become the most important element in the flourishing liberal doctrine. Now it was argued that the power of the State should be restricted to a minimum – that of seeing that no one endangered another's life or liberty. Apart from this, neither it nor society had a right to dictate what a man did with his life; it was up to the individual to fashion his own life (providing he did not harm others) – this was the only way he could live as a man, fulfil himself as a man. This concept of freedom emphasizes the importance of removing external impediments to action, impediments in the form of legislation, or State interference which prevents men acting freely. It was not accidental that a doctrine of this kind found expression in the context of *laissez-faire* capitalism. Its supporters saw society as a wonderful economic mechanism where hidden laws operated to create wealth, a mechanism which should be left to function naturally unimpeded by State interference. Into this context the idea of men as free beings, acting independently but harmoniously in unison if only restrictions on their actions were lifted, fitted neatly and easily. If this creed with its insistence upon the rights of free speech, publication, and association was instrumental in curbing the powers of the State and in making it easier for the unrepresented and underprivileged to campaign for representation and an improvement in their lot – both important in themselves – it was at the same time a curiously one-sided idea of freedom which, for those who did not benefit from the *laissez-faire* economy, was in other respects a hollow mockery. It was not simply that the way in which freedom was interpreted by the State and courts seemed to differ depending upon whether one was rich or poor, supported the *status quo* or demanded radical change, but rather that the exercise of this 'freedom' by some deprived the rest of any scope to make use of their 'theoretical' freedom. For a man who could not find work, for a woman at sweated labour in a factory, for a child who went down the mines or up a chimney at the age of eight, there was, in a very real sense, no freedom of action. They were free to eke out a miserable, stunted existence or starve.

The liberal doctrine was strong on the importance of curbing the State's powers, on the value of free speech and assembly, but in its emphasis on the individual it ignored the fact that the social and economic ordering of society gave some individuals power over others, produced gross inequalities and severely limited the freedom of the underprivileged in any practical sense.

The Marxist Critique and the Bolsheviks' Task

It was these aspects of the *laissez-faire* or capitalist economy that Marx, in contrast, emphasized. Society, as he saw it, was divided into two opposing classes, classes whose interests must necessarily conflict – those who owned the means of production, the property-owners, and those who did not. He did not deny, on the contrary he applauded, the productive nature of such an economic mechanism and one as highly developed as industrial capitalism with its unprecedented capacity for producing material wealth; nor did he belittle the 'democratic' rights won after a struggle with the crown – civil liberties, equality before the law, etc., were a definitive advance on a more arbitrary system of government. But what he did argue was that, as long as the present system of property relations existed, society would be split in two, material inequality would increase, and the minority would continue to benefit at the expense of the majority. Only when the majority seized power and abolished private property could class conflict disappear, inequality be abolished, and men become really free to develop as individual, creative beings, restricted neither by an oppressive State nor by material and cultural circumstances.

Here then the State, although seen as an oppressive force, is not considered the primary enemy. Instead its existence reflects the more basic oppressive economic relationships in society; it upholds and supports them but does not create them. The main enemy is property which creates power for some, inequality, injustice and an inevitable clash of interests within society. The socialist movement which spread during the nineteenth century, absorbing some of Marx's ideas, emphasized the existing inequality and the degradation suffered by men, women, and children. The socialist, like the liberal, was concerned with freedom – with creating a society in which men would be free (able) to live as men, as creative social beings. But, unlike the liberal, he argued that this was impossible within the confines of capitalist society and hence he was less interested in the differences between one capitalist society and another (an autocracy versus a republic) because, although these made a difference to campaigning rights and organization, they in themselves could never produce equality, justice, or freedom. For similar reasons he was less interested in spelling out the political forms of the new society. It was assumed that the vast majority would take power from a minority of capitalists and Marx had suggested that force or coercion would be necessary initially to crush their opposition. But before long, it was assumed, the need for rule, coercion, for a State of any kind would disappear.

The extent to which different sections of the labour movement accepted or interpreted the Marxist analysis varied from country to country as economic and political conditions varied from one to another. We have already mentioned the unique position in which the Russian Marxists found themselves and described their attempts to produce an analysis and a plan of action that accorded with it. But now they were faced with a far more difficult task: that of creating an alternative economic and social mechanism to *laissez-faire* capitalism and a different type of democracy –

a classless, socialist republic. In the new society poverty and need would disappear, all would participate in administration, in productive and creative work and each individual would be able to develop as a creative human being.

To lay the foundations for such a society it was necessary to destroy old institutions, economic, cultural, and political, and to create new ones. This meant staying in power which in turn depended, at least in large part, upon Bolshevik ability to destroy old institutions (thus undermining the structures which provided their opponents with power) and the ability to create new institutions which would both strengthen the Bolshevik position and further their aims. Whereas it may not be difficult (at least in principle) to abolish the old, any revolutionary party is likely to be faced with a far from easy task in creating alternative institutions. It may be that conditions in the country will be such that there is little conflict between the type of institution that will best enable the revolutionary party to remain in power and the type that will best accord with the long-term aims of the revolutionaries, but usually, historically at least, revolutionaries have been faced with a conflict of this kind. It is imperative that they remain in power for any of their aims to be realized, yet it may be impossible for them to stay in power without, at least in the short-term, taking actions that conflict with their long-term aspirations. The problem is not so much that a temporary 'undesirable' measure has to be taken but rather that the taking of such measures may have consequences which make it *harder* in the long-run to achieve the original objectives. To say this is not to say that revolutions are doomed to failure or that revolutions are therefore 'undesirable' in some sense, but it is to say that revolutionaries should be aware of the problem. In some respects the Bolsheviks were acutely aware of it; in others they failed to see the potentially dangerous consequences of temporary expedients. Let us now look at their attempts to resolve the contradictions between staying in power and creating a socialist society. Although again the two are connected, for simplicity's sake we shall first look at their economic and social policy, then at the political reforms, and in conclusion bring the two together.

First Steps to Socialism

In the days following the revolution the new government passed
a series of decrees aimed at making their position clear not only
to the masses of the people in Russia but also to the proletariat
in Europe. It was after all hoped, or rather assumed, that the
example of a socialist revolution in Russia would spark off
revolutions in the west. A decree on land proclaimed that henceforth the land belonged to the people: the peasants should organize themselves, take over the land, and distribute it among
themselves. Industry was not immediately nationalized wholesale,
but a decree on workers' control placed decision-making in the
hands of workers' committees and provided a structure of district
and regional councils of delegates. Education was to be free for
all, of whatever age, and schools and local Soviets were to work
out curricula. Discriminatory legislation against women was
abolished – they were to have equal rights with men; marriage
and divorce were to become simple civil proceedings. Capital
punishment was abolished; wealth confiscated from the rich.
There was to be no oppression of the national minorities.[4]

But before these decrees could be realized in practice, peace
had to be achieved. All were agreed that an end to the war was
essential (indeed, this had been one of their first announcements)
but, when it came to deciding how this was to be achieved, the
Bolshevik leadership split. It was one thing for Trotsky, as
Foreign Minister, to publish the secret treaties, refuse to repay
foreign loans, and declare that the Workers' Government would
not bargain with an imperialist power, it was another to refuse
to agree to the German terms when the alternative was a German
advance into Russia. Lenin argued that the terms must be accepted, Bukharin and the left argued that the new Workers' State
could not deal with such a government. The terms were not accepted, the Germans marched, driving any opposition backwards,
and finally Lenin's argument prevailed. The Soviet government
signed the new, significantly worse, terms which meant that the
western territories (part of Poland and the Ukraine) were lost.
Temporarily peace was secured. But barely had this been achieved
than civil war broke out. Those opposing the Bolsheviks consisted

of a number of disparate elements – generals, officers, and troops loyal to Kerensky or to the Tsar, landlords and industrialists anxious to regain their property, SRs, Czech prisoners of war – these, usually in uncoordinated efforts, backed by troops, money, and advice from the allies now moved against the Bolsheviks. For the next three years civil war raged across the countryside.

One important reason for the Bolshevik victory was the support of the peasants or, rather, the peasant preference for the Bolshevik over a returning ex-landlord. It was the Bolsheviks after all who in October 1917 had passed the decree on land. This first decree, simply awarding the peasants the land and the right to distribute it, was taken from an SR programme, which in turn had been based on peasant demands in the summer. The land was not made 'State' property, except for a few large estates which were kept intact: it was simply handed over to the peasant communities or remained in individual peasant hands. Although on paper the government passed a further decree which did in words 'nationalize' the land, in practical terms the distribution and cultivation of the land was left to the peasant communities themselves. An immediate problem was caused by the food shortage in the towns. The disruption in the countryside and the civil war reduced even further the supplies of grain to the towns. Faced with starvation in the towns, where lay the basis of their support, and determined to end black-market speculation in grain, the Bolsheviks sent troops to requisition grain and forbade private trade. But this policy of forced requisitioning was inevitably hated by the bulk of the peasantry (and thus weakened peasant support for the Bolsheviks) and did not solve the food shortage: a peasant who is going to lose his surplus grain will simply reduce the amount he grows. Peasant and industrial discontent and the breakdown of the trade network persuaded the government to rethink its policy at the end of the civil war. In an attempt to stimulate agricultural production, improve relations with the peasantry and between industry and agriculture, the Bolsheviks substituted a tax in kind for grain requisitioning, introduced State prices for grain, and allowed private trading. In other words the peasant was to be allowed to produce and trade as a private individual. This was essential, Lenin argued, if the alliance between worker and peasant was to be maintained and the devastated economy rebuilt. In the next chapter we shall look in more detail at the problems surrounding the 'worker–peasant alliance'. Here it is sufficient to indicate not only that it was going to be far from easy to introduce a system of socialized agriculture but that, in order to stimulate agriculture, the Bolsheviks resorted to measures which were going to encourage those very petit-bourgeois peasant attitudes they wished to stamp out.

In industry the situation was rather different but no less difficult. The Bolsheviks came to power on a wave of workers' enthusiasm and industrial anarchy – workers' committees were taking over the plants, removing old owners, tearing down the old institutions. In their decree on workers' control the Bolsheviks both recognized and authorized such a situation. But in the prevailing conditions industrial production was grinding to a halt: the breakdown in the trade network (made worse later by the civil war) meant that factories were unable to get supplies; large sections of the labour force, relatively new recruits to industry, left to return to the countryside where land was being distributed and there were hopes of something to eat; some of the trade unions were openly hostile to the Bolsheviks, and the specialists and engineers refused to work or were scared to work under workers' management.

Some system of coordinating the use of resources and industrial production was necessary – if only to provide goods for the war effort. Socialism, Lenin argued, lay in coordinating, managing resources, organizing production in such a way that productivity increased; in Soviet conditions of the time that meant strict organization and discipline. Hence, in place of autonomous workers' committees, what was needed was a plan for the economy and a management strong and capable of realizing it. With these objectives in mind the government set up an administrative body to be responsible for coordinating supplies and production at a national level (at least in theory), nationalized enterprises, and replaced workers' control by a system of collegial management – an appointed manager plus representatives from the factory committees, or, as it became, the trade union. The recalcitrant unions were brought over to the Bolshevik side by a mixture of persuasion and force, and the workers' councils were absorbed into the trade-union structure. Organizationally, at least, the Bolsheviks had replaced the semi-anarchic system of workers' control by two national structures subordinate to the government – an administrative management network and the trade unions. Of course during the civil war much of industry simply had to be managed on an *ad hoc* basis and much simply failed to function at all. Quite apart from the problem of creating some system to run industry and keep supplies flowing, there was the problem of the labour force. It was not only that industrial workers were leaving for the countryside but also that the best and most willing recruits for the new Red Army or party and government posts came from among loyal industrial workers. The Bolshevik leaders found themselves in the uncomfortable situation of having to weaken still further the basis of their support – the industrial workers – by calling for their aid as soldiers at a time when this was almost a certain passport to death. To win the civil war this was necessary but, as was said with despair, when the civil war ended the best of the working class would have gone and how should socialism be built without them?

A decision which provoked considerable opposition within the party was that to employ the 'bourgeois specialists' at relatively high salaries. At the time of the revolution the number of those who came over to the Bolshevik side was negligible and industry was suffering without them. Lenin argued that they had to be 'bought' back although this was a departure from the principle of equal pay. Following the revolution the government had limited the pay of government officials to that of skilled workmen, and the trade unions themselves began a campaign to equalize wages within industry. To pay bourgeois specialists high salaries seemed to many a retrograde step and a particularly unwelcome one, given that it was the *bourgeois* specialists who were to benefit. The leadership agreed that it was a departure from socialist principles but, they argued, it was only a temporary policy, the differential was not nearly as great as it had been before the revolution, and the specialists would work under the strict control of the workers' organs.

At the end of the civil war in 1920, against a background of inflation, industrial stagnation, and peasant discontent, the Bolsheviks had to rethink industrial policy. Just as in agriculture private incentive was to be granted a role, so, in industry, did the emphasis shift. Small-scale industry was denationalized, State industry was to be run in a profitable way, and, it was hoped, trade agreements with capitalist countries would provide both finance and foreign expertise. The communist, Lenin stated bluntly, must learn to be a businessman. As might be expected, the combination of agricultural and industrial 'concessions' (termed the New Economic Policy or NEP) dismayed many who had fought the civil war in the belief that the economic policies of what came in retrospect to be called 'war communism' were proper communist policies which would herald in a new era. Disillusionment within the party might have found expression in more direct criticism of the policies had it not been for two factors. First, as the new policy was being announced at the March 1921 Party Congress, rebellion broke out at Kronstadt, the naval base near Petrograd which had been a stronghold of Bolshevism. The sailors now demanded a return to 'Soviet democracy', freedom for other socialist parties, freedom of elections and the press, the end to grain requisitioning, etc. Red Army troops moved against the sailors and the rebellion was put down, but this served as a signal to the party of their potentially weak position within the country. Party unity seemed essential at such a time of crisis. Secondly, in the preceding months, party unity had been severely strained by a bitter debate over the management of the economy. Trotsky, in charge of the railways, had introduced martial discipline and a dictatorial system of management in which the unions had no part; he had argued that in time of war this was essential and furthermore, he argued, since the Soviet republic was a Workers' State, the workers could need no protection against their own government; trade unions in the traditional sense were no longer necessary, they should be absorbed into the State machinery as part of the mechanism responsible for seeing that industry ran in a disciplined, organized fashion. Not surprisingly this attitude – and it was only the most extreme statement of what in practice tended to happen in some other branches too –

provoked opposition both from the trade unionists and from some party members. A group was formed within the party calling itself the 'Workers' Opposition' which argued that the workers were being deprived of any control and that a new bureaucratic administrative mechanism was taking over the Workers' State; this group argued that the unions should swallow or absorb the administrative and managerial structure; the unions, through a series of councils, should be responsible for all industrial policy; only then would the interests of the workers be safeguarded. In the final stages of the debate a compromise platform was accepted: according to this, the unions should be granted a role in the Workers' State but not that of overall control; they should participate in major policy decisions, defend the workers' interests when faced with bureaucratic mismanagement or administrative narrow-mindedness but not interfere in management functions, and play an educative role among the labour force – instilling communist ideas, teaching skills, hygiene, raising the level of literacy. Thus a compromise was reached (but one which did not really solve the problem) after a period of the bitterest public infighting the party had known. No one was in the mood for another fight of this kind over the new agricultural and industrial proposals.

These early attempts to find an industrial policy and the debates that accompanied them reveal some of the basic problems facing the Bolsheviks. They were confronted with the task of finding an alternative to private ownership and market relationships (difficult enough in itself) under conditions of scarcity and disruption. Because of the unfavourable situation, they accepted the need for certain temporary departures from socialist principles: unequal rates of pay, concessions to private ownership in agriculture and industry. But, whereas these might be seen and recognized by all as 'departures', socialist principles did not in themselves always or even often provide set answers. There could be (and was) endless argument over what was and what was not a proper socialist policy – not merely what was the 'proper' or 'best' policy in the circumstances but what it was the party should be striving for. The conflict over the way in which the economy should be run was not simply an expression of the peculiarly difficult situation in which the Bolsheviks found themselves, it was also an early attempt to establish what 'power' and 'authority' might mean in a socialist context.

The Constituent Assembly

Before October the Bolsheviks had upbraided the Provisional Government for delaying the calling of the Constituent Assembly and, when they took power, still referred to the forthcoming Assembly as the body which would determine how Russia should be governed. Initially the Bolsheviks assumed that they would win an electoral victory – both because it was they who had realized the popular demands for all power to the Soviets, peace, and land and because, by their other decrees, they were proclaiming policies which had the support of the masses. But by early December the Bolshevik leadership began to fear this was over-optimistic: the intelligentsia and wealthier classes were openly hostile, the Mensheviks still had the support of sections of the labour movement and, more important in terms of numbers, the SR party had much the strongest ties with the peasantry, ties which would probably count now that the peasants had got the land. Again the party leadership and its supporters were divided on what to do: some were for cancelling the elections altogether, some for excluding the right, others for holding new elections (polling was already underway) and others for dispersing the Assembly when it met. Eventually it was decided to arrest leading members of the Cadets but to allow the rest of the deputies to meet. The date set was 18 January 1918, and a Third Congress of Soviets was called for the 19 January.

The election results gave the combined SR groupings approximately 55 per cent of the seats, the Bolsheviks 21 per cent; the remainder were divided between Mensheviks, Cadets, and small national groups. Approximately 400 of the 800 deputies managed to attend the opening ceremony at which Chernov, the leading figure of the SRs, was elected President. The Bolsheviks then walked out. The Assembly began to discuss peace and land. Late that night the Bolshevik guards asked the deputies to leave and shut the building. The following day there was a demonstration in support of the Assembly which the troops dispersed, and thus ended the Assembly's existence.

How did the Bolsheviks justify their action? Here, argued their opponents both at the time and since, was a genuinely democratic election in which, for the first time in their history, the people of Russia (and the other Tsarist lands) voted for their representatives. The Bolsheviks found themselves in a minority – how then could they claim to be representing the people? It is worth giving the Bolshevik counter-arguments because in them they begin to spell out their ideas on democracy. On the one hand they argued that the election results did not reflect the true feeling in the country. Lists of candidates had been drawn up as far back as September, but since then the SRs had split into a left and a right wing; however, SR candidates tended to be of the right and in many districts peasants had no left candidate to vote for. Whereas delegates to peasant Congresses[5] tended, by the end of December, to split roughly equally between right and left, right SRs far outnumbered those of the left in the Assembly. Also, the Bolsheviks argued, in many districts voting had taken place too soon after the revolution for the policy of the new government to have become known or understood. (One could also add that the results did not correctly represent right-wing sentiment in the country, since by this time sections of the right had decided to join the generals in order to fight the Bolsheviks rather than vote.)

In producing these kinds of argument, for which there was certainly justification, the Bolsheviks were meeting their opponents on their own ground, that is, claiming that it was not a democratic election because it did not represent majority opinion. (The supporter of parliamentary democracy does not necessarily consider that it is the task of an election to provide an assembly which 'represents' voters' preferences. In the British system, for example, the winning party may poll, and on one occasion has done so, fewer votes than its unsuccessful rival, while the Liberal Party may get very few seats relative to the total number of votes cast for it. As a system proportional representation more properly reflects opinion in the country as a whole. But this does not invalidate the Bolshevik argument because their critics' accusation was that the Assembly *was* representative of public opinion; it was this the Bolsheviks denied.) But if we accept that the composition of the Assembly did not reflect public opinion – and that this is what a 'democratic' assembly should do – then, as some Bolsheviks beforehand and other socialists afterwards argued, it should have been abandoned and a new election should have been held. To this the Bolshevik answer was twofold. Trotsky suggested that the idea of an assembly reflecting or representing public opinion is a myth because opinions are always changing. This, in some absolute sense, may well be true but taken to this extreme is an arid argument. As Rosa Luxemburg pointed out, if taken seriously it would make any attempts to be guided by the majority, any attempts to reach democratic decisions, meaningless. The main thrust of the Bolshevik argument was rather different: there was nothing particularly sacrosanct about this type of bourgeois election – *Soviet* democracy was a more meaningful type of democracy because under it people did not simply elect representatives who served in a national assembly, unaccountable to the electorate, for a period of years, instead they elected delegates to a Congress whose job it was to make policy and then return to the locality to execute it; the people elected local organs in which large numbers participated; the delegates served for short periods, could be recalled at any time, and a rapid turnover ensured that as many as possible participated in the business of government. Here then the argument has shifted; it is now based on a different concept of democracy, one in which participation, control, and as close an adherence to shifting public opinion as possible are stressed. Here the Bolsheviks were attacking the idea that one-man, one-vote and 'free' elections between competing parties are a sufficient condition for democracy.

The Bolsheviks produced one other argument, different yet again, against submitting to the SR majority. When Lenin asked 'How could democracy abolish classes, without which we cannot achieve socialism?' he was suggesting that an adherence to majority opinion could not solve the social conflict in the country and that the primary aim should be to do precisely this. It was because the Bolsheviks believed that class antagonism based on private property was the major source of conflict that they sought to end private ownership. The industrial workers, it was argued, saw the connection between property and social conflict; the countryside – whence came support for the SRs – was backward in comparison, still strongly influenced by ideas of private property, and to allow 'the countryside to lead the town' would be to encourage rather than to abolish class conflict, inequality, poverty, and oppression. It was now for the workers, with the help of the poor peasants (the 'proletariat of the land') to lead, educate the mass of the peasantry towards socialism.

We find then a number of different, not necessarily consistent, strands in Bolshevik thought of the time: most notably an adherence to the belief that popular or majority opinion is important coupled with the argument that it is justified for a minority to rule in the interests of the majority. The stress upon making participation more than a matter of casting a vote every few years would probably receive more sympathy from the liberal democrat of today (given his experience of the apathy often engendered by this aspect of parliamentary democracy) than it did from his counterpart of the twenties. And, understandably, to many the achievement of universal suffrage seemed in itself enough to presage a radical change in social policy.

In another respect too Bolshevik criticism of the inability of formal mechanisms in themselves to achieve desired political or social ends makes them much more 'modern' than those in the twenties who believed in the almost magic properties of constitutions. Lenin argued: 'Either the dictatorship of Kornilov . . . or the dictatorship of the proletariat – there is *no other* choice for a country which has gone through an extremely rapid development with extremely sharp turns and amidst terrible chaos, created by one of the most terrible wars in history.'[6] Although it is impossible to predict what would have happened had the Bolsheviks bowed themselves gracefully into the wings and allowed the SRs to form some kind of a government and constitution, the likelihood of Russia shifting peacefully into constitutional democracy (which is what many critics have suggested was the alternative) does seem extraordinarily far-fetched. For one thing the SRs had never espoused the idea, for another the right, already collecting its troops, had no liking for SR policies and was, by this time, determined to put an end to all these socialist notions. The experiences of the preceding year alone had split society into such antagonistic groups that it is difficult to see how any peaceful solution could have been achieved. A right-wing military dictatorship would probably have won the day, although how long it could have held power is another matter. It is only if one tries to see the situation as it was that one can understand the actions of a political party that wished to end the rule of the few over the many. The Bolsheviks had hoped and assumed that they would have the support of the masses; when they found that this was doubtful they were not prepared, given the alternative as they saw it (and they were probably correct), to yield ground. Compared with a Kornilovite dictatorship, they were after all the more 'democratic' of the two.

The Bolsheviks were concerned that the people, the masses, should participate directly in government, organize their own lives, be equal in the sense that all should be decision-makers, none should have power over others because of a graded hierarchy of officials. They attempted to find forms that would encourage this. Only those forms which could fit with man's requirements as a conscious, rational, and creative being could be called 'democratic'. This kind of emphasis or attitude was, of course, nothing new. The French revolutionaries had attempted to create new forms to correspond with their views on the purpose of man's existence and, although liberal spokesmen of the nineteenth century had argued for representative government and participation (admittedly limited) in government on utilitarian grounds, they had done so with a passion that suggested they considered man a thinking, creative being who required a particular environment to develop as an individual. But by the 1920s this kind of concern with the underlying purposes or rationale behind governmental forms was being replaced in the minds of liberal democrats by a concern with the forms themselves: the proper division of power between legislators, executive and judiciary, electoral systems, and the suffrage. The Bolsheviks were not guilty of this but, in their very proper concern with 'essential' or basic questions and their disgust at the inadequacies of parliamentary democracy, they tended to ignore certain valid parts of the liberal democratic creed. Earlier we commented on the liberals' concern with the curbing of State power, of the executive; the distrust of an authority which could not be held responsible for its actions; and the emphasis on the importance of criticism and dissent (free speech, etc.) and an independent judiciary. We also noted that Marx himself recognized these bourgeois liberties and rights as being of great importance. Now in 1917, when the Bolsheviks came to power, they too came as champions of free speech, press, and assembly and of a government responsible to the people. It was not long, however, before they had passed a decree limiting the freedom of the press and suppressed their political opponents of the right. Relations with the other socialist parties were strained over the civil-war period – at some times opponents were actively suppressed and at others some kind of a compromise was reached – but by its conclusion no other political party was allowed to exist. The leadership did not take these actions casually – they provoked bitter discussion and disagreement and the decree on the press was seen at the time as a temporary measure – for the very reason that the Bolsheviks felt uneasy about denying these basic liberties. In this sense they were heirs to the European democratic tradition. But they found themselves surrounded by enemies, with a precarious hold on power – a situation in which the existence of these liberties meant a very real threat to their position – and they were well aware that their opponents, by and large, would not grant them these benefits were the situation to be reversed. In such a situation it was not difficult to argue that, in order to ensure liberty for all, it was desirable to curb it now for some; that the Workers' State must be saved at all costs. And it was relatively easy to suggest that the quite proper concern with curbing the power of a bourgeois State and safeguarding the liberties of its citizens did not apply when the State was a dictatorship of the proletariat acting in the interests of the great majority of society. It was for these reasons that they sanctioned the existence of a new security force, the Cheka, which applied the concept of revolutionary justice in a crude and primitive fashion. This is something we come back to in a later chapter.

This was the line the Bolsheviks took, and on these grounds they denied their opponents the right of opposition. Those who took the decisions were at least partly aware of the dangers, but they underestimated the extent to which such a stance would make it progressively easier for them both to justify the suppression of any opposition or criticism and to open a way for a future 'irresponsible' government. Once the element of accountability to the people is removed and dissent denied, one important safeguard against the emergence of an arbitrary government acting in its own interests is lost. But, perhaps more important, to act for the people is to deny those basic elements in the democratic ideal – participation by people, creativity, etc. – that one had set out to ensure. What might be recognized by the leaders as temporary expedients, undesirable in themselves but necessary, could well be interpreted (as they were) by those new recruits to the Bolshevik cause as perfectly proper long-term measures. In such a situation much will depend upon the circumstances in which the ruling party finds itself and the way in which circumstances affect the attitudes and behaviour of new recruits to the cause. What we must now look at, is what was happening to the party and the Soviets.

The New Workers' State

When the Second Congress of Soviets met in October 1917, it elected a Central Executive Committee and ratified a new government, the Council of People's Commissars. Delegates to the Congress, it will be remembered, were sent by factories, regiments, and towns. In the country and towns of Russia Soviets were being formed, only to be displaced by Committees of Public Safety (opposed to socialist notions) and then to re-emerge. Some had a Bolshevik majority, some a Menshevik, others an SR. By 1918 the White Army and then the Red swept over the country, putting down resistance, setting up their own supporters, until the next outburst of violence put the opposing side in. Under these circumstances the government could do little more than produce a framework for Soviet democracy which was very far from being realized in practice. Yet it is worth outlining the proposals so we can see how it was meant to work.

In October it had been proposed that the Congress should meet every three months, as part of the notion that people should choose new delegates at frequent intervals. But it was clearly impossible to assemble delegates from all over Russia so frequently, and in 1918 it was decided that the Congress should meet once a year. This Congress should be a united one – peasants and workers. The franchise was both restricted – landlords, industrialists, army officers and priests were excluded – and unequal – the countryside provided fewer representatives per head of population than the towns. The local Soviets – set up by the people in their place of work, or district, or village – should elect delegates to attend regional conferences which in turn elected delegates for the national Congress. This body should pass the laws and elect an Executive Committee which should elect a government (the People's Commissars), and be responsible for legislation when the Congress was not sitting.

Quite what the relationship between the central government and the local Soviets was to be was not clear. In the early days, with their belief in participatory democracy and their desire to end bureaucracy and the rule of officials, the new Commissars tended to see their role as one of laying down general plans or directions by way of guidance, while leaving it to the local organs, the Soviets, to implement them in a creative way. For example, Lunacharsky, the Commissar for Education, thought it sufficient to outline the government's aim on abolishing illiteracy (approximately 80 per cent of the population was illiterate), making education free for all, of whatever age, an education that should combine learning with practice, and develop people's potentiality rather than force instruction upon them. It was then up to local Soviets and schools to create the educational system – not for officials of the Commissariat to give orders and tell them what to do. As can be imagined, it was far from easy to achieve the desired results. The teachers themselves only gradually moved from hostility to acquiescence, and the lack of funds to pay their wages did not help matters. There were hardly any printing presses still at work and very little paper. Local school committees had little idea what they should be doing and could be faced with a popular demand to turn the school-house into a hall so that theatrical performances could be given. Bands of homeless orphans roamed the country in search of food and shelter. The university staff and students harassed the few Bolshevik supporters among the staff and resisted attempts to introduce courses for working-class students. And all the while a civil war was raging.

Using education as an example, we can pick out certain phenomena that affected the new system of government in most aspects of its activity. First, there was a desperate shortage of resources – both materials and men. In their attempt to husband the material resources, to organize their distribution carefully between all the bodies competing for them, and to ensure wide participation in decision-making, departments, coordinating departments, councils, and committees were set up which proliferated to produce a bureaucratic tangle in which no one knew who controlled what. At the same time a job in a government department, party or trade-union organization provided the best guarantee of a ration-card and food. There was no shortage of applicants for jobs and, as might be expected, it was often the old civil servants who now crept back and were taken on because they had at least some 'office' skills. The government apparatus began to swell. As this happened, the number of loyal party members who were needed to take over administrative jobs – overseeing the proliferating organizations, checking on the specialists, coordinating the mushrooming institutions – multiplied. The party itself was changing from being a party of industrial workers to one of administrators – both because those who were industrial workers by profession had now moved into government or party posts and because white-collar personnel were joining the party in an attempt to preserve or obtain a job.

Secondly, the principle that Soviet democracy meant people in their local communities taking affairs into their own hands, creating new forms and methods of social existence without officials ordering and inspecting their lives, began to suffer. For most people during the civil war there was the struggle simply to survive – to find enough to eat, to keep a roof over one's head. For people who were often near starvation, not counting those who did starve in town and country, the tasks of running enterprises (when there were no raw materials), creating new forms of education, amenities to free women from domestic drudgery, and running a community often seemed idle dreams. Even under ideal conditions this would have represented a huge leap forward in social consciousness for people who for centuries had been accustomed to living under Tsarist rule, were illiterate, unaccustomed to taking any but the simplest decisions. This was particularly true of the peasants. Ignorance and apathy further encouraged the tendency for the Red Army and the government to organize for people, to order them. Government and party officials who went on fact-finding expeditions would return depressed and disheartened at the rapidity with which early attempts to effect changes foundered or faded away. Yet, while it is important to refer to this, it is equally important not to forget the enormous amount of initiative, energy, and idealism in the face of tremendous odds, which was displayed by the poor, hungry, and uneducated in trying to organize schools for all ages, women's organizations, children's homes, hospitals, and to end the old inequalities of wealth and privilege.

But under civil-war conditions the local Soviets or trade-union organizations often owed their existence to the Red Army. Too often they became the creation of the victorious army rather than representative bodies chosen by the local community. What seems to have happened is that small executive committees of the Soviets began to replace the larger Soviets as the decision-making bodies (it was a time for action rather than repeated election and discussion) and increasingly these became dominated by those whose loyalty was strongest, in other words, Bolsheviks. In time of war those suspected of possible disloyalty were best excluded. The opposition parties – SRs and Mensheviks primarily – found themselves harried, members arrested and finally forbidden.

This in turn influenced the attitudes and behaviour both of the Soviet 'officials' and of the Red Army. The former began to consider that they occupied their position as a right, became used to taking decisions and giving orders. The Red Army itself, particularly those recruits who fought for the revolution and received their training as party members in its ranks, became accustomed to giving orders, making appointments, crushing any opposition with force. In March 1917 the Bolshevik party had numbered

perhaps 20,000, 60 per cent of whom were industrial workers.
A year later the party had grown to ten times its 'underground'
size. In 1921 it was reckoned that approximately 85 per cent of
the now 700,000-strong party had entered during the years 1918–
21. In other words the overwhelming majority of the party that
now held power and was faced with the task of building a socialist
society out of the ruins left by the First World War and the civil
war had joined after the revolution and received their first experience as party members during the civil war.

The slogan 'whoever is not for us is against us' became, under
civil-war conditions, interpreted more and more crudely. It affected the party's attitude to opposition within the country and
without. The danger of the peoples of the non-Russian Tsarist
lands – the Ukrainians, Georgians, Armenians – making use of
their newly won independence to produce governments hostile
to the Soviet republic (as happened in the Ukraine) turned
'national independence' into 'national independence for the socialist movements' in those countries and finally into support for
those sections of the socialist movements that were Bolshevik.

If, at the bottom, participation, decision-making by the people,
suffocated beneath a network of departmental agencies, over-
worked officials, and a desperate effort to survive, at the top
party and Soviet democracy became more centralized and less
democratic. Initially, it will be remembered, the Congress of
Soviets was to meet frequently and between sessions the Central
Executive Committee was to legislate and see that decisions were
executed. The Council of People's Commissars, the cabinet as it
were, consisted largely but not wholly of Bolsheviks. The Left
SRs held some ministerial posts. As the lower Soviets became
increasingly Bolshevik-controlled, and the other parties were
suppressed, the composition of the Congress became more heavily
Bolshevik and the non-Bolshevik delegates, representing no particular party, less and less important. In itself the Congress as an
institution lost importance. It met once a year, but important
decisions were taken throughout the year and, as the Bolshevik
party began to dominate decision-making more and more at every
level, it was overshadowed by the annual *Party* Congress. The
Soviet Central Executive Committee too began to lose influence.

It grew in size – 300 members in 1920 – was too large and un-wieldy to act as a single decision-making body, itself became increasingly Bolshevik-dominated and, similarly, overshadowed by its counterpart in the *party*, the Party Central Committee. The Council of People's Commissars continued its existence as the government of the country, but by now it was exclusively Bol-shevik and could not really be considered a non-party body. Its leading members were leading party figures – party and govern-ment had become merged into one at the top. But the party organization still kept itself separate. The annual Party Congress elected a Central Committee, which in turn elected smaller com-mittees – the Politburo, Orgburo, and Secretariat – to direct decision-making and organization of party matters. It was here that the most important decisions tended to be taken.

Thus at the top the party and Soviet apparatus to all intents and purposes merged and, as the party began to dominate the Soviets at lower levels in the hierarchy, the Soviets became less important than their corresponding *party* organizations – local committees, regional bodies, up to and including the Party Con-gress and Central Committee. These now became the place where large-scale policy decisions were debated. From henceforth it was the party that reflected the social conflicts, new and old, and the contradictory aspirations of the new society.

Problems and Bolshevik Solutions

What the Bolsheviks were attempting to create was a social and political framework which could both cater for participation in decision-making, initiative from below, and local control *and* produce an allocation and coordination of resources that would meet needs and increase social wealth. This is a formidable task under any circumstances; in Russian conditions of the time it foundered.

In anything but small, self-sufficient communities it is necessary to have some kind of a mechanism which provides for goods and raw materials to get from A to B – for example, from producer to manufacturer to consumer. Simply to maintain current levels of output, there has to be coordination between the different elements involved. The Bolsheviks were faced with a situation where this coordination had broken down and output was well below previous levels. It was essential to provide some overall guidance or direction – which it was felt the workers' committees were incapable of doing – and to raise labour productivity if only to regain the previous level of output. It was with these considerations in mind that the Bolsheviks evolved a national administrative structure and centralized the trade unions, finally opted for greater management control (and began to appoint and train management specialists) and brought the old specialists back with higher pay. This raised two problems: how do we make social control – i.e. by manual workers, the proletariat – meaningful in such a situation and how do we prevent those old distinctions of decision-makers versus others, specialists versus non-specialists, and rich versus poor, re-emerging. The unease felt in the party at the failure of the new methods to remove these distinctions was reflected in the debates of the period. The official answer was that the party, representing the working class and including in its ranks the best elements of that class, would carry out a controlling function and prevent the old distinctions from having their previous undesirable consequences. It was from the ranks of the workers that the new administrators and managers should be drawn and they, endowed with an honest proletarian consciousness, would have the interests of the workers at heart and not develop narrow administrative or specialist interests. Party workers would watch over the old bourgeois specialists. Thus, although formally parts of the administrative or decision-making structure might be hierarchical and exclude collective decision-making by the manual workers, it was rule by the workers because the administrators were proletarian by origin and acted in the interests of the latter. But, although this was the general justification, the leadership was well aware of failures in practice. Hence the attempts to get party workers to return to the bench for a spell as factory workers and the repeated insistence on the need to weed remnants of the old bourgeoisie and petite-bourgeoisie and career-seekers out of the party.

The Bolsheviks were uncomfortably aware of the tendency for a new administrative stratum of decision-makers to emerge and escape from control from below. But their proposed solution – to rely as far as possible on administrators who came from a proletarian background and to set up commissions of workers and peasants to check government activities – was no real answer to the problem. Nowadays it is accepted that in large-scale organizations – be they governmental, party, or private – it is no easy matter to prevent the leadership from becoming oligarchic, removed from its supporters and often independent of them; all too often, despite contrary intentions, the organization becomes bureaucratic, and a hierarchy seems to stamp itself upon the members. This phenomenon was the subject of serious analysis by a few writers of the time (Weber and Michels in particular) but in general attracted little attention. (Although at least one of the Bolshevik leaders, Bukharin, studied Weber's and Michel's work.) Whereas western constitutional theorists ignored it altogether, the Bolsheviks believed that as a phenomenon it was relatively easily overcome. In this they were wrong and they underestimated the way in which the Bolshevik party, for example, as it grew and developed a formal organizational structure with a hierarchy of committees and paid officials could become a party in which the leadership and officials would dominate and limit the influence and participation of the lower bodies.

The Bolsheviks too overestimated the extent to which a person's background is sufficient to fashion the role which he is called on to play. They assumed that to put a worker in a management position would transform the management–worker relationship into one where both pursued or advanced the workers' interests. Not that they were naive enough to believe that the 'personal' factor alone was enough, but they did attach greater weight to it than, again on the basis of what we have learnt since, we would today. We now know that there is a very strong tendency for people to adapt to the roles they are called upon to play: they adjust remarkably quickly to a new environment, and display attitudes and behaviour that accord with their new position. What is less well understood is under which circumstances the job will transform the new incumbent and when, on the contrary, background or past training is going to prove more important. It seems reasonable to suggest that when the role is a firmly established one, set and fixed, it will strongly influence the new incumbent whereas, when it is not clear what the job consists of, the background of the incumbent will be important in determining what the job becomes. If this is true, then one could argue that the Bolsheviks were correct in stressing the importance of proletarian consciousness or background in the years immediately following the revolution, because that was a time when roles, jobs, authority patterns were ill-defined, and when persons would consequently mould or create new roles. It is possible to argue that the Bolsheviks were right in this, but that what they tended to underestimate (although they were aware of and worried by it) was the effect of the civil war on this 'proletarian consciousness' and the pressure that the hostile and unfavourable environment would exert upon those in authority. Here we return to an earlier point: those who graduated from the civil war had served a party apprenticeship which consisted of fighting, giving orders or obeying them, crushing opposition. The 'leather-jackets', as they were called, were ready and able to forge new roles, but not always in the way the leadership expected or hoped for.

In theory the principle that constant criticism and supervision by workers and peasants could keep officialdom and administrative decision-making in check seemed satisfactory. In practice it foundered on two obstacles. First, it is difficult for *ad hoc* bodies to control or oppose decisions from above, especially when it is not easy to find out where decisions originate, since they pass through different instances, bureaux, and departments. Secondly, and probably more important, the suppression of criticism that began with that of the openly hostile right-wing circles and by the end of the civil war included the Mensheviks, SRs – anything that questioned Bolshevik authority in any respect – affected the whole climate in which criticism could be made of government policy and decision-making. In 1921, as was already mentioned, the party itself was split into wrangling factions. Lenin's solution, which was adopted with misgivings as a temporary measure, was to prohibit the organization of factions and to insist again on obedience to decisions once they had been taken. The effect of this was to restrict the circle within which debates were fought out to the leading party organs, and to make it easier for those in lower positions to stifle discussion and criticism at local level by suggesting that it was unconstructive or anti-party policy. On the one hand the leadership was arguing that only criticism, initiative and action by the working people could destroy the bureaucratic features of the proletarian State, on the other it was providing weapons which could be used to prune both healthy and unhealthy growth.

Part Two
Political Change

4 Industrialization and Collectivization

If the main concern of Part I was twofold – to contrast different conceptions of what is a desirable social and political system, and to describe the way in which one attempt to introduce a new social and political order was affected by the circumstances in which the revolutionaries found themselves, by the problem of agreeing on what were appropriate methods to use, and by the foreseen and unforeseen consequences of their actions – in this second part the emphasis shifts to a rather different set of questions. We have already outlined Bolshevik aims: the replacement of private ownership and the market mechanism by cooperation and equality under a system of social ownership and self-government. Now, if we turn our attention to the late thirties, we find not only had the goals not been achieved but, on the contrary, a dictator ruling by means of a large apparatus of officials and coercion, and a combination of policies which – admittedly under a system of social ownership – encouraged and applauded many of those phenomena the Bolsheviks had set out to eradicate. Whereas, for example, the party leadership in the early twenties had reluctantly agreed to wage inequality as a temporary necessity, in the mid-thirties ever-widening differentials were pronounced to be desirable; whereas the growth of the central party and state apparatus had been a subject for concern, by the late thirties it was no longer a topic for discussion. An important question is how or why this should have happened. It is, after all, odd when men's endeavours in one direction produce such opposite results. Our first concern will be with this question and with some of the answers people have given to it. The answers differ depending upon people's views on what it is that determines or influences political and social change. Hence we shall not be attempting merely to provide an answer to one particular case but also to evaluate different approaches to the question of political change.

The Stalinist system itself is a second topic that we shall deal with in some detail. In outlining its features we shall try to show why it deserves to be treated as a political system different from what went before and what comes afterwards. Implicitly or explicitly this raises the question of what is meant by a political system – when, in other words, is it useful or enlightening to contrast structures of power, to call them 'different' and when does it make sense to talk of them as being similar? This question is barely distinguishable from one which asks 'what constitutes political change?' And the answer to this will in turn affect an account of how political change occurs, as we shall see when we look at some different interpretations.

Explanations Past and Present

In 1927 a decision was ratified at the Party Congress to move ahead with the expansion of heavy industry. A five-year plan for the economy was drawn up for the period 1928–33. In November 1929 Stalin (who had emerged from the factional infighting within the leadership after Lenin's death as the dominant figure in the Politburo) gave the go-ahead for widespread collectivization of agriculture. As a result of these two measures (and we shall discuss the relationship between them in a later section), the character of the Soviet economy was changed. By the mid-thirties not only had the remnants of private industry disappeared but the foundations of a gigantic heavy industry, directed and controlled by the State, had been laid; the bulk of the land no longer lay in the hands of individual peasant families but, instead, was the property of either State or collective farms. Social ownership and the industrial transformation of the country had become a reality. This was the revolution from above. Not surprisingly the implementation of such a revolution *from above* entailed the transformation of the central organs of government in whose hands lay responsibility for the social and economic changes. New industrial commissariats or ministries sprang into being, the party apparatus (faced with new tasks of directing, cajoling, and supervising the gigantic industrial and agricultural enterprise) expanded, the NKVD (or secret police) was used in the collectivization campaign to deport perhaps five million 'rich' peasants and their families. All worked according to plan or rather to directives which, covering every facet of social life, emanated from on high. Thus there was now central direction, a burgeoning, centralized administrative apparatus to organize and direct the masses of the people who threw themselves in a frenzy of either enthusiasm or fear into the great struggle to industrialize the country. By 1938 Stalin and the NKVD had sent millions of people – from eminent old Bolsheviks and high-ranking generals to artists, writers, workers, and peasants – to their deaths before firing squads or in labour camps. For two years, 1936–8, the country was subject to mass terror, a terror which then subsided but continued, in a subdued form, until Stalin's death in 1953. From 1936 until his death, the Soviet Union was ruled by a dictator with the help of the NKVD, the party, and ministerial apparatus. The Soviets, debate and discussion, innovation and experimentation, were all dead.

We have now to answer two separate questions. First, how or why was it that by the mid-thirties the Bolshevik party had created a social and political system, so many of whose features conflicted with their earlier ideals or aspirations? Secondly, how can we explain the kind of dictatorial rule, backed by terror, that existed from 1936 to 1953? The second question begs a third: what was the relationship between the decisions of 1927 and 1929 and the Stalinist dictatorship that emerged in 1936? Were dictatorship and terror a necessary or perhaps likely consequence of the industrialization and collectivization campaigns or do they require a separate explanation? Let us look at some of the answers that have gained widespread support.

One common answer has been to deny the need to ask such questions. Towards the end of Stalin's rule both western writers and Soviet theorists tended (for different reasons) to emphasize the continuity of Soviet development from the revolution, through the twenties and thirties, up until the present. It was argued that, although some changes had occurred during the years of Bolshevik rule, they were relatively minor: essentially the system had remained the same. We shall look at these views (which are still held by some today) later on. But first it is worth reminding ourselves that hindsight often bears little relation to perceptions of the time.

Nowadays in the west it is customary to look upon the thirties as the most brutal and horrifying period in Soviet history. The violence associated with the collectivization campaign and then the purges casts a shadow over the decade. Yet at the time opinion in the west was perhaps as favourable to the Soviet Union as it has been at any time, except during the allied effort of 1942-5. It took two major events – the Great Depression and the rise of Nazism – to produce a reassessment of the 'Bolshevik menace' which had been an object of hatred and scorn in the twenties. Now, against the background of mass unemployment, economic chaos, and misery in the west, the Soviet planned economy claimed attention. Both intellectuals and the labour movement were impressed; even business men were fearful. Conditions in the west not only swelled the ranks of the continental Communist parties, and turned more than Clydeside red, but also persuaded the more reformist left-wing parties that they should look to the Soviet Union for solutions.

In addition Nazism appeared as a threat to parliamentary democracy, and one more powerful and nearer home, while the USSR joined the League of Nations (1935) and produced a new Constitution (1936). The United States at last recognized the Soviet government. This is not to say that the governments of Western Europe and America lost their old fears, but rather that Stalin appeared as a more moderate and sensible leader than his revolutionary predecessors. The liberals and labour intellectuals went further: Soviet democracy worked, the new Constitution showed what could be achieved. Beatrice and Sidney Webb, Fabian leaders who had had little sympathy for the revolution, now toured Russia and produced a huge volume, entitled *Soviet Communism: a new civilization*. Both old western specialists, such as Bernard Pares who had been horrified by the revolution, and emigre Mensheviks, such as Dan, became supporters of Stalin and the new regime. The great treason trials of the old Bolsheviks in 1936–8 were accepted by many as proper trials in which the guilt of the accused was proved.

In part the difficulty of getting information – the restrictions on correspondents, the lack of reliable statistics, and the success with which the Purges were hidden – was responsible for the claims made in defence of the Soviet system. But, as in earlier and later periods, this was less important than the wish to believe and the need to fit the USSR into an accepted conceptual framework. Trotsky's attack on the Webbs for producing 'Bolshevism for the Cultural Bourgeoisie', his argument that bureaucracy was producing a society rent by contradictions, and his criticism of the trials in dispatches to the *Manchester Guardian*, fell largely on deaf ears. The desire to see the Soviet system as a viable democratic alternative to the economic and political chaos prevailing in the west was too strong. In one respect Trotsky, the conservatives, and less consciously the moderate left, all agreed – the revolution was over. According to some the early revolutionary ideals had been betrayed; according to others, dangerous utopianism had been replaced by sensible policies. But, however different their evaluation of the present, all agreed that there had been a change and they tended to see the late thirties as a consolidation or continuation of policies adopted at the beginning of the decade.

Inside the Soviet Union itself it was clear to all that the policies of the late twenties and early thirties represented an important change. Again the evaluation of the change varied. For some the 'revolution from above' was creating socialism, for others the twenties became in retrospect a golden age. The events of the late thirties – the Great Purge – provoked plenty of 'unofficial' disagreement, as we shall see when we deal with them in Chapter 5, but by this time the 'official' explanation stressed the continuity between past and present.

Not until Khrushchev's secret speech of 1956 (given at the Twentieth Party Congress but never published in the Soviet Union)[1] did the Soviet leadership admit that certain excesses had occurred under Stalin and that Leninist and Soviet democracy had suffered in the process. Khrushchev made a distinction between Stalin's actions before 1934 and afterwards: Stalin's defeat of Trotsky and then of Bukharin and the Right, during the twenties, and his leadership of the party during the first five-year-plan period and collectivization deserved nothing but praise; it was only after 1934 that his megalomania and suspicious nature led him to make mistakes. Although the Soviet leadership has since modified the criticism, it has never been suggested that Khrushchev was mistaken in his evaluation of Stalin's pre-1934 role. Individual writers and historians may have tried to query some aspects of collectivization or suggest that it contributed to later excesses, but the official line has always been that the decisions of 1927 and 1929 were the right ones; that they were properly implemented and had only desirable consequences. In official eyes, then, developments up until 1934 were a continuation of the revolution; the first five-year-plan years were the Great Construction Period when socialism was built; there was no contradiction between revolutionary ideals and the new social and political order. Hence to the official Soviet spokesman of today our first question is a non-question and, while he would agree that some things went wrong after 1936, he would deny that they were related to or the consequence of the new order that emerged as a result of industrialization and collectivization. His counterpart in the Stalin period would have denied equally vehemently that there was anything wrong with or any real difference between the years before and after 1936 – except in so far that after 1936 socialism was firmly established and everything was better than before. Purges, terror – minor phenomena, exaggerated by hostile bourgeois critics. For him the period 1917 to 1953 had a beautiful unity or progression about it: the revolution flowed into victory in the civil war, the strengthening and cleansing of the party, the spread of Bolshevik ideals which triumphed with the construction of socialism in 1936; despite the adversities of the Second World War, the Soviet people continued to march forward 'along a motor way paved with sugared asphalt'[2] under the wise leadership of comrade Stalin.

As was mentioned earlier it was not only Soviet commentators who, in the late forties and early fifties, saw the Stalin period as the natural outcome of the revolution in 1917. Western writers too, although from a very different point of view, tended to stress the continuity of the Soviet system. The Bolsheviks had come to power, imbued with something called Marxist-Leninist ideology, which drove them to refashion society regardless of the population's desires or needs, to create an industrialized, totally regulated, conformist society in which individual freedom was suppressed. The Stalinist system did not contradict any revolutionary ideals; on the contrary, it embodied them. This approach, still found today in bland assertions of the type 'since the main aim of the Communist elites was the maximization of industrial and military power', shares with its Soviet counterpart a curiously cavalier attitude towards history.[3] It is a convenient attitude of course. It makes the task of explaining events or phenomena much easier if we simply assume that they accord with the intentions of the actors. It is convenient but bad history. A more sophisticated approach, which shares some points in common with the above, but deserves serious consideration is that which suggests there was a natural (although not necessarily conscious) progression from Leninism to Stalinism. This view does not deny that the early Bolsheviks had some 'utopian' ideals (although it skims over what these were in a very cursory fashion) but it argues that the total product-mix of Marxism-Leninism plus the concept of a united obedient party paved the way for the Stalinist dictatorship. Sometimes Stalin as an individual, seeking power ruthlessly and unscrupulously receives most of the blame; sometimes it is suggested that an individual of his type was bound to emerge as leader. Here there is a tendency to concentrate on political forms as the main determinant of future social and political phenomena: a militant revolutionary party will tend to crush all opposition in order to retain power; then, as a single party, unaccountable to the electorate, it will tend to turn into an absolute dictatorship. Not surprisingly this kind of argument is advanced by those who are the staunchest defenders of the 'constitutional' aspects of liberal democracy. Implicit in such a view is the suggestion that we must beware of all militant revolutionary parties because, once in power, they will develop into dictatorships backed by terror.[4]

Recently there has been a shift away from this kind of approach to one which places greater stress on economic and cultural conditions·as determining factors. In the attempt to offer explanations of the political change that occurs in underdeveloped countries as they embark upon 'industrialization', western commentators have outlined certain social, cultural, and political phenomena which (they argue) make up something called the process of 'modernization' and accompany the industrialization and urbanization of an underdeveloped economy. In accordance with this view the Bolsheviks become the 'agents' of modernization, of some almost inevitable social process. They and what they did are seen as 'responses' to a particular stage in social development. 'The comparative study of communist systems must be given a sense of unity through the realization that in communist ideology, party rule and the experience of totalitarian methods of control . . . there is combined a distinct and unique response to *the demands of contemporary society*'[5] (my italics) . . . Their commitment to 'industrialization' plus their 'authoritarian political culture' (itself presumably a product of their environment) was enough to ensure certain consequences.

The trouble with this is that the key concepts are vague. What are 'the demands of contemporary society', what indeed does it mean to talk of the 'demands' of any society? 'Industrialization' is little better. Industry presumably can be developed in very many different ways and forms. Hence to talk of the *necessary* consequences or social and political phenomena that accompany 'industrialization' is unsatisfactory. Either specifically, or rather vaguely, advocates of this and the previous approach are implying the existence of limiting or constraining factors, consequences that follow from certain types of action and, clearly, if one is to pursue any goal, it is important to know what chance it has of being achieved. (Although one may still pursue an unrealizable goal on the grounds that, although it will not be reached, the attempt will improve existing conditions.) Similarly, if one is trying to explain why certain things happened, it is important to look at the relationship between the goals of those concerned, the means they adopted to achieve them, and the circumstances in which they found themselves. But it will not do to prejudge the issue by ignoring or perverting the goals or talking of 'necessary' consequences.

Bearing this in mind let us see if we can explain the Bolshevik decisions of 1927 and 1929 and assess the consequences of those decisions.

Aims and the Environment

To understand the decision of 1927 to embark upon a rapid acceleration of investment in heavy industry, we must begin by remembering why it was that the Bolsheviks were so concerned to change the existing economic structure and what that economic structure was. Socialism, and even more so communism, pre-supposes a level of social wealth sufficient to satisfy men's needs for food, housing, clothing and to provide health, educational, and cultural facilities – in other words a situation in which men, all men freed from material worries, will be able to develop their potentialities. Under communism the abundance of material and social goods will end the need for payment or the distribution of goods according to any other criterion than that of a man's needs or requirements. Marx had argued that the amount of social wealth engendered by advanced capitalism was sufficient to pro-vide the basis for a socialist society. It was clear that the poor countries of Asia and Africa had not yet reached this level of development, but, argued Marxists, the world as a whole was ripe for a socialist revolution. The reason for this was twofold: in the advanced capitalist countries, the existing relations of production were now actually holding back the development of resources; and international trade had made the world one econ-omic unit. In order to free the vast potential for further develop-ment, it was now both feasible and necessary for society to take over the means of production and produce plans to ensure the creation of wealth rather than the present chaotic waste of resources. Since the poor countries formed part of the world-wide capitalist system – they provided raw materials, were affected by world prices and booms or slumps in Europe or America – a socialist revolution in the advanced countries would necessarily affect them, but this time to their benefit. Instead of robbing them, holding back their own attempts to break out of a primitive agricultural system, the experience, resources, and talents of the advanced countries would be at their disposal.

In 1917 in the middle of a war which had swept Europe into a senseless holocaust of destruction and suffering, the Bolsheviks had thought of the October revolution as the spark which would ignite the world socialist revolution and destroy the system which had produced such a terrible war. They had defended their revolution, anxiously awaiting the support of a socialist Europe. Their relative backwardness would not matter once socialism triumphed in the industrial giants to the west. 'Relative' is the key word here. Compared with the countries of Africa and Asia (compared with China in 1949), the Russian empire was not underdeveloped: it was one of the leading industrial countries of the world, with heavy and light industry, an exporter of manufactured goods, with some of the largest and most 'modern' plants in the world. But, as was mentioned in Chapter 1, 80 per cent of the population still lived and worked, in a primitive fashion, on the land. The combination of these two types of production did not produce anything like a level of social wealth which could satisfy even the most basic needs of the population. When the harvest failed, famine followed. The strong arms of the European proletariat and resources from outside would be necessary to overcome the backwardness of the countryside, to develop industry, and thus to provide essential goods and services. In this sense industry was seen as the key to social wealth.

Initially the prospects for a European revolution looked good but by the early twenties the Bolsheviks had to reconcile themselves to being the single socialist survivor in a hostile capitalist environment with no prospect of an imminent revolution. Simultaneously they had to reassess the future of their revolution. They had come to power on the basis of an alliance between the industrial workers and the peasants, or rather by supporting a peasant revolution with the seizure of power by the industrial workers. This was not the kind of socialist revolution expected in the west where the dominant class, numerically, was the industrial workers. In 1921 the party leadership recognized that, although the Red Army had defeated the immediate threat of counter-revolution by the Whites and the allied powers, and had the strength to put down either peasant risings (directed against forced requisitioning) or a Kronstadt rebellion, there was no way in which a devastated economy, lacking the prerequisites for a socialist order – either a highly developed industrial base *or* help from outside – could be transformed administratively into socialism. It was one thing to requisition grain from the peasants if the alternative was the end of the Soviet republic or if it seemed that massive aid from the west would be forthcoming to revolutionize rural life; it was another to continue with such a policy when it became clear that no such help was immediately forthcoming and that industry was dependent upon food from the countryside. Some compromise with the peasants was necessary.

The compromise, already mentioned in the preceding chapter, was the New Economic Policy, or NEP. Requisitioning was replaced initially by a tax on grain, then by the State's purchasing grain at fixed prices. And, as a further stimulus to agriculture, the leasing of land and equipment and the hiring of labour were allowed. In industry the State retained control of all large-scale concerns, but small, primarily light-industry, plants reverted to private ownership. And, most important, private trading was permitted – to provide a mechanism for exchange between town and country: food for the towns, consumer goods for the peasants.

This policy, variously described as a 'breathing space' or 'a temporary retreat', was bitterly resented by some sections of the party. They found it hard to accept the injunction to turn themselves into businessmen, to learn to trade. Even though they might see that there was no alternative at present, it was difficult to accept that after three years' civil war they had to adopt a policy which encouraged those very tendencies – private property, the quick profit, speculation – they had fought to eradicate. They feared the emergence of a new NEP petite bourgeoisie which would care nothing for equality but only for the scarce consumer goods. And it was not difficult, in such a situation, to blame the peasant for endangering the revolution.

Yet what was forgotten here was that without the peasant (both in his army greatcoat as a Soviet delegate and as a peasant woman sacking the lord's manor-house), the Bolsheviks would not have come to power. In this very real sense the revolution was the result of an alliance between workers and peasants, an alliance which gradually broke down, until the Bolsheviks could count on only the poorest peasants as their supporters. It is tempting to suggest, because it simplifies the problem, that in introducing NEP the Bolsheviks recognized the incompatibility of the aims of workers and peasants, that NEP was the recognition of a revolution won by two different classes, whose interests were different, whose attitudes were bound to cause conflict once the old owners had been expropriated. Such an explanation assumes that we know what peasant attitudes were in 1917 and it assumes, furthermore, that the peasant's primary desire was to become a property owner and enrich himself. But it is better to admit, on the basis of the scanty evidence, that peasant attitudes at that time were conflicting, contradictory – all shades of opinion were represented – and that it was not at all clear which were going to dominate. The peasants supported the Bolsheviks against the White landlords, they were with the Bolsheviks in tearing down the edifice of Tsarist officialdom and replacing it with local self-government. Other parts of the Bolshevik programme – education, the attack on religion, equality for women – provoked support and opposition. To talk of the peasantry as wholly conservative, superstitious, interested in private gain, does not fit with their actions during the years of revolution. What we can suggest is that, even in ideal circumstances, it would have been a hard struggle for the peasants to combat the weight of traditional ways and beliefs. Civil-war conditions where Bolshevik authority became synonymous with forced requisitioning, where famine swept the land and peasants were engaged in a desperate struggle for survival, provided an environment in which certain attitudes tended to flourish: the desire to grab and hold on to one's own source of survival, the view of the government as something hostile and alien, the need to live as best one could and not get involved in dangerous matters of politics, to blame fate and appeal to God for help. Without the civil war it is hard to know what would have happened to the alliance between peasants and workers. As it was, it snapped. The peasants now wished to be left alone, to live a little.

The slogan for the party now became 'cooperation with the peasants'. Lenin argued that although at present the aims of workers and peasants were contradictory (the peasant wanted high prices for grain and cheap consumer goods, the industrial worker wanted cheap bread), it should be possible gradually to bring them together, direct them towards a common socialist goal. This involved restoring peasant confidence in the government, a slow process of education, and the gradual introduction of cooperative methods of farming or State farms, by means of which the peasantry would come to see the material advantages of a modern socialist agriculture. Cooperation was essential if industry was to be rebuilt and the Soviet republic to survive. But the problem was that 'cooperation' in fact meant allowing the peasant to live and work as an individual proprietor. Few resources were put into State or cooperative farms (not that there were many to spare in any case) which had no appeal for the peasant who was managing to work his land at all profitably.

During the twenties there was endless debate and disagreement over what was happening in the countryside. It was usual to talk of three categories of peasants: the poor peasant, the middle peasant, and the kulak or rich peasant and to analyse changes in social stratification in these terms. But the interpretation or definition of the terms differed from one specialist or politician to another, which makes it difficult to talk with any confidence of changes in the countryside. It is certainly true to say that the peasantry as a whole did benefit from NEP (i.e. they were living better under it than they ever had done) and probably true that the more prosperous peasants benefited most. But for our purposes the actual situation is less important than the perception of it by party and industrial workers. It was not difficult, with food shortages in the towns, unemployment and insufficient resources for industry, to see the peasant as the main beneficiary of NEP and to accuse the 'capitalist' kulaks of holding the towns to ransom.

So there was a breathing space: a breathing space while the ravages of war were repaired. It took the period from 1921 to 1926 to restore industrial production to its pre-war level. Very little new investment took place. Instead the existing plants and mines, the rolling stock and railways, damaged by war, were being repaired (a much less costly operation) and incomes were being spent on consumption, which encouraged light rather than heavy industry. But even while this was being done, and more particularly once pre-war levels of output had been reached, the question was always present: how can one build an industrial base, without which even basic needs will remain unsatisfied, in an isolated, peasant-dominated society? There was no easy answer to this question, a question which today has become commonplace (although no less difficult to solve) for all those interested in the countries of the Third World, but at the time the Bolsheviks were working in the dark. They were the first government to attempt such a transformation of society and the debates on how to attempt it bring out some of the problems. It is not surprising that in the late fifties the Soviet 'experiment' of the late twenties suddenly became of interest to western academics while the newly independent countries of Africa began to look to the Soviet model of industrialization in their desire to solve the problems of their own backwardness.

By the middle twenties it was clear to the Bolsheviks that the only way to achieve within the foreseeable future a level of social wealth that would satisfy even basic needs was by investment in heavy industry. Heavy industry would provide the power and machinery without which the provision of everyday amenities and the consumer goods industry would crawl forward. Given the international situation, resources for investment were going to have to come from saving. (Despite the government's efforts, credit from abroad was disappointingly small.) To put it crudely, in order to build a heavy-industrial base in such a situation, investment or savings are necessary. Instead of spending all one's income on consumer goods, some must be saved to finance basic industries. The benefits of new coal-mines, dams, steel-mills and blast furnaces are not felt for some time – it will take several years to build them or to build and start production in enterprises making machinery and equipment for other factories – and, in the case of the armaments industry, the consumer never 'consumes' the products. Hence the question arises – how is the 'saving' to be done? It is very unlikely that voluntary saving by the population as a whole is going to provide the answer. If the majority of the population is engaged in agriculture, little 'saving' can be expected from those who can barely make ends meet, while the more prosperous peasants – given a choice between consumer goods now and consumption at some later, indefinite date – are unlikely to choose the latter. The working class which is the only one that might be expected to be willing to tighten its belt is by definition the minority class and hence it is doubtful that its savings will be sufficient. Furthermore it seems unlikely that the working class will be prepared to make these sacrifices without some corresponding effort on the part of the peasantry. The alternative is perhaps to find a tax system which will be acceptable to the peasants. By 'acceptable' is meant one which will still provide them with an incentive to produce more, one from which both government and peasant will benefit. But this is very difficult to devise.

This then is a situation which if left to itself is not going to produce a change in the investment/consumption ratio in favour of investment. The primary producing units, the farms and factories, are not going to come up with an 'answer', nor is a Congress representing all. A government which does decide to go for investment is going to have to rely upon more than voluntary cooperation; it is going to have to take 'unpopular' decisions. If voluntary cooperation is not going to produce the savings and investment in industry, what other measures are, theoretically, possible? These would seem to range from what might be called 'direct coercion' (that is, slave labour, forced requisitioning of agricultural output) to 'indirect coercive or administrative' measures (that is, rationing, taxation, withdrawing resources from consumer production, holding down wages). The question which then arises is: which, if any, of these will produce the desired result? This in turn can only be answered if the 'nature of the desired result' is spelt out. To say 'the creation of a heavy-industry base' or even 'a level of social wealth to satisfy basic needs' is far too vague. One has to be specific and suggest the rate at which investment should be undertaken, the speed at which a heavy industry accounting for x per cent of total output could or should be built, the extent to which present consumption should be held down. The answers to these questions will partly be determined by and will partly determine the methods chosen to achieve the changes. For example, more stringent measures may make it possible to effect more rapid change; the refusal to use them may mean slower growth; the final decision will depend upon an assessment of their feasibility and desirability which in turn will be influenced by views on the relative desirability of rapid and slow growth.

It is not only investment/consumption decisions that are involved. Any structural change in the economy (from one type of production to another) entails changes in the distribution of labour. Again the question arises – how is this to be achieved? (Even in an advanced capitalist economy which underwent a socialist revolution this question would require an answer: there might well still be conflicts between community decisions to make changes and the willingness of individuals to change their occupations so as to effect the changes.) If voluntary cooperation is absent or insufficient, then the other options are to use coercion (the direction of labour), to make a situation sufficiently unpleasant for people to want to move or to use material incentives – wage inequality. Decisions of this kind and indeed the prior decisions on investment and consumption necessarily entail decisions on the mechanisms by which total economic activity should be coordinated. We suggested earlier that the Bolsheviks saw their task to be the introduction of an alternative to the market mechanism because of its irrational and inequitable distribution of goods and resources, and we outlined some of the early disagreements over what was and what was not a 'socialist' alternative. In the discussions and debates of the mid-twenties very little agreement was reached on what was to be the 'alternative'. It was accepted by all that, at some stage, private property in the countryside would be replaced by cooperative farming (although there was no agreement on what type of cooperative farming was best); it was accepted that there would be planning authorities to plan and coordinate the activities of the different economic units. It was clear that, in Soviet conditions, even with the abolition of private property, all the individual units if left alone were not going to produce the desired level of output; hence some aggregate decision-making and a means of ensuring that the primary units acted in accordance with these decisions was necessary. What was not clear was what means were to be used: a hierarchical system of directives (and, if so, in whose hands was authority to lie at the different levels), the use of price and other 'economic' mechanisms, an incentive system?

We have tried to show that to talk of 'industrialization' as though it has one 'form' and must therefore have one particular set of social or political consequences will not do. Equally to talk of a Bolshevik commitment to 'industrialization' as though that explained the kinds of decisions taken at the end of the twenties is a non-explanation. Depending upon the goals, tactics, and methods adopted, 'industrialization' will take quite different forms. That there are problems involved in trying to shift from a predominantly agricultural economy to one with a highly developed industrial base by 'socialist' means with or without help from outside is undeniable. Whether the obstacles are insurmountable without help from outside was one of the questions that occupied the Bolsheviks and one which still requires an answer today. The decision to make such an attempt in isolation certainly reduces the options available but it does not predetermine a particular course of action. As we shall now see, the Bolshevik leadership came up with their own answers.

The Debate over the Way Forward

The relationship between the means of financing investment in heavy industry and the speed at which it should be developed was central to the whole debate. As early as 1923 Trotsky was arguing for an expansion of heavy industry financed by heavier taxation of the wealthier peasants and a curbing of wages for the industrial workers who, he argued, would accept the necessity of such a measure. A start should be made now on the building of a heavy-industry base. This was part of the programme of what came to be known as the Left Opposition. He was defeated by a majority of the Politburo. The introduction of such a policy at that time, it was argued, would endanger the still fragile links that had been forged between industry and agriculture, and between party and peasants. The way to move forward for the time being was by providing the peasants with the incentive of consumer goods which would encourage grain production and the development of the agricultural sector; this would provide food for the towns, an increasing supply of raw materials for industry, and a steadily larger surplus to be exported in return for industrial goods. Any such tax measures would reawaken old hostilities which would make it more difficult to encourage participation in cooperative farming and, as important if not more so, would act as a disincentive to produce. Bukharin, at this time and for the next two or three years, was the strongest advocate of the 'slow-growth' policy, symbolized in his famous statement 'riding into socialism on a peasant nag'.

Theoretically it would have been possible to continue in this way – relying on peasant consumption to stimulate light industry, with heavy industry developing slowly in its wake – but such a policy meant delaying, if not endangering, a future socialist order. To creep slowly forwards would take decades. This had several disadvantages. First, the longer NEP was left in operation, the stronger it was feared the peasantry would become and the greater their attachment to private property. A class of sturdy individual peasant proprietors would be a threat to the revolution. Secondly, to rely on imports from abroad for heavy industrial goods had serious drawbacks. The goods had to be paid for and the amount of grain the government had available for export was small; even had the government the money to spare, to rely upon hostile capitalist countries for basic industrial commodities was an un-attractive proposition. The international situation was yet another factor which told against leaving heavy industry to develop slowly. The Soviet Union was in no position to defend herself against the military might of the capitalist powers; to guard against attack from outside, the armaments' industry must be built up.

As can be imagined, as NEP continued and particularly by 1926 when pre-war levels of output had been reached, these kinds of arguments began to carry more weight. We have already referred to the antipathy felt towards NEP by many in the party. This was not the kind of society they had fought to achieve, either in terms of class relationships or the material and social well-being of the population. NEP did not provide the resources for a decent standard of living, for schools, housing, leisure and culture facilities, and what there was was unequally distributed. The desire for change and nostalgia for the civil-war period grew. At the same time the party had grown in size, primarily from an influx of industrial workers. These new recruits, crash-coursed through an elementary programme on Marxism, had little time for brilliant theoretical debates. They had grasped that the October revolution had established a dictatorship of the proletariat, but one which was slow in bearing fruit; there was unemployment in the cities, the standard of living was no better than in Tsarist times while some – new and old officials, the NEP-men or private traders, and the peasants – were benefiting.

By 1927 the party leadership, Bukharin included, had decided that a change should be made: a definite commitment to heavy industry. At the Party Congress of that year it was agreed that the five-year plan should incorporate this. Investment was to increase by 150 per cent during the period 1928–33. Finance would be needed both for the materials for the new projects and to pay the larger industrial labour force, for whom additional food would be required. It was hoped that rationalizing and reducing costs within the industrial sector, issuing state bonds (that is, borrowing money from the population), raising taxes for the wealthiest peasants, and a small shift to collectivized agriculture would provide the finance; and more food for the towns from a more efficient agriculture.

In the spring of 1928 it became clear that there were difficulties ahead. After a bad harvest the amount of grain that the government had managed to buy from the peasants was less than that of the previous year. It was going to be hard enough to feed the towns, let alone have any in reserve. It was at this point that Stalin introduced or raised the possibility of financing industrial investment by rather different means. Accompanied by a few supporters, he set off for Siberia and, backed by army units, used direct force to squeeze the harvest out of the peasants. Grain was collected at gun-point, wealthy peasants were expropriated for hoarding supplies, and Stalin returned to face a censure from the full Politburo. These, it was agreed, were emergency measures, not to be repeated. But the question of how the government was to meet its commitment to the programme for industrial development, which was already underway, had to be squarely faced.

Stalin argued that the peasants must pay part of the cost, they must pay a 'tribute' to industrialization. Everyone recognized that the situation as regards grain procurements (the amount the government bought at state prices annually from the peasants) was unsatisfactory: even during the good years of NEP the government had been unable to build up reserves; each year there was anxiety whether there would be enough to feed the towns. Now Stalin produced figures which suggested that, although gross output of grain had reached pre-war levels, the amount that the State managed to buy from the peasants was less. In other words he suggested that, although the grain was there, the peasants were refusing to part with it (they were living better while the industrial workers suffered). Furthermore, under the old regime, it had been the large estates which had sold the highest percentage of their produce; now that there were small individual proprietors, less was being put on the market; it was the collectives and State farms who marketed the highest percentage of produce. Hence, he argued, if the structure of landownership could be changed from one of small owners to large collective farms, equipped with machinery, agriculture would become more productive and more would be sold to the State. The original plan of collectivizing 15 per cent of sown area by 1933 should be revised upwards and simultaneously the kulaks, the wealthy peasants, who were hoarding grain and selling at high prices when it was scarce, should be taxed much more heavily. Even the middle peasants, the relatively prosperous, should contribute by increased taxation.[6]

The Right, led by Bukharin, argued that the problem of grain procurements could be solved by raising the State prices for grain. They suggested that an important reason for the government's difficulties was that the price for grain had been lowered which made it less profitable for the peasant to sell. If prices were raised, more grain would be forthcoming. They agreed that the kulaks should be taxed but insisted that to tax the middle peasants would alienate the bulk of the peasantry. Such a policy would mean an end to Lenin's 'cooperation with the peasantry'. Collectivization must be attempted with caution and there must be no repetition of the Siberian methods which were a regression to the period of the civil war, the wounds of which NEP had barely healed. Socialism could not be built by force.

Although Bukharin was right in criticizing the government's price policy as an important factor in keeping procurements low, it is doubtful that his suggested raising of the price could have solved the problem of financing heavy industry. Higher prices for grain would have meant more food for the towns and perhaps reserve stocks; they would have also meant more money in peasant pockets to be spent. Unless the output of consumer goods was increased to meet this demand (and the emphasis in the plan, it will be remembered, was on putting resources into heavy industry), there would be more money chasing the available consumer goods which would push their prices up, and the peasant would be no better off than before. The following year he would view the new 'higher price' as no better in real terms than the original one. Only if the government could persuade the peasant to save some of his increase in income, or tax him in such a way that he still had an incentive to produce more, would the policy work. Unfortunately it was clear that State bonds were going to bring in very little money, and as already mentioned it is extremely difficult to devise incentive tax systems for peasants.

The Campaigns Themselves

While the arguments continued, the pace of industrialization quickened. Those in favour of a more rapid advance suggested that the targets laid down in the first variant of the five-year plan were too modest and could be exceeded. Targets were pushed up, projects started on little more than basic raw materials and unskilled labour with shovels. A fever of speed, output, results began to spread from one sector of society to another. The trade-union leadership watched this development uneasily. It was true that unemployment was disappearing but management was interpreting the emphasis on investment as a signal to halt wage increases (which was causing unrest at shop-floor level) and, against union opposition, management was pressing for greater wage differentiation between skilled and unskilled. Legislation on safety and working conditions was conveniently forgotten in the desperate attempts to meet or beat plan targets. It was not only in industry, in the planning and party offices that this output fever took hold. The writers' and artists' organizations were calling upon the party leadership to give them social directives, a five-year plan for the arts in the Great Construction period; in all circles there were those who raised the old civil-war cry 'whoever is not with us is against us'.

It was against this kind of background that the debates of the top were fought out, and Bukharin and the trade-union leadership – the moderates as we can call them – were outmanoeuvred and defeated. In the spring of 1929 Stalin again resorted to 'emergency measures' to bring in the grain, and by April the Bukharin group was excluded from decision-making. The trade-union leadership was replaced by one which was willing to give its whole-hearted support to the industrialization drive.

It does not seem that Stalin was convinced of the feasibility of an all-out collectivization campaign until the autumn, but the expeditions and the defeat of Bukharin indicated that he could get support for using force if necessary, and several pilot schemes to persuade peasants to join collective farms were carried out during the summer. (Under the collective-farm system, as opposed to other forms of cooperative agriculture, the peasant household joined by putting in its land, livestock, and any heavy equipment; these then became the collective property of all the participants, who were meant to elect a chairman and administration. The family kept its house and implements.) By November Stalin had decided. In a speech, which was interpreted as a call to action, he claimed that the middle peasant (that is, the solid bulk of the peasantry) was joining the collective; here lay the solution to the economic problems. As a result, a campaign was waged throughout the country by party officials, backed by the NKVD and army where necessary, to create the collectives. The campaign sent perhaps five million kulaks and their families to their deaths or to Siberia, and transformed the countryside once again. But in March 1930, with more than half the peasant households collectivized, Stalin called a halt. Peasant opposition, expressed in the slaughter of livestock and a refusal to work once within the collective, meant that agricultural production was going to be seriously affected. Somehow the spring sowing had to be done. Local officials were blamed for 'excesses' and peasants allowed to leave the collectives. By June less than a quarter of peasant households remained in the collectives. However, the principle of mass collectivization in the near future was not discarded. Thereafter the campaign was renewed, more cautiously, and by 1934 90 per cent of peasant households either belonged to collective farms or worked in State farms.

Meanwhile industry was being built. The original targets had long since been thrown to the winds and with them went the hoped for coordination between resources, output, consumption, and the size of the labour force. The industrial labour force, swollen far beyond what had been planned by the influx of urban unemployed, women and peasants from the countryside, trebled during the period 1929–35. This destroyed the original consumption targets. It was not until the mid-thirties that grain supplies began to rise, and the disastrous slaughter of livestock at the beginning of the collectivization campaign affected meat and milk production. 1932 was a year of famine in the countryside and hunger in the towns. Meanwhile resources intended for light industry and for agricultural equipment were swallowed by voracious heavy industry. Out in the steppes vast dams, blast furnaces, steel mills – whole new settlements were springing up; in the old established centres big industrial combines were growing from old. Both industrial labour and the peasantry were paying for industrialization by being forced to tighten their belts and work long exhausting hours in poor conditions.

We suggested earlier that there are several different aspects to an 'industrialization' process and so far we have dealt primarily with that of financing the new investment. Another (which bears on the nature of a socialist society) is the organization of the production process, something which itself has many different aspects. In agriculture the market mechanism had been destroyed; through a mixture of coercion and persuasion, the central authorities had produced a network of State and collective farms which now had to work as productive units. Faced with peasant hostility, apathy, and bewilderment, the State took on responsibility. The State farms operated in the same way as industrial enterprises: they were granted certain resources, given output targets, and the labour force was paid fixed rates. The produce went to the State. The collective farm was ostensibly a self-governing unit, responsible for managing its own affairs, except in so far as it received an output quota from the higher authorities. This it had to meet before it could dispose of any remaining produce. It was responsible for its own investment, upkeep, seed, etc. and for any payments to its members. Thus in one sense it retained control over its own affairs but this was severely limited by the higher authorities' control over what it produced (in the form of planned quotas) and by its reliance on the State for the use of heavy machinery kept in neighbouring 'machine-tractor stations'. In a very real sense the State 'took over' agriculture.

In industry the control authorities were responsible for planning and directing the movement of resources. The form this took was the following. The leading party bodies – the Politburo in particular – made the major policy decisions on the direction the economy was to take and the methods to be used. A central planning agency was responsible for drawing up an economic plan which spelt out the combination of the different resources necessary to achieve the general targets. As we have already mentioned, the first five-year plan was replaced by a new more ambitious plan which, given the unforeseen consequences of collectivization and the fever which gripped the country, itself soon became meaningless. When in 1933 Stalin declared that the five-year plan had been completed, this was true only in one sense. The output targets for much of heavy industry had been achieved (and in some cases surpassed) but the planned relationship between inputs and outputs, between consumption and investment, between heavy and light industry, between the size of the labour force and goods produced, had gone by the board. Henceforth the Soviet Union has had what is often referred to as a 'planned economy'. It is more enlightening to say that it has had one particular type of a planned economy. One can imagine an ideal type of planned economy in which the economic activities of all the units are carefully coordinated to produce an exact, desired pattern of outputs; in such a situation, there would be no room for exceeding targets, or rather to do so would be a crime since it would throw the whole delicate mechanism out. Planning in the Soviet Union has (for obvious reasons) never even approximated to this. The kind of system introduced by the first five-year plan was much more limited.

The central planning agency drew up a plan, specifying the relationship between major items – investment, consumption, agricultural and industrial output, labour and wages – in accordance with the general policy line decided on by the political authorities, and then, within this framework, attempted to produce plans for the most important industrial sectors. Even here, and still more for the less important sectors, the estimates of the necessary inputs for the required output were crude. Now a mechanism was needed to translate these plans into activity on the part of the producing units themselves. That which was introduced – although introduced is not quite the right word because it implies something which is the result of a conscious, premeditated decision – was a curious mixture. One important feature was the use of 'administrative methods': direction became a keyword, direction from above. Orders were issued, to be implemented without question; failure meant at the least demotion, at worst arrest for counter-revolutionary activity. The old commissariats remained, but they were now joined by new industrial commissariats (or ministries) responsible for different sectors, often headed by leading party men. To them fell the task of breaking down the overall plan for their sector, and issuing plans to the enterprises under their control. Here then was a hierarchical system of central authorities issuing directives, appointing personnel, and responsible for the activities of their subordinate units. With the proliferation of government departments – industrial ministries, ministries responsible for labour, finance, transport, construction – competing for resources and for jurisdiction over the affairs of enterprises and plants, the load upon the party apparatus increased. Not only was the party apparatus, a strong centralized organization, called upon to lead the industrialization drive but it also received the task of coordinating the activities of the different units, adjudicating between them, and finding remedies for failures. Increasingly the party apparatus, itself growing, became the single clear line of authority to the centre. In these circumstances the Soviets withered away.

This was incompatible with autonomy of decision-making at the work-place. The manager, appointed from above, became the executor of a plan issued by the higher authorities. He in turn rejected the participation of trade union or workers' representatives in decision-making as unnecessary interference. It will be remembered that in 1929 the hesitant trade-union leadership had been replaced by one willing to work wholeheartedly for the achievement of plan targets. Equal wages, wage rises, safe or healthy working conditions all became of secondary importance: a luxury to be forgone for the present. The task now was to transform the enormous, new, raw, unskilled labour force into an industrial labour force, capable of increasing productivity. Different methods were adopted. Again there were administrative methods, bordering on coercion: the direction of some peasant labour, stringent penalties for absenteeism, lateness, sleeping on the job, and drunkenness, the whittling away of workers' rights (granted in the early twenties) and trade-union rights. Simultaneously material incentives were introduced as an important means of achieving the required distribution of the labour force, raising the skills of the labour force, and improving productivity. Wage equalization, something the unions had fought for in the twenties, was denounced by Stalin in 1931. Wage differentiation – of all kinds – was a proper socialist tool; payment must be in accordance with the value of the work done. What this meant was that those working in key industries – coal-mining, steel, machine-building – were to be paid higher rates than those in the less essential or less 'socially valuable' consumer industries, and hence labour would be attracted to those sectors. Furthermore, within each industry, rates were to be related to skills with the highly skilled receiving substantially more than the unskilled, thus providing an incentive to the individual to improve his qualifications. And, in addition, a graduated piece-work system was to be introduced wherever possible to provide an incentive to individuals to increase their output, to raise productivity per man-hour. Thus an incentive system came into existence alongside a hierarchical administrative system as a means of ensuring that resources were distributed in accordance with the policy-makers' objectives.

It was not only in industry that hierarchical administration, specialization, and differentiation became hall-marks of the new order. Whereas the early Soviet leadership had tried to stress the importance of people undertaking many different activities, and the breaking down of barriers between different aspects of social life (people should be workers, poets, soldiers simultaneously; education should be wide, embracing all types of activity and synthesizing them; decision-makers should return to the bench; all should take turns in administration, etc.) there was now a quite different emphasis. Professionalization, the acquiring of a particular skill, and a particular place in an organization devoted to a specific end with its own hierarchy became institutionalized. The writers were organized into a single union – their job was to write, just as the task of all those in the steel industry was to produce steel. Education was the business of the teachers; defence lay in the hands of professional armed forces. Occupations were institutionalized and each had its own graded hierarchy, with its own system of income differentiation. It was no longer the task of the individual to concern himself with the different facets of social life; he had his own particular job to do.

The description of the ways in which a new social and economic order came into being would be incomplete without mention of what we can call 'moral incentives' as opposed to material incentives. The dissatisfaction felt by many in the party with NEP, the desire for 'positive' change, and the clamour raised by a vociferous wing of the intellectual community for direction from above were instrumental in persuading the leadership that drastic measures were feasible. Equally the acceleration of change, the adoption of higher and higher targets cannot be understood without reference to the enthusiasm and conviction of this vocal group that socialism could be built and built rapidly by the Soviet republic on its own. Countless party enthusiasts threw themselves with enthusiasm and fervour into the 'second revolution' which would forever remain with them as the greatest and most exhilarating period of their lives. But its appeal was not limited to party youth, nor even to youth alone. Some former oppositionists (supporters of Trotsky, and Zinoviev and Kamenev in their unsuccessful campaigns for an industrialization programme in the mid-twenties) came out in support, foreign socialists and even emigres came back to help. Consciously or unconsciously Stalin had the ability to lead the campaign in such a way that he could capture the support of different sections of the community. For those at the top, party intellectuals and activists old and new, there was the claim that collectivization would not only provide the State with a steady supply of grain but would produce a modern mechanized agriculture which would be much more productive and bring for town and country alike a rise in living standards. The horrors of collectivization appalled some but once begun, they could argue, it was best completed and then the positive consequences would be apparent. It was the civil war again but a civil war which would result, not in a devastated economy, but in, at last, a material base of a socialist kind: heavy industry and cooperative agriculture under social ownership.

On a less intellectual level, by emphasizing that the Soviet republic was facing a crisis, a crisis engineered by the kulaks who were growing rich at the expense of the workers, Stalin fanned old hostility towards the peasant, provided a scapegoat for present ills, and held out the promise of a better future without the kulak. It was not only the peasant who became a useful target. The dislike and hostility felt towards bourgeois specialists (whether in industry or the arts) and even towards some older party intellectuals by the new aggressive party activists and intellectuals was expressing itself in strident tones by the end of NEP. Stalin attacked the bourgeois specialists (thus ensuring the support of the new group in the party), who found themselves accused of sabotage in industry or anti-Soviet interpretations in art and the social sciences. Not only did they provide a convenient scapegoat for current failings, but, it was made clear, they must either accept the Great Construction period and its imperatives or they would suffer. However, they were welcome to participate, and they would be rewarded handsomely if they did. By 1930 Stalin was claiming that what the party needed was 'the best representatives' of each social class or group – all were needed in the great campaign. This was the beginning of a policy, continued ever since, to recruit administrative, professional, and skilled personnel into the party instead of relying upon party watch-dogs to control their activity. Party membership jumped from one and a half million in 1929 to three and a half million in 1933. Despite what has just been said, worker representation in the party was higher than at any other time in the Soviet period: 65 per cent of party members were workers by origin in 1932, 43 per cent were still workers by occupation. This was the consequence of a 'worker-recruitment' drive in the latter half of the twenties and the overall expansion at the beginning of the thirties.

The tasks of running and organizing the social transformation of the country meant that there was room to absorb the new, the up-and-coming, and yet a need to retain all the skilled personnel available. This was the objective situation which made the different policies possible. But what was remarkable was Stalin's achievement in phasing them in such a way that he met the demands for an attack on bourgeois specialists and intellectuals while simultaneously absorbing them into a new administrative elite. Now all were paid more and all were party men.

As part of the campaign to attract all and sundry from the youth to the emigres, Stalin emphasized, somewhat cautiously at first, a grand vision of *Russia*. It is worth contrasting two quotations, one from Lenin and one from Stalin, in which we can see how a basic idea has subtly acquired a new emphasis.

Lenin (1922): Russia cannot be saved only by a good harvest in a peasant economy – or only by the good condition of light industry which supplies articles of consumption to the peasantry – that also is not enough; *heavy* industry is indispensable ... Heavy industry needs subsidies. Unless we find them we are lost as a civilized state – let alone as a socialist state.

Stalin (1931): One feature of the history of old Russia was the continued beatings she suffered ... All beat her – for her backwardness: for military backwardness, for cultural backwardness, for political backwardness, for industrial backwardness, for agricultural backwardness. She was beaten because to do so was profitable and could be done with impunity ... Do you want our socialist fatherland to be beaten and lose its independence? If you do not want this, you must liquidate our backwardness . . .[7]

Stalin conjures up old Russia by repetition of the verb 'beat' (the knout or whip symbolized serfdom to many); he recalls the defeats she suffered as a national power, introduces the word 'fatherland', and suggests that *Russia* could again suffer defeat and become a subjugated nation. In this way he plays upon patriotic feelings. Again it was no coincidence that some, of different political opinions, who had opposed the revolution and either emigrated or remained as domestic 'emigres in spirit' now renounced their earlier opposition and returned to play their (often tragic) part in creating a new and powerful Russia. Simultaneously Stalin stressed the danger of the capitalist threat: the Soviet Union must build up its military strength, surrounded as it was by hostile regimes. But this was accepted by almost all – Right and Left – and had been an important factor in the decision of 1927.

Another Look at the Causes

We began this chapter by asking how it was that a party should have embarked upon a course which resulted in a social and political order so different from that spelt out in its original programme, and we referred to some commonly held explanations. In the preceding section we have tried to show that the answer does not lie in something called 'Marxism-Leninism' nor in 'a commitment to industrialization'. If one looks at the different solutions put forward by leading Bolsheviks during NEP, their attempts to grapple with the problems facing them, and the seriousness with which the arguments were conducted, it is clear that all 'Marxism-Leninism' provided them with was a framework of analysis which stressed the interconnection of economic, social, and political relationships and a conviction that some attempt must be made, at some point, to move towards a system of social ownership and a more industrialized economy. We have also tried to show that a 'commitment to industrialization' is, in itself, a meaningless phrase and that there was nothing predetermined about the actual decisions taken by the Soviet leadership nor the means they adopted to achieve their aims.

The consequences of adopting such policies and methods will be treated in the following chapter but one or two points remain to be made before we leave the campaigns themselves. In an earlier section we suggested that in certain circumstances the choice of particular goals limits the methods available for achieving them. For example, if one wishes to raise labour productivity when resources are limited, some division (or specialization) of labour is an obvious method or, to take another example, if the re-allocation of labour is necessary to achieve a desired output and coercion is unacceptable while moral incentives are not sufficient, then it is difficult to find an alternative to the use of material incentives. It is one thing to say this, it is another to conclude that a particular pattern of specialization or wage differentiation which was in fact introduced has therefore been 'explained' or was to be 'expected'. Just as the term 'industrialization' needs to be given a content before any conclusions can be drawn as to its consequences, so do terms such as 'functional differentiation', 'specialization', and 'differentiation'. This point needs to be made because of the unfortunate tendency on the part of certain 'modernizers' to talk as though there exists a 'natural' process of industrialization which entails an 'increasing' degree of functional differentiation, specialization, etc., and to assume that a particular level of productivity or GNP per capita could only have been achieved with the existing pattern of differentiation. It is only true that 'industrialization' is accompanied by these phenomena if the term is defined so as to include them, but then of course they cannot be consequences. Furthermore it might well be possible to have a higher level of productivity or GNP per head by decreasing the extent of wage differentiation or functional differentiation that exists in a society at a particular time; similarly, better results might well have been achieved in the Soviet Union in the period in question had there been less reliance on these methods.

All we can say is that the Soviet leadership seem to have assumed that specialization and wage differentiation were appropriate methods for obtaining a certain pattern of output, and that the greater use of them, the greater (correspondingly) would be the returns. This attitude – that, if a particular method can be shown to have certain consequences, a more extreme variant will produce even better consequences (which does not follow) – seems to mark all the policies of the period. It is not simply that the Soviet leadership used coercion, the issuing of directives down a centralized hierarchical apparatus, material incentives and moral incentives, but that in all cases the form these took was extreme. We have tried to indicate the nature of the problems facing the leadership and the pressures which led to their adopting a combination of these different measures. But one can still be surprised that they were adopted so completely. To understand this we have to return to the party and the party leadership as it had become by the late twenties.

This brings us back to the argument that a militant, centralized party, which allows no opposition, will 'lead' to a dictator and extreme policies and that, in this sense, Stalin's actions over the five-year period were not unexpected, perhaps even the natural outcome of 1917. Hopefully the foregoing analysis has shown that such a view is far too simple. It is true that the kind of political situation which had come into being by the late twenties was one which allowed for extreme actions on the part of the leadership, but there was nothing inevitable about such a situation or about the actual decisions taken. The infighting between Lenin's heirs – Trotsky, Zinoviev, Kamenev, Bukharin, and Stalin – that marked the twenties and the way in which it was conducted had serious consequences for party democracy. All were guilty (from fear of splitting the party and from a certain arrogant assumption that it was for the party to follow where they might lead) of trying – until it was too late – to keep discussion limited to those at the top of the party; all tried to smear each other with past misdemeanours; each tried to claim the mantle of Lenin and helped in the creation of a Lenin cult. It was this lack of agreement at the top, this inability to agree upon solutions, that made it possible for Stalin, the man who took care to build up a party machine of supporters, to defeat the others and gain support for a policy which promised change at last. It was not that a centralized party with a militant ideology led to a dictator and collectivization; on the contrary it was the infighting within the party, the hesitancy over what to do, that made the emergence of a single leader, with a centralized apparatus, possible and brought support at last for almost any policy as long as it promised a way out of the present standstill. Support for Stalin there certainly was and it was not restricted to docile followers or unscrupulous careerists, as is sometimes implied. Men at the top who at a later date opposed him, when they had far more to lose, were staunch supporters of the industrialization and collectivization campaigns, and this excitement spread right down the ranks.

5 Stalinism

In 1934, the year of the Seventeenth Party Congress, the party existed as the organization which had directed and controlled the huge campaigns of the previous five years. The Congress, hailed as the Congress of Victors, was the occasion for this powerful organization to celebrate its achievements and decide on the future. It was the unquestioned authority in society and Stalin, its leader, owed his position to the strength of the party.

Five years later, the Eighteenth Party Congress was held. Only fifty-nine of the delegates had participated in the Seventeenth Congress. Of the 1,966 delegates to that Congress 1,108 had in the meantime been arrested. Seventy per cent of the Central Committee (or ninety-eight persons) elected at the previous Congress had been arrested or shot. And, of the seventeen newcomers to the Politburo during the years 1926–37 (that is, those who had been the staunchest supporters of Stalin's policies) seven had been liquidated by 1939; four more were to die in the next two years. In effect the leading core of that victorious party which had celebrated in 1934 had been destroyed. And with the destruction of personnel went its power. Formally the party was as before the dominant political authority in society. In reality its position had been undermined by the secret police. Now Stalin stood above the party, a dictator who could use it as an instrument of rule when he wished, or ignore it.

Not until 1952 was another Party Congress called and that Congress met in an atmosphere of fear. Reconstruction had been completed: the devastation caused by the Second World War had been repaired and the economy rebuilt. Yet the Congress did not convene to discuss new policies. The ageing dictator, more suspicious than ever, was surrounded by lieutenants whose fear paralysed their ability to formulate policy. Policy directives came from Stalin, and Stalin had nothing new to offer, unless it were another purge. The newly elected Politburo and Central Committee had no collective authority. They were merely collections of individuals who, fearful for their own future, sought safety in praising Stalin and carrying out the policy of the moment.

Important as the use of police power was in making Stalin an unchallengeable dictator and keeping him in that position, Stalinism meant far more than that. Stalin's rule from 1936 to 1953 was associated with a certain kind of policy and a certain kind of policy-making process. To put it crudely, the short-term aims and methods of the first five-year plan and collectivization became transformed or sanctified into correct policies to be repeated year after year. Discussion of policy alternatives ceased. A large, fragmented, bureaucratic apparatus, devoted to the completion of tasks set from above, emerged. And at the top stood Stalin, around whose person and deeds a cult developed that elevated him far above the ranks of ordinary mortals. This kind of policy and ordering of society became not merely a stage in the Soviet republic's path to communism, the consequence of its unique position and social development, but something of universal application to be imitated by any country which aspired to socialism.

In this chapter our task is to analyse the Stalinist system as it existed from 1936 to 1953 and to try to see how it was related to the campaigns of the first five-year-plan period. One great difficulty in dealing with the period is the paucity of materials – the lack of reliable statistics and the absence of any serious internal analysis of economic, social, and political phenomena. In this respect, as in many others, it is very different from the twenties. But let us begin by saying what we can on the consequences of the 'revolution from above'.

Social Consequences of the Revolution From Above

Although the Seventeenth Party Congress was ostensibly a victory celebration, it was in effect the swan song of the Bolshevik party. We shall argue that the kind of social and economic order, brought about by the industrial and collectivization campaigns under the aegis of the party, undermined or at least posed a serious threat to its continued existence. This is not to say that Stalin's destruction of the party as the central political authority in society was 'inevitable' or even the most likely result; it is to say that it is difficult to imagine the existing political structure continuing unchanged.

The means used during the first five-year-plan period – coercion, centralized direction of the economy by means of different hierarchies, specialization, and differentiation – had the effect of splitting society vertically and horizontally. Ostensibly, taken together, they coordinated social activities; in fact they did nothing of the sort – they pitted sector against sector, unit against unit. Let us look at this from a number of different angles. Targets in heavy industry had been met or surpassed but at the expense of consumer goods, agricultural investment, and the standard of living in town and country. Stalin had argued for collectivization on the grounds that it would (a) ensure the State a steady supply of grain (b) raise agricultural productivity by the introduction of mechanized farming and therefore (c) make a better life possible for the peasants. Unfortunately the force with which it was effected and the subsequent emphasis on the priority of heavy industry meant that only the first of these aims was realized. Collectivization provided the government with a steady supply of grain for the towns (and even that only after a famine of horrifying proportions) but not a more productive agriculture nor a better life for the peasants. The investment required to provide mechanical equipment, fertilizers, farm buildings, and roads was swallowed up by heavy industry. Since it was short of grain, the government simply took all there was to be had, thus depriving the peasantry of any incentive to produce more – even had they so desired during the first years of shock and bewilderment following collectivization. Thus, instead of being aided by a highly productive, prosperous agriculture, the State found itself directly responsible for organizing and managing a poverty-stricken, backward peasantry.

While agriculture lagged, industry forged ahead but this in itself was not a smooth process. It was not simply that heavy industry advanced while light industry stood still but that within industry the contrasts between administrators and workers, and within the ranks of the workers themselves, sharpened. A new stratum of management personnel, engineers, designers – hastily trained but well paid – emerged, as did a thin layer of skilled and 'shock' workers. These were the privileged, beneath them – given the influx of new unskilled labour and the shortage of machines, instruments, and tools – was a mass of unskilled, uneducated workers, earning low wages. Not only was sector competing against sector for scarce resources; not only were divisions being created within the work-force but also the administrative and incentive system set the lower units in each hierarchy against the top. Those at the top – the commissariats and departments – had to spread scarce resources between the enterprises under their jurisdiction; they wanted results in terms of output. The enterprises found themselves engaged in an endless battle to get more resources out of their commissariats or a reduction in output targets. At the top the commissariat and departmental chiefs were simultaneously engaged in a struggle against each other – to get more resources for their individual branches, to stake claims for labour, transport facilities, or energy. They had to devote their energies to their own particular branch – judged as they were by its success – regardless of the effect their activities might have upon the rest of the economy. Instead of industry advancing with agriculture, instead of one industrial sector complementing another, they were torn apart and benefited at each other's expense.

We have already mentioned, in the last chapter, how this division of activities was not restricted to the economic sphere, how the different professions – teachers, writers, soldiers – became institutionalized with their own hierarchies and reward systems, again under centralized control. Here too their function was narrowed to that of carrying out a specialist task, decreed from above: to write a certain type of book, to teach a specific curriculum.

Their Effect on the Party

This kind of 'sectionalization' of society – both in terms of social activities and social groups – that was occurring placed the party under strain. It was intended that the party, as a centralized organization with branches in all types of institutions, should be the body to supply the necessary direction and coordinate the activities of all the separate units. It, containing the best representatives of the different social groups, was to be the architect of the building and the cement to hold it together. But the problem was that the different party bodies were subject to the sectional pressures existing in society; nor was it clear whether there was a policy which could reconcile the interests of the different elements. Materials on the history of the party in this period are few and far between but we can try to piece together the scraps that do exist to show the way in which the party was affected.

The demands that each sector meet its target, and the identification of leading party members with the individual sectors, meant that within the top ranks of the party the different sectional interests jostled against each other. For those in charge of heavy industry the progress of their sector became identified with the 'social good' while those in charge of consumer goods or housing disagreed. It was not simply at the top levels of the party that sectional interests emerged. Even in the twenties the Red Directors (the new enterprise managers) had been noted for their defence of management interests; now new and old, all within party ranks, could press for their interpretation of management functions 'necessitated by the new tasks'. Regional authorities and district authorities found themselves in competition one with another, rather than in coordination. In the countryside at least some party workers openly inquired what had happened to the original goals behind collectivization. They had gone to work in the countryside, to help establish and run a new productive agriculture which would, among other things, benefit the peasant. Instead they found themselves expected to execute a policy which gave the peasant no incentive to produce and left him destitute. Appeals were made to the central authorities but to no avail: the signatories were recalled from their jobs. But whose interests were being furthered by such a policy? Was the present emphasis on investment at the expense of consumption necessary or desirable? It was not only among party activists in the country that these questions were being asked as the first five-year plan came to an end. It seems that unease over the extent to which present consumption had been sacrificed to future benefits was strong enough for there to be disagreement over the shape of the second five-year plan. Some argued for a continuation of the same pace, others for a slower tempo. The former argued that the Soviet Union's military potential was still weak, the latter countered with the argument that when war came it would be better to have fewer tanks and a population more united behind the government. The arguments of the 'moderates' prevailed in that the second five-year plan did specify a relative increase in consumption but this in itself did not solve the problem that the planning and incentive system compelled each unit to work for itself, regardless of how this activity affected others.

As far as is known, Stalin himself did not take up a strong position on either side. The debate itself was a slightly awkward one in that demands for a more moderate policy could, although they did not necessarily, imply criticism of the chief architect of the previous policy. Indeed the whole question of the role of the leadership and its relationship with the lower party organs was, not surprisingly, the other topic of the period. We have referred to the party leadership's taking over responsibility for directing and administering the economy, and the use of directives from above down through the party hierarchy. This administrative or command system, with its similarities to the civil-war period, was welcomed by some as an indication of the leadership's drive and purpose but there were others who were concerned at the accumulation of power by the leadership and the denial of rights to the lower party bodies. Were the lower party bodies simply obedient executors of decisions from above? Even for those who were less concerned with the possible consequences of granting the leadership almost unquestionable authority the situation seemed somewhat unsatisfactory. On the one hand they were being asked to carry out dictates from above, on the other they were being asked to play a constructive and creative part in building a new society: they were the leaders who at every level should show initiative, guide and direct the people. When the attempt to do the two produced a conflict (as, for example, the party men found in the countryside), it was disconcerting – to say the least – to find one's own experience and efforts ignored by the central authorities. To get the job done demanded initiative, independence, yet this in itself was liable to bring censure from above.

Criticism of the role of the leadership inevitably became entangled with the question of Stalin's role, so much did he dominate the party during the period. It was not perhaps surprising that there was a tendency for those who were critical to see him as responsible for the shortcomings. It was already a situation in which men's eyes were fixed on the leader rather than on the whole complex of phenomena which gave him his position. And once this happens the leader's position is strengthened, rather than weakened, because the scope of criticism is narrowed.

During the years of crisis that followed the initial collectivization campaign, many felt that whatever his personal faults Stalin was the strong leader needed to direct the party. There is no evidence that any of the leading Politburo members who had supported him against the Right queried his leadership. Sporadic attacks from groups lower down the party did, however, occur. Circulars were distributed criticizing his autocratic leadership and the lack of party democracy, and demanding his removal from the position of General Secretary. Those involved were expelled and exiled. In one case Stalin demanded the death sentence for the ring-leaders but was outvoted by a majority of members of the Politburo who were not prepared to countenance this most extreme of measures for party offenders. But, by 1934, whether from anxiety at the enormous power Stalin had concentrated in his hands or from concern that the strains of the past few years, both political and personal (the work-load he had undertaken plus his wife's suicide), could affect his judgement, it seems that his removal from office was considered as at least a possibility. And there was one man, Kirov, secretary of the Leningrad party organization since Zinoviev's defeat in 1926, one of Stalin's men of 1929, popular within the party, who as an advocate of a more moderate economic policy was an obvious candidate. At the Seventeenth Party Congress, where he received an ovation as long as that given to Stalin, he was appointed to join the central party Secretariat in Moscow. We shall come back to him in a moment.

Stalin's power at this time consisted of the following elements. He was the undisputed leader of an organization which produced policies and directed their execution; as leader of this organization he had considerable control over appointments and influence on policy decisions. But there was more than this: over the past few years he had taken on responsibility for a wide range of policy matters (thrown up by the campaigns) and through the creation of his personal secretariat was fast becoming a government within the government. Even minor matters of policy awaited his approval. By way of an example of both the scope of Stalin's concerns and attitudes towards him, an incident involving Mandelstam, a poet of repute but long out of favour, is illuminating. Mandelstam was arrested in 1934 after reciting a satirical poem about Stalin to a small group of acquaintances. He was interrogated and sentenced to exile. His wife, upon his arrest, went immediately to Bukharin who in the past had helped Mandelstam, but Bukharin was unable to exert his waning influence apart from telling Stalin that people were dismayed at the case. Stalin then rang Pasternak and asked for his opinion of Mandelstam; Pasternak defended Mandelstam as a poet and a friend, and was curtly told by Stalin that the matter would be looked into. Thereafter Mandelstam's sentence was changed to one which merely prohibited his residence in major cities. His widow, who recounts the incident, notes that the attitude even among Mandelstam's friends who were not loyal party people was one of gratitude to Stalin, of praise for his beneficence and his care over an individual: he had deigned to interfere and remedy an injustice. As she rightly points out, what should have been criticized was a system which allowed poets to be arrested for satirical poems and then let their fate depend upon the inclinations of an individual.[1]

But even she accepts without question her personal audience with Bukharin: the special position of or attention awarded to 'known' individuals. Mandelstam as a poet of repute, personally admired by Bukharin, could seek and hope for protection where a lesser poet or an unknown individual had no such opportunity. This 'personalization' of decision-making was a marked feature of the Soviet system and one which strengthened the position of a leadership prepared to encourage it. By 'personalization' we mean the taking of decisions not in accordance with rules which applied to all cases of a particular kind, but on a much more *ad hoc* individual basis. When they came to power the Bolsheviks had argued that decision-makers should be accessible to all and, in the confusion and difficulties of the early years, party leaders and commissars were inundated with personal requests, grievances, demands for decisions. Since it was not clear who, at lower levels, had the authority to do what and there were disputes over what should be done, it was clearly best to get a decision from as important a body or person as possible. This pressure from the periphery encouraged the centre to issue directives, revoke decisions, and interfere in local matters which in turn encouraged the growing body of officials, caught in the crossfire between the central government and local bodies or individuals, to pass the decisions on up.

Although it was possible to argue (and rightly so) that Stalin with his personal secretariat and penchant for policy-making on large and small matters was accentuating the centralization of decision-making, the widening of the scope and power of the centre, and the consequent reduction in party or Soviet democracy, more than his removal would have been necessary to remedy these features themselves. Was party or Soviet democracy compatible with the type of policy, methods of execution, and social order embodied in the industrialization and collectivization campaign? Some thought that it was, arguing that a new Constitution could establish new political relationships to accord with the now socialist base. It was to Bukharin that the task of devising such a Constitution fell. Its main provisions were as follows: the abolition of the discriminatory and unequal franchise and indirect voting; in their place a Supreme Soviet composed of two chambers, one elected by a direct one-man-one-vote system from equal electoral districts, the other composed of an equal number of representatives of the different nationalities; the Constitution reaffirmed the basic rights of the citizens and referred to the communist party as the leading organization in society.[2] If Bukharin or others hoped that with its introduction in 1936 a new era would begin for the Soviets as bodies reflecting public opinion and influencing policy; that a healthy Soviet democracy could cure the evils of over-centralization, bureaucracy, and personal power, they were sadly mistaken. They were mistaken not only in the sense that they were too late – by 1936 the Great Purge was already underway – but also and more importantly in the sense that Soviet democracy was incompatible with the type of policies being pursued and the whole structure of decision-making and execution. Industrialization and collectivization had produced a material base for socialism (the end to private ownership of the means of production) but social relationships that were far from socialist. It was a divisive policy rather than the reverse: one which kept agriculture and the bulk of the peasantry poor, which split the working class into rich and poor, and set sector against sector. Opportunities for social advancement were opened up but accompanied by marked income differentiation and the introduction of other privileges in the form of housing, consumer goods, and leisure facilities. Decision-making was centralized, and relied for its execution upon hierarchies of officials, leaving little scope for autonomy at local level. Under such a system what scope was there for Soviet democracy and whose interests was the party to represent?

We mentioned earlier that the historian of the period suffers from a shortage of materials. By the mid-thirties few statistics were being published, social-science journals had ceased publication or become empty in content, there was no longer any critical public discussion of social or political phenomena. This was not surprising. Peasant opposition to collectivization was too violent to be publicly admitted; the drop in living standards in the towns too marked. The drive for production at all costs which undid much of the progressive labour legislation, and rule by order from above, were difficult to reconcile with earlier claims on social relationships under socialism. If there had been the kind of serious analysis and criticism that existed in the twenties, it would have been increasingly difficult to argue that a socialist society was emerging. The way out of the dilemma was to deny the validity of critical discussion.

Here then was a social and economic transformation effected by a number of different means which called into question the whole concept of party rule as it had existed in the twenties. Stalin found a 'solution' to the problem by destroying the party. This is not to say that such a 'solution' was inevitable or necessary; it is to say that the party was caught in a situation which it was either going to have to alter radically – if it was to continue to play its previous role – or it was going to find itself cast in a new mould of some kind or other.

The NKVD

In writing of collectivization we made only a brief reference to the NKVD or Commissariat of Internal Affairs. It was this institution that Stalin used to break the party in the years 1936–8.

In December 1917 a special organization, called the Cheka, had been created. The task of this commission, which existed at central level and had local branches under the local Soviets, was to discover and suppress any attempts at counter-revolution. Imprisonment and later the death penalty were the weapons it used. As can be imagined in civil-war conditions the meting out of justice was a rough and ready matter – social origin was enough to make a man a victim – and the Cheka became a feared organization. Even those who supported the Bolsheviks and recognized that their overthrow would mean no lessening of terror and civil strife saw in the Cheka a hydra that would prove difficult to control. Victor Serge, who grew up in exile in France, became an anarcho-socialist, and returned to Russia in 1919 to become a critical supporter of the Bolshevik regime, described the situation thus:

Since the first massacres of Red prisoners by the Whites, the murders of Volodarsky and Uritsky [Bolshevik leaders] and the attempt against Lenin (in the summer of 1918), the custom of arresting and, often, executing hostages had become generalized and legal. Already the Cheka (the Extraordinary Commission for Repression against counter-revolution, speculation, and desertion), which made mass arrests of suspects, was tending to settle their fate independently, under formal control by the Party, but in reality without anybody's knowledge. It was becoming a State within the State, protected by military secrecy and proceedings *in camera*. The Party endeavoured to head it with incorruptible men like the former convict Dzerzhinsky, a sincere idealist, ruthless but chivalrous, with the emaciated profile of an Inquisitor: tall forehead, bony nose, untidy goatee, and an expression of weariness and austerity. But the Party had few men of this stamp and many Chekas: these gradually came to select their personnel by virtue of their psychological inclinations. The only temperaments that devoted themselves willingly and tenaciously to this task of 'internal defence' were those characterized by suspicion, embitterment, harshness, and sadism. Long-standing social inferiority complexes and memories of humiliations and suffering in the Tsar's jails rendered them intractable and, since professional degeneration has rapid effects, the Chekas inevitably consisted of perverted men tending to see conspiracy everywhere and to live in the midst of perpetual conspiracy themselves.

I believe that the formation of the Chekas was one of the gravest and most impermissible errors that the Bolshevik leaders committed in 1918, when plots, blockades, and interventions made them lose their heads. All evidence indicates that revolutionary tribunals, functioning in the light of day (without excluding secret sessions in particular cases) and admitting the right of defence, would have attained the same efficiency with far less abuse and depravity. Was it so necessary to revert to the procedures of the Inquisition? By the beginning of 1919 the Chekas had little or no resistance against this psychological perversion and corruption. I know for a fact that Dzerzhinsky judged them to be 'half-rotten', and saw no solution to the evil except in shooting the worst Chekists and abolishing the death-penalty as quickly as possible . . . Meanwhile the Terror went on, since the whole Party was living in the sure inner knowledge that they would be massacred in the event of defeat; and defeat remained possible from one week to the next.

In every prison there were quarters reserved for Chekists, judges, police of all sorts, informers and executioners. The executioners, who used Nagan revolvers, generally ended by being executed themselves. They began to drink and to wander around firing unexpectedly at anybody.[3]

After the civil war attempts were made to bring the organization more closely under government control and to define and limit its powers. Accused were to come before the courts. It became part of the Commissariat of Internal Affairs, then an independent agency, and by 1934, the time that concerns us, again part of the NKVD. But it remained as before, although not so obviously so, an agency against whose actions there were few safeguards and one which included many of the worst elements in Soviet society. It was this commissariat or ministry that was responsible for internal and external security. Its officials held posts in all important organizations – other ministries, the army, enterprises, and institutions – and a network of paid and unpaid informers existed. Nominally the NKVD and its head were under the jurisdiction of the Council of People's Commissars, but by 1934 Stalin was responsible for the appointment of the Commissar, who at the time was Yagoda, and received reports direct from him. Over the past few years NKVD activities had increased: the disaffection in the countryside, the campaign against bourgeois 'saboteurs', had 'demanded' increased vigilance and more personnel.

In November 1934 Kirov, the party leader seen by some as Stalin's successor, who at the Seventeenth Party Congress had been elected to the central party Secretariat, was back in Leningrad preparing to move to Moscow. On 1 December he was assassinated in the party headquarters in Leningrad. The circumstances of the murder were suspicious, suggesting possible complicity in high places and, after Stalin's death, Khrushchev hinted that Stalin himself might have been responsible. Whatever the truth of the matter, Stalin used the assassination as a means to strengthen police powers and harass old opponents. NKVD agencies were requested to speed up the investigation of those accused of complicity in acts of terror or sabotage. Special boards of NKVD officials and a Procurator were to be set up to sentence offenders. The Procurator, an official of the Commissariat of Justice, was there to see that legality was observed. This was the only link preserved with the legal system. These boards could sentence offenders to exile or corrective labour camps; by 1936 they could impose the death sentence and no appeal was to be allowed. Simultaneously, following Kirov's death, a call for vigilance within the party was made. The assassin himself, a young man called Nikolayev, had been a party member and much was made of this. Old Trotskyites and other oppositionists who had been re-admitted to the party were again suspect, and Zinoviev and Kamenev were arrested and sentenced to imprisonment (on the flimsiest evidence) for having influenced Nikolayev by their views. Any indirect connection, however indirect, now became treated as a cause of subsequent behaviour. Later it became sufficient to argue that the accused's actions *could* have led to someone else's behaving in a treacherous fashion, although no one had actually done so. Sentences became based on hypothetical events.

The Great Purge

It was against this background that the Great Purge began in 1936. The next two years saw the publicized trials of leading party and government officials, both old Bolsheviks and Stalin's supporters of the twenties. There was the purge of the officer corps in the armed services, and the equivalent 'officer' corps of the party, ministries, and intellectual community. And accompanying all this, the almost indiscriminate arrest and sentencing among all sections of the population. In order to understand how Stalinism operated, how it affected the attitudes and behaviour of those living under it, and much of what happened after the dictator's death, we must devote some attention to the Great Purge. Quite apart from this, it deserves our attention as a social and political phenomenon which is neither easy nor pleasant to have to explain. Persecution, police terror, false confessions, and incrimination, accompanied by passive popular acquiescence or active collaboration have been a feature of many different kinds of societies and regimes. To explain this recurrent or persistent phenomenon is beyond the scope of this book, but any attempt at explanation must take what happened in the Soviet Union into account.

Briefly the main events were as follows. In August 1936, suddenly, without even the knowledge of most Politburo members who were away on holiday, Zinoviev, Kamenev, and other old Bolsheviks were accused of forming a terrorist bloc at Trotsky's instigation with the aim of assassinating leading party officials. All except one confessed to their guilt and were executed. In their confessions they implicated other leading party members, including Bukharin. A month later Yagoda, the Commissar of the NKVD, was replaced by Yezhov and it was he, nicknamed the dwarf, who gave the period its name: the Yezhovshchina.

In January 1937 more leading Bolsheviks, Radek, Pyatakov, and Sokolnikov, who at one time or another had had links with Trotsky but who had stood firmly behind Stalin in 1929 and taken a leading part in the Great Construction, came to trial. They were accused not only of plotting assassinations but also of sabotage, of links with enemy agents, and desiring the restoration of capitalism. There is some evidence that this prompted a last stand by some members of the Central Committee who, at a meeting, attempted to oppose Stalin. The attempt came far too late – by now Stalin and the NKVD could break any opposition. Bukharin was arrested and their arrests followed. March 1938 saw the last Great Trial – Bukharin, Rykov, and Krestinsky (all members of Lenin's Politburo), Yagoda, and others of Stalin's Commissars. Espionage, sabotage, plotting to end the Soviet State and restore capitalism were the charges. All were again sentenced to death.

The public trials were only the tip of the iceberg. Shooting of old oppositionists, already in the camps, began in late 1936 and by the spring of 1937 the purge of party organizations, government bodies, and institutions was in full swing. According to Solzhenitsyn a few public trials were held in the provinces in 1937 but, because of the local feelings aroused and the inability of the prosecutors to make the charges stick, open trials were quickly abandoned.[4] In June came the amazing indictment of the Red Army generals for treason and then the purge of the upper ranks of all the armed services. And side by side with this went the almost arbitrary arrest of individual workers, peasants, teachers, artists and NKVD officials themselves.

Since no proper figures have been published, any estimates of either the numbers or categories involved must necessarily be open to doubt, but we can say something about those social groups who were hardest hit. Anyone holding an official post was in danger, and the higher the post, the greater the danger. Specialists or intellectuals, particularly those who had had connections with foreigners, party members who once had had links with old opposition groups, representatives of national minorities, diplomats or army personnel, artists and writers, were the groups who perhaps suffered most. In more general terms the male urban population of over thirty was worst hit. It has been reckoned that perhaps 5 per cent of the population, or eight million people, were under arrest in 1937-8. Perhaps 10 per cent of those arrested were shot, the rest went either to labour camps (from where few returned) or into exile, or remained in prison.[5] The figures are so large that they defy the imagination. To begin to grasp the reality behind them, it is essential to read either the autobiographical accounts or the novels of those who survived.

By the summer of 1938 the worst was over. Yezhov was replaced by Beria. In 1939 Stalin officially announced that the need for a *party* purge no longer existed and admitted that individual mistakes had been made by overzealous officials. But there were no rehabilitations or recriminations: a successful operation had been performed and those who had taken part could feel they had done well. At the same time there was no dismantling of the NKVD apparatus nor lessening of its powers: it was now a huge organization, responsible for perhaps 10 per cent of the labour force which, in the camps, was engaged in construction projects, lumbering, mining, etc. Although the Great Purge was over, the use of police power, arbitrary arrest, and forced labour was not. At the outbreak of war several small nationality groups were deported to the east. After the war the camps received more recruits – foreign prisoners of war, Red Army soldiers who had surrendered to the Germans, and Soviet citizens who had remained in the zones occupied by the Germans. And, during the last years of Stalin's rule, Jews, intellectuals, and people of all ranks were still being arrested.

Whatever the right figures may be, the magnitude of the Great Purge and the continued existence of terror is not in doubt. How then did it happen and what were its after effects? When Khrushchev referred to the Purges in his secret speech to the Twentieth Party Congress in 1956, he suggested that Stalin's suspicious nature was largely responsible and that unscrupulous persons in the NKVD or party played upon his fears and suspicions. It is interesting to compare his explanation with those that went round in the camps or prisons where the question 'why am I here?' demanded some kind of an answer.

Some, in particular party members, were convinced that their own arrest and that of a few others was a mistake (and hence appeal would eventually bring release) but that in general the sentences were correct. This was in fact the official line. When Stalin referred to the Purge in 1939 he referred to it as a correct and positive undertaking accompanied, unfortunately, by a few minor excesses. Others, and there were many who were convinced of this, argued that it was the work of the upper echelons of the NKVD who both misled Stalin and kept the truth hidden from him: if only Stalin knew, he would put it right. Many believed that there were enemies of the people (under fascist or capitalist influence) but they differed in their estimation of how large a proportion of the arrested these were. The process had snowballed, some argued, as NKVD officials attempted to fill quotas, to overfulfil them, in the usual spirit of beating targets or because they were afraid that if they did not make arrests they would be accused of lack of vigilance.

A rather different kind of analysis came from old oppositionists and some of the intellectuals who tried to find social explanations for this strange phenomenon. Some of these argued that Stalin had risen to power on the back of a new police-party bureaucracy which was alienated from the mass of the party: he now had to destroy what was left of the old proletarian party because it was a threat to the new bureaucratic caste. Others suggested, that on the contrary, the leadership was attacking this new bureaucratic group (which was attempting to consolidate its position) and using the lower echelons of the party and popular hostility to the new office-holders to try to dislodge them. It had to do this to prevent any group consolidating its position and becoming a conservative force. This last theory was elaborated on in the late forties by some western specialists. They suggested that in a one-party State, where there are no formal or constitutional mechanisms to replace office-holders, the only way to replace the old with the young and to preserve social momentum is by repeated purges.

In trying to 'explain' the Great Purge, it is as well to identify what it is that we are trying to explain. We may want to distinguish the question 'how could it have happened?' (that is, what were the pre-conditions that made such a phenomenon possible) from the question 'why did it actually happen?'. And we should specify what the 'it' refers to here. Do the different elements – the trials of the old Bolsheviks compared with the indiscriminate arrest of unknown people – require a single or different explanations? Do we need one explanation for its beginning and another for its continuation? Khrushchev attempted to provide one basic explanation: all that happened could be attributed to Stalin's paranoia and megalomania, and the unscrupulous behaviour of certain party and NKVD officials. Yet clearly this will not do. Other monarchs or presidents have suffered from similar psychological traits and had unscrupulous advisers without this leading to a reign of mass terror. This is not to say that these factors were unimportant. It is difficult to find an explanation for the Great Trials that does not take into account Stalin's desire to wipe out any possible threat to his own position and it is certainly true that he became increasingly suspicious of all who surrounded him or held leading positions as time went on. Certainly too he found active support from leading NKVD officials and party officials. They encouraged his fantasies, obeyed his orders with alacrity, and themselves discovered 'culprits' thereby proving to Stalin that he was 'right.'

But, if Stalin the individual and some of those who surrounded him must in this sense be held responsible for the execution of the leading old Bolsheviks and many of his own men of 1929, we must introduce other factors in order to explain why it was they were able to do this – the pre-conditions for such actions. We must refer back to the political situation: the accumulation of power in Stalin's hand; the attitudes towards him, both the adulation *and* the unease felt in some party circles (the former was important in that people were loath to believe he could be wrong, the latter was important in that it encouraged Stalin to act before the unease turned into an actual threat); the existence of the NKVD as an institution, its history of finding 'internal enemies', and its subordination to Stalin. In the previous section we tried to show how some of these political phenomena were related to the changing social environment and, in this sense, we can agree that the Purge was related to the incompatibility of the new social and political order and the 'proletarian party' –

which Stalin consequently set out to destroy. But it is insufficient to talk simply of a conflict between a new bureaucratic-police stratum and the old party as though this in itself were an explanation. One has to introduce the peculiar political forms that accompanied such a conflict without which there is no reason to believe that it would have necessarily resulted in the Purge; the outcome could well have been quite different. And even then it is not as though the Great Purge, even in its early stages, was directed only against erstwhile political opponents in the party. Officials at all levels in the party and government machine who had obtained their position as loyal Stalin men went too. The new administrative stratum suffered badly. But the contrary argument – that the Purge was a mechanism to dislodge new bureaucratic incumbents and preserve social momentum – is even less convincing because rapid industrialization was in itself creating enough new jobs to maintain a high level of social momentum. In the attack upon administrators, as in the case of the officer corps in the armed forces or the NKVD leadership, we must see Stalin's fear, whether justified or not, of any potential opposition at work.

To explain the 'snowballing' effect we can point to certain phenomena specific to the Soviet Union of the thirties. First, a police network existed that was accustomed to finding counter-revolution and whose officials were rewarded for so doing. It was operating in an environment where target-fulfilment equalled success, and where its power and control over resources depended upon the success of its officials in finding enemies and expanding penal institutions. Secondly, the Purge benefited many – all those who stepped into dead men's shoes, took their jobs and apartments. The mid-thirties was the period when the benefits of belonging to the political, administrative, or intellectual elite became really apparent and acceptable – apartments, holiday trips, and scarce consumer goods were now being distributed openly to those with status. In such a situation where the rewards were great and the penalties for not participating in the campaign for vigilance even greater, it is not surprising that there were many who denounced neighbours or colleagues, either out of envy or through fear. And, of course, there were the honest collaborators who, in an atmosphere of official hysteria about hidden enemies and the daily 'discovery' of them, began by suspecting colleagues and acquaintances, and ended by denouncing them in all sincerity. More generally the pressures that can persuade a people to participate in a campaign of denunciation (or to collaborate with an occupying power), and the reasons why they do, are many and complex. A complete explanation would require more than the specific conditions mentioned above.

The whole question of cooperation with the official policy is a very difficult one. Khrushchev argued that, with a few exceptions, everyone believed in Stalin and acted in good faith; they had no knowledge of the true situation. In saying this, he was inflating one element of the truth. Both from accounts of people in the camps and from later explanations it does seem that for many Stalin remained above reproach and that the guilt of those arrested was accepted. (Khrushchev suggested that after the war he and other party leaders began to doubt Stalin's sanity but that by then there was nothing they could do: any opposition by them would have been seen by the population as evidence of their being traitors. Stalin could not be wrong.) But it is very difficult, if not impossible, to draw a line between honest support and support accompanied by twinges of doubt and guilt. When, after 1956, accusations began to be levelled against those who had actively participated in denunciations, it was often suggested that these people did not sleep soundly at night or, despite their conviction that in general they had done what was right and necessary, there were small incidents which they tried to forget but which refused to be wholly suppressed. Although there probably are many such people, it is too easy a way out to press the point too far. For each one who does feel some guilt, there are probably several who do not. The need to justify one's behaviour, if only to oneself, is very strong. Most people are remarkably good at doing this, whatever the circumstances, and official policy both at the time and afterwards has encouraged this natural reaction.

The question of individual responsibility is never easy. In one sense, all who survived must bear the responsibility; in another, those who acted for personal gain or from fear, or who knew that 'mistakes' were occurring at every level on a scale that brought the whole policy into question, must bear a greater share. It does seem that the closer one's connections with the political, police, or intellectual elite, the greater the awareness that something had gone wrong. Khrushchev was trying to persuade his audience that no one (apart from Stalin and a few accomplices and perverts) was really responsible, because they had all acted in good faith, and that the top echelons in society were in the same position as ordinary people. In 1962 Ehrenburg, a Soviet writer, suggested in his memoirs that many had felt that something was wrong but had gritted their teeth and kept silent. This provoked an attack upon Ehrenburg and an official rebuttal because, if accepted, such a suggestion could lead to criticism of the present authorities' behaviour at the time.

In the west Khrushchev has often been praised for condemning the Purges and criticized for dodging the question of responsibility. And, of course, in some moral sense, the criticism is justified. But, on a political level, it is naive. What we have to remember is that those who in 1956 occupied the leading positions in all spheres of social life were people who owed their positions either to their active support of the Purges or to their silent collaboration. By condemning the Purges and Stalin's leadership of the country, Khrushchev was in effect announcing that they had been following a false god for nearly twenty years. This was a blow bad enough. But to admit, in addition, that they should take responsibility and accept that they had no right to their present positions would have been to demand the voluntary suicide of the present political and intellectual elite. Those in authority do not willingly sign their own death warrants. The odd individual might shoot himself, but for most it was far easier to accept that they had been misled, that they had honestly done what they thought was their duty, and that no good would come of recriminations. Recriminations would damage the reputation of the country's leaders and hence the country itself; wounds, best plastered over, would break open in daylight; all existing authority, in whatever sphere, would be questioned. Half-truths were difficult enough to face, what might be the consequences of telling the whole truth? And, one should add, no one, even with the help of the archives, knew what that was.

Those who had been arrested early on, and survived, and there were few of them, and those, at the other end of the scale, who felt the Purges had been justified and they had played an honourable part in them, were the two extremes. In between stood the vast majority torn between feeling shame and horror at what had happened and a desire not to have to examine their own consciences too closely. The political leadership could and did take this uneasy attitude into account in deciding what line to take. From time to time since 1956 there have been demands by individual writers or citizens and even on one occasion by Khrushchev for a proper examination of the past, for the punishment or at least removal from office of those who won their positions by their actions in the Purges. But, although the political leadership may have used such appeals to justify the removal of important individuals on occasions, it has always firmly rejected this as a general policy and, were a public opinion poll to be taken, the results would probably be in favour of such a stance.

Stalinist Dictatorship

From 1936–7, until Stalin's death in 1953, the economic mechanism introduced by the earlier campaigns continued to exist under the aegis of a personal dictatorship. The divisive effects of that mechanism were held in check by a political framework which allowed them no overt expression. There was now one policy-maker, Stalin, one 'wise' leader who stood above all the competing factions; he (who was unaffected by sectional interests) could discover the correct policy, that which served the social interest as defined by him. There was no longer any proper forum for debate, any discussion of alternative policies, which would have set the different 'interests' one against another and renewed the debate over consumption versus investment. Instead Stalin decided policy and, not surprisingly, he tended to repeat existing policies.

There were a number of reasons for this. First, the economic mechanism was relatively good at achieving certain simple goals: the growth of the major branches of heavy industry and armaments. The planned diversion of resources to these branches plus the system of directives down to enterprises and an incentive system geared to increase output of these goods, plus the pressure on party branches to make this top priority – all combined to send heavy industry forging ahead. By the time of Stalin's death, despite the terrible destruction of the Second World War, the USSR was an industrial and military power second only to the United States. This success was achieved at a cost. The growth of heavy industry (and the emphasis on output at all costs) was accompanied by the weak development of light industry, stagnation in agriculture, the ignoring of new technological developments and new types of production (new sources of energy, plastics, chemicals), and the waste of resources in the form of breakages, damaged and poor-quality goods. But it was not simply that Stalin considered that the achievements outweighed the costs and hence he continued with the original policy. His taking on of responsibility for policy in itself had certain consequences. Since only the leader was responsible for defining what were socially desirable goals and deciding what was the best way to achieve them, subordinates concentrated entirely on their specific tasks and ignored any wider questions. Their world was limited to their little (or big) empire; their position depended upon its importance and its success in fulfilling tasks set from above. This encouraged those below Stalin to think within existing limits. Furthermore, since the leader alone was responsible for initiating policy, to propose a change implied a criticism of previous decisions; it was in one's interest to suggest that all was well. It was dangerous to suggest that available resources were insufficient or that targets were not being met; it was equally dangerous to suggest innovation and change. This was not restricted to those who reported direct to Stalin; their subordinates in turn were fearful of reporting the true state of affairs or of acting independently. Hence Stalin tended to live in an unreal world of falsified statistics and, if Khrushchev is to be believed, a world in which happy and prosperous peasants ate and lived well. As a consequence the dictator would and did produce the same package deal, unless faced by a drastic situation which could no longer be hidden from him. Since, too, it was physically impossible for one man to follow or take an interest in all aspects of policy, Stalin tended only to intervene in an emergency or to innovate in a purely arbitrary fashion – for example, there was his proposal to plant a forestry belt round the USSR to prevent erosion and his contribution to the theory of linguistics. But these sudden excursions into different policy areas were important in one sense. They strengthened the idea that wise, all-seeing Stalin was aware of what was going on and that at any moment, without warning, he might act. Officials at all levels were desperate lest they might be the next to come under scrutiny (and who knew who was whispering what in Stalin's ear) and thus the system retained its blind momentum.

Existing institutions strengthened their position and existing priorities hardened. The temporary aims of the first five-year plan – notably the relation between investment and consumption and the stress on heavy industry – became untouchable principles of socialism; the aim of securing grain reserves for the State became the be-all and end-all of agricultural policy. Hierarchical administration in institutional empires, income differentials, the existence of a privileged stratum of administrators – all these became accepted as the right and proper (indeed the only) characteristics of socialism. This is not to say that the situation remained unchanged since 1934. As the number of primary units (the enterprises) grew, so – although not so fast – did the number of ministries and their departments. (The Commissariats were renamed 'ministries' in 1946.) But, as they grew bigger and more numerous, straining and pulling one against another, advancing their own interests and concealing activities where desirable, it became increasingly necessary to provide some kind of coordinating mechanism and control over their actions. Whereas originally it had been the party apparatus that had directed and administered policy, now the NKVD participated *and* checked the work of the party; those who headed the apparatus carried no greater weight with Stalin than the NKVD heads, or indeed than individual ministers. Central party departments with overall supervision of either a number of ministries or certain aspects of their work still existed – or rather were created, then abolished and refashioned in a different form – but they shared their function of supervision with other ministries or agencies (the Ministry of

Finance, the Bank, planning agencies) and with the NKVD which now had an economic empire of its own. Throughout the period there was continued administrative reorganization – prompted by Stalin's desire to cope with the problem of emerging sectional interests and to prevent independent bases of power becoming established. At the bottom the enterprises were hemmed in by regulations, red-tape and controlling agencies whose status *vis-à-vis* each other was not always clear; at the top the different departments and agencies were caught up in an administrative tangle.

In such a situation, the only decision one could be sure of was one which came from as high an authority as possible in Moscow. In a centrally planned economy, especially where resources are stretched, the best place to be is at the centre where decisions are made. Not surprisingly all the big institutions had their head-quarters in the capital and there was an endless stream of officials arriving from and departing for the provinces. But this 'centralizing tendency' was accentuated by the administrative structure and by the atmosphere produced by the Purges. Bureaucracy and red-tape had been a feature of the Tsarist civil service and a phenomenon much criticized in the twenties. But the Purges made the cultivation of 'bureaucratic attitudes' (bureaucratic in the sense of a dislike of taking decisions without official backing from higher up) a *sine qua non* for survival. Officials avoided taking decisions where possible, demanding countless documents, and tried if they could to pass problems on to their superiors. This increased the load falling on the shoulders of those right at the top and slowed down the whole process of administration.

It was a centralized system, extremely centralized in the sense that there was one policy-maker ruling by means of a number of huge institutions, each of which had branches or subordinate enterprises all over the USSR and which together controlled all aspects of economic and social activity, overlapping one with another. But it had no one dominant hierarchy or institution to guide and direct the rest – instead there was a tangle of overlapping and conflicting agencies and organizations in which clear lines of command had become blurred.

In the twenties the party had been concerned with major issues, major in the sense that their resolution, one way or another, had far-reaching social and political consequences: inner-party democracy, relationships between town and country, between consumption and investment, coercion versus cooperation. At that time the party existed as a political organization which saw itself as responsible for deciding policy and justifying decisions not only to itself but also to the rest of society. But by the early fifties all this had disappeared. The party no longer existed in this sense. It was still there, with a membership of six million, three quarters of which had entered during the Second World War. But by now holding an administrative position in almost any field entailed party membership: there was nothing special in being a party member at this level because all one's colleagues were party men too. This dilution of the significance of party membership had been accompanied by the decimation of the original apparatus. The existing apparatus was larger, staffed with new recruits, but without the original's power and authority. There was no party organization responsible for making policy, no forum where discussion could take place. During the war Stalin had created an 'inner cabinet' of advisers which was not a party body; afterwards, despite the formal existence of a Politburo, Stalin took decisions after discussion with one or two individuals or with a small group called together to discuss the issue in question. The Politburo as such did not function. It was Stalin who decided who should participate in policy-making. This is not to say there was no political infighting at the top, no disagreements between Stalin and his subordinates, and between the subordinates themselves. It does seem that the occasional disagreement arose over economic planning, modernizing village life, or party recruitment, but such disagreements were not made public at the time, nor did they become the subject of debate among any but the few individuals involved. In other words it was a period when issues did not exist, when problems were not allowed to exist. But since people in a position of authority must find problems and make it clear publicly that they are doing something about them (as part of stressing their indispensability, the need for their services), those who fail to find them in certain spheres will discover them in others. And furthermore part of the Stalinist credo was that the existence of 'dangers' lurking within Soviet society required a strong and vigilant leadership to protect society. The distribution of resources, the distribution of power were at this time excluded from a possible 'problem-field'. So where were the problems and dangers? They turned out to be the cultural and ideological shortcomings of a section of the artistic intelligentsia. Zhdanov, one of Stalin's lieutenants, led an attack on the artistic world. The charges ranged from producing pessimistic, satirical literature or too many western plays to belittling the role of the party in the war or writing modern music. Thence the attack shifted via the dangers of cosmopolitanism and the presence of foreign agents to one on the Jews. These were the official issues of the period. They afford a good indication of the leadership's preoccupation with the trivial in its desire to avert its own and the population's eyes from fundamental questions.

Different Explanations

This account of the Stalinist system has attempted to describe its economic and political characteristics and to show how they were interrelated. Implicit in the analysis is the suggestion that they cannot be understood one without the other or, to put it more strongly, that in talking about Stalinism one is talking about a phenomenon in which the 'political' cannot be separated from the 'economic'. If one tries to separate the two, one runs into problems of trying to explain how Stalinism worked or what provided the system with its momentum. Perhaps this is best seen by looking at the inadequacies of certain commonly accepted analyses which concentrate on Stalinism as either an 'economic' or a 'political' system.

To the Marxist it is the relationship between classes that acts as the dynamo of change. Furthermore political relationships are part of the superstructure, determined by the base – the economic relationships in society. The State pursues the interests of the ruling class. In a later chapter we shall look in more detail at Marxist critiques of the Soviet system, here we are merely concerned with showing how this kind of analysis (if crudely applied) is unsatisfactory when it attempts to explain the Stalinist system in terms of a superstructure determined by the base. One explanation put forward by some Marxists of the time (and afterwards) was that the momentum of the system lay in the conflict between 'the bureaucracy's' pursuit of capital and wealth at the expense of the working class; the State, therefore, pursued the interests of the bureaucracy.[6] We suggested earlier that this type of 'explanation' is unsatisfactory in that it does not, in itself, explain why 'the State' should have taken the peculiar form that it did – and this is surely worth explaining. It does after all matter whether millions of people are being sent to labour camps; whether freedom of association and speech are allowed; what forms a class struggle may or may not take as a result of the political organization of society. But here the point to be made is that by to all intents ignoring the form the State assumed the analysis of the class relationships and the economic 'base' is weak. To what extent does it make sense to say that the 'interests' of the 'bureaucracy' were being furthered by the economic relationships or that the bureaucracy's pursuit of its own interests provided the system with its momentum? If one asks who was benefiting in a material sense, which were the privileged groups, the answer is political and government officials of the higher ranks, officers, skilled specialists, scientists, artists, skilled workers in key industries, etc. It will not really do to call these 'the bureaucracy' without perverting the meaning of the term. But, more materially, although these groups may have received a greater share of society's wealth than the rest, the overall low level of consumption – the lack of goods and facilities, even for those with money – makes it difficult to talk in any meaningful sense of the system serving their interests. A handful at the very top certainly did live well but the great majority of the privileged income-groups could do little more than put their money in a post-office savings account, and hope for but probably not obtain a new apartment. In a non-material sense it is even more difficult to talk of the State serving the interests of the 'bureaucracy': during the Purges, and even afterwards, officials at all levels and the privileged groups in society were in a more precarious position than workers and peasants, and suffered worst.

This view tends to ignore the effect the State had upon social and economic relationships and, in its desire to offer a classic 'class analysis' of the role of the State, tries to squeeze the Stalinist phenomenon into categories which do not apply. This was not a society with well-established classes (how could it be, given the upheavals of the past twenty years?) nor, consequently, one in which the relationship between superstructure and base was similar to that under mature capitalism.

The Stalinist interpretation was very different. By the early thirties Stalin was arguing that, with the revolution from above, the State had taken on a guiding and directing role: the relationship between base and superstructure was different from that under capitalism. Under socialism the State determined social and economic relationships; instead of withering away, it became more important. The State now provided the momentum for social change. This followed from the Stalinist analysis of class relationships under socialism. With the social ownership of the means of production, there could no longer be class conflict; instead there were two harmonious classes – workers and peasants – and a stratum of the intelligentsia, all of whom shared the same common interests. No analysis of social and economic relationships was necessary; by virtue of social ownership there could be no conflict of interests within society. It was the State that now controlled the future destiny of society and hence what became important was proper organization – indeed politics became reduced to questions of appropriate organization and leadership.

We leave a discussion of this type of 'class' argument until a later chapter – except to point out that since it excludes any attempt to analyse existing relationships and ignores the political methods used by the State it is singularly unhelpful in 'explaining' Stalinism. But it is interesting in quite another sense. Whereas the Bolsheviks of the twenties saw political relationships to be embedded in society and incapable, in themselves, of transforming social relationships, by the late thirties the political superstructure had, in theory, become 'independent'. Elevated above society stood the political leadership, or rather the supreme leader who 'discovered' the correct policies and was responsible for finding the best form of organization which could execute the policies. The image presented of society is very simple: a wise leader, a political organization carrying out commands, and a social base affected by policy but not, in itself, affecting the political superstructure. Everything now becomes a matter of organization. The structure of society is taken as given; all that remains to be done is to improve the institutional framework; any small problems that occur can be solved by improved organization.

This transformation of the Soviet approach is not surprising when set against the background of the political transformation that had occurred since the late twenties. In some ways the approach had become similar to the constitutional approach of the west: both took social and economic relationships as given, and thought of politics as the creation of a correct framework, existing almost independently of society. In its view of the State as a benevolent repository of wisdom, paternalistically guiding social progress along well-established lines, the Soviet approach reminds one of Bismarckian concepts of the State. And indeed the similarity is not accidental. The vision of society as a socially harmonious whole, the idealization of existing relationships, and the view of the State as a benevolent authority representing the interests of the whole, is one shared by what one might call progressive conservatives from Burke to Bismarck and beyond. This shift to a conservative vision by the Soviet leadership took its own unique path, and the result was also unique. Certain elements, such as the increasing stress placed upon nationalism and patriotism, and the attempt to link the present with the past as part of a glorious tradition, are part of the armoury of conservative politicians past and present. But, because it was very difficult to reconcile the debates, policies, and ideas of the twenties with the present, the past had to be falsified, myths were created which suggested a continuity, a coherence. History was rewritten.

Perhaps the most important of these was the myth of the party; now seen as a body which had always been united round a leader whose pronouncements were always right, a body whose unity and strength depended upon the possession of something called Marxist-Leninist ideology which ensured the right decisions were taken. Such a suggestion would have been anathema to the early Bolshevik leaders. Lenin never argued that being a Marxist or leader of the party ensured the correct choice of policy; that knowledge of the scientific laws of Marxism provided any concrete answers. The most he would have claimed is that, as a Marxist, prepared to analyse complex situations from a class point of view, one stood a better chance of understanding social developments and reacting accordingly. The leadership could be wrong. But, under Stalin, whatever the leadership did was, by definition, right and policies needed no justification in terms of an analysis of the present and their probable consequences. In order to stress the continuity with the past, quotations from the holy fathers of Marx, Engels, and Lenin were used wherever possible. The ideas were emasculated but the words remained, part of a framework which justified the present and suggested its deviation from a revolutionary past.

A very curious element, but an important one, of the Stalinist image of a socially cohesive society, was the myth surrounding the leader. To stress the importance of leadership and organization is one thing, to suggest that the leader is supremely wise and good is another. Stalin and his subordinates assiduously cultivated the Stalin myth in a manner reminiscent of Louis XIV and his court. Stalin was thanked, praised for each and every event; all achievements were attributed to him. If one reads the hymns to Stalin, the references to his greatness and goodness by any public speaker or writer, one is forcefully reminded of the eulogies made, at all levels of society, to the Sun King. This phenomenon, that of sincere adulation by large sections of a society, is something that is hard to comprehend; something that seems to fit, in some sense, into a period when people still believed in the Divine Right of Kings, but is out of place in twentieth-century Europe. Yet it happened, and added another dimension to the strange combination of old and new ideas that made up the theory of the time.

By the time of Stalin's death then, the Soviet approach to its own society and politics had changed. In the west too people were beginning to write about politics in a rather different way, less about constitutions (the experience of the Weimar republic had shown that constitutions may not guarantee democracy), more about political parties, pressure groups, voting patterns – the informal structure of politics in a western democratic society.

At the same time the emergence of Nazism in Germany and Stalinism in the Soviet Union demanded some kind of an explanation. After the war, with the changed balance of power, the Soviet Union became a potential threat. The Cold War developed. Now it became important to know what was going on inside the USSR and to predict the future. In the United States, government money poured into Russian studies, which experienced a rapid expansion in the atmosphere of the Cold War and McCarthyism.

The kind of analysis that was being used to treat politics in western democracies did not seem very appropriate for the Soviet system. At the same time there was a desire to make as much of a contrast as possible between western democracy and fascism or Stalinism – to stress how different they were, how good the one, how bad the others. As a result, the USSR now became a proper subject for study, indeed a vital one, but a subject that was quite separate from the rest of politics. There could be little common ground between specialists studying Britain or America, and those, the new Sovietologists, who now studied Communism.

In an attempt to explain or simply to describe the phenomenon of Nazism and Stalinism (and the two were classed together), the specialists produced the 'totalitarian' image or model.[7] Although different writers stressed different aspects, all agreed that the following were crucial elements: (a) a single party dominated by one leader (b) a militant ideology which sought the transformation of society in accordance with certain higher 'laws' (c) police terror and repeated purges (d) the destruction of all intermediate social groups or autonomous institutions in order to produce an atomized population (e) central control of communications and mass propaganda. Here, in sharp contrast to the Marxist type of critique mentioned earlier, attention is focused primarily on certain political forms. This is not surprising in that its advocates wished to emphasize the difference between political structures under western democracy and in the Soviet Union or Nazi Germany, and in that their intellectual background was one which tended to treat political phenomena as separate from and independent of economic and social relationships. It is true that some linked these kinds of political form with the abolition of private ownership and a free market economy, but the connection between the two was not spelt out clearly – indeed it could not be, since in the German case private ownership continued to exist. What was seen as crucial was the existence of a militant group, armed with an ideology (taken to mean a set of dogmatic beliefs) regardless of what that ideology contained. In an age of mass communications and advanced technology, it was argued, the coming to power of such a militant group would result in totalitarianism.

We already suggested in an earlier section why this kind of explanation cannot account for the kinds of change that took place in the Soviet Union and it should be clear from the analysis of Stalinism why such a description is inadequate. It is interesting though to reflect how similar in some respects the totalitarian image was to the Stalinist image. Both depicted the Soviet period from 1917 to 1953 as one in which aims remained unchanged, both saw the party as somehow still the same party because its 'ideology' (that is, the rhetoric of Marxism-Leninism) remained the same; both emphasized the guiding nature of something called 'Marxist-Leninist ideology' and granted Stalin almost superhuman powers of control over society.

Part Three
The Contemporary Political System

6 New Approaches

This part of the book describes and analyses the political system that has replaced Stalinism. We shall be trying to fit together various elements – the type of political leadership, the way in which policy is made and the nature of that policy, and the methods of rule that are used – in order to understand one configuration of power or, in other words, the form the State assumes and its relationship to society. We want to know who and what determines policy, who participates in turning decisions into action or prevents their realization, and who benefits from this type of policy and way of making decisions. We want, after all, to gain some idea of the consequences that follow from the existence of a particular type of political system.

But before offering the reader our account, we need to outline the changes that have taken place in the description and assessment of the Soviet system over the past twenty years. Compared with the post-war period when the totalitarian view held sway, queried only by those Marxists who supported Stalin and a few Marxist critics, today there is considerable variety in the analyses of the system. In this chapter we try to show how and why this has occurred, and to spell out what it is that these new approaches have to say.

The Changing Environment

In the immediate post-war period those in the west studying politics tended to argue that the following were the major features which distinguished the Soviet from the liberal-democratic political process: (a) the policy makers were not subject to regular elections (b) there was no legalized active opposition able to criticize and defeat government proposals (c) indeed there was no freedom of speech (d) in a State-owned economy and society, controlled by one party, there were no autonomous sectors or pressure groups to exert pressure and to be bargained with (e) once policies were made no organized opposition or pressure for change was permitted. It is one thing to state these kinds of difference, it is another to infer the consequences that stem from them. Usually this kind of analysis was accompanied by the suggestion, implicit or explicit, that hence the government had 'a free hand' in making policy, it could produce unpopular 'minority' policies regardless of majority opinion; no individual or group was safe. Furthermore, ran the argument, since people were unable to discuss policy alternatives freely and to campaign for change, they were unable to exercise choices and to influence the process. At its crudest the image was one of a government free to impose policy upon a captive audience who had no option but to applaud and carry it out. The western framework in contrast, it was suggested, enabled people to choose on the basis of information and discussion, to protect or advance their rights and interests; and ensured that government decisions taken broadly over time were responsive to the wishes of the majority. This approach, very little different from that of the twenties, took certain traditional liberal values and assumed that the political arrangements of parliamentary democracy embodied them. The totalitarian arrangements in the Soviet Union embodied quite different principles and hence there could not be, nor was there, any common ground between them.

It was in the mid-fifties that people in the west began to question the simple contrast between multi-party democracy and totalitarian rule that had satisfied an earlier generation. The reasons for the shift were several and can be grouped under four headings: events in America after the end of the Korean war; developments in the Third World; events in the USSR after Stalin's death; and, interacting with these, partly caused by them, partly as a result of developments in other academic disciplines, a change in the preoccupations of those studying politics.

Inside America the end of the Korean war led to seven years' economic stagnation while the belief in American technological superiority was shaken by Sputnik and claims of Soviet strategic capability. As in the thirties, although in a less extreme form, the poor performance of capitalism was accompanied by a questioning of the belief in its inherent superiority and that of the values that went with it. From the mid-sixties on, the ghetto riots in the big cities, the disillusionment with the Vietnam war, and the inability of the government to cope with urban problems, poverty, and inflation destroyed the unthinking faith of an earlier period in the unequalled capabilities of the American political system. As important were developments in the Third World. By the late fifties unfortunate things were happening in the newly independent African States: 'democratic', multi-party states were turning into one-party States or suffering from coups. In Latin America dictatorships replaced one another: Cuba had a revolution without Soviet help; Asia and the Near East provided a bewildering mixture of authoritarian regimes, growth in communist party memberships, and anti-western sentiments. All this was taking place against a background of US–Soviet competition for the allegiance of the new States: while the United States was struggling to preserve the boundaries of the free world, the USSR was presenting itself as a superior development model for the underdeveloped countries.

With the ending of terror in the USSR and the successful curbing of secret-police powers by the political leadership, one of the main props of the totalitarian model began to crumble. However the Soviet system did not collapse. There was a bloodless change of government in 1957; the impressive rates of growth continued, standards of living rose; concessions were made on censorship, criticism, and freedom of discussion. This seemed to suggest that it was misleading to talk of purges and terror providing either the dynamo or an essential element of the system. For all these reasons the fifties and sixties were a period of self-doubt in America. This atmosphere encouraged the already more sociological approach to politics which those, beginning to query the supposed properties of formal institutions, had begun to employ. And the new writing on American and in turn British politics affected, although not always in a direct and obvious fashion, the approach towards the Soviet Union. Let us then look briefly at what happened to the study of liberal democracy.

The Study of Liberal Democracy

Political scientists in America had begun to develop an interest
in what we can call the mechanisms of government – the way in
which people choose a government and the way the government
makes policy – as opposed to formal procedures. A number of
studies of voting behaviour and attitudes towards voting or
towards the political parties themselves did not support the view
of the voter as an active citizen who thought deeply about the
alternative programmes offered by the political parties, made
conscious decisions which he could defend with rational argument, or indeed that he always took his electoral responsibilities
very seriously. On the contrary, ignorance of and apathy towards
the electoral system were marked among a substantial section of
the community. Quite apart from this, it was not difficult to show
that, although legally the right to organize a political party or
branches of one existed, in practice social pressures made this a
hollow right in certain communities. Furthermore, studies of the
political parties themselves produced evidence of organizations
which were far from 'democratic' in the way in which the leadership at national or local level was chosen and then ran party
affairs.

Simultaneously the existence and activities of organized
'pressure' or 'interest' groups were commanding attention. It
became apparent that organizations, representing sometimes
large, sometimes small, sections of the community (the unions,
big business, the farmers, doctors, etc.), spent considerable time
and money enlisting support for themselves from elected representatives, government officials, and the Press. To what extent,
people began to ask, was the real business of government – the
formation of policy – the result of a process of bargaining, influence, and the activities of organizations or officials which
represented only some sections of the community and were not
democratically elected? The assumption that with free elections
and competing parties an active citizenry chose its representatives
who then pursued its interests began to look shaky. Having the
vote did not seem to ensure that one's interests would be taken
into account in any meaningful way. It was difficult to argue

convincingly that the government or political parties must be
responding to most of the wishes of most of the people or they
would lose their support when it was not clear who else there was
to support. (Although this was not to deny that governments
might and indeed sometimes did respond to the pressure of public
opinion on particular issues.) And although the existence of
pressure-group politics was seen by some to 'save' democracy –
if people's interests were being ignored, they formed autonomous
groups to press their case, and this healthy 'pluralism' ensured
that people's interests were taken into account by governments –
it was difficult to ignore the fact that the apathetic and unorganized tended to be the poor and underprivileged, and that the
voices of some relatively small sections of the community appeared to carry inordinate weight when decisions were made.[1]

While it was becoming clear that the claims made for democratic institutions would require some rethinking, a more sharply
critical attack upon western or American democracy appeared.
Marxists in Europe and America had always claimed that bourgeois democracy was class rule but they had been ignored as
misguided fanatics. Neither had the writings of those continental
theorists – Mosca, Pareto, or even Weber – who in the early
decades of the century had attempted to find an answer to Marx's
analysis of society found an audience, let alone a receptive one,
in America or Britain. Mosca and Pareto had argued that
although Marx was right to talk of a ruling class both he and
naive democrats were wrong to imagine that the division of
society into the rulers and ruled could be done away with. There
is, they argued, a ruling class in every society; this is natural and
necessary because not everyone can participate in decision-
making. The fact that the rulers form a relatively privileged class
(using the term loosely, *not* in a Marxist sense) or stratum – in
terms of wealth, status or opportunity – is natural or unavoidable.
If the ruling class becomes too inbred, too rigid in defence of
itself and its progeny, erects too many barriers against aspiring
and capable newcomers from below, this will lead eventually to
weakness. But, if the system allows for mobility up into the new
ruling class, the absorption of vigorous representatives of new
social forces, there is no reason why society should not evolve

peacefully with one ruling class or elite being gradually replaced by another. These 'elitist' theories began to attract attention in the late fifties as the study of politics became more sociological, but it required a contemporary critical attack upon American democracy to bring the subject out into the open. This was provided by C. Wright Mills's *The Power Elite*, an analysis of American society which owed something to Marx, and something to Mosca and Pareto.

Mills argued that in America decision-making lay in the hands of top echelons in the government, big business and military; those who held these offices came from a small, wealthy, 'social' group; they acted in concert to produce policies – regardless of the wishes or interests of the 'rest' who were excluded from decision-making – and to maintain recruitment of their own kind. Here we have a classical account of an elite: there is a correlation between power or decision-making and socio-economic status; a small privileged group recruits from among those with a similar background and perpetuates its own rule, a rule which is the prerogative of the few. Note that this is not a 'class analysis' in the Marxist sense, because Mills does not argue that the relationship to the means of production is the cause of this phenomenon (although he does deal in some detail with the important part that ownership of property plays in securing elite status and has 'big business' as one of his three links in the chain of power) and he is less concerned with demonstrating that the powerful produce policies which are in their own interest than with showing that they operate as a closed circle of decision-makers. In this respect his criticism is a good nineteenth-century liberal one: benevolent despotism is as great an evil as malevolent despotism; men are not men unless they are free to choose their own destinies. But, implicitly at least, Mills does seem to be arguing that the policymakers are prompted by a vision of the world which puts a low premium on the wishes or interests of the majority of the population.

The two major criticisms that have been made of the Mills-type analysis (and other attempts to define the power elite) are that they ask the reader to accept that they have identified the most powerful without offering him any proof and that they assume the powerful work in unison without, again, supplying the necessary evidence that this is so. Consequently critics of Mills have endeavoured to show that disagreement among decision-makers is as marked as a common set of interests, and that pressures from outside have an important effect upon actual decisions. Although the debate remains inconclusive (and must do so as long as there is disagreement on what might constitute a power elite) it has had its effect upon those seeking to explain and justify democratic institutions. Theorists have recognized that those active in politics are a small minority of the community and that decision-making is the prerogative of the few; furthermore those who do participate and particularly those in positions of authority fare better on the criteria of wealth, status, and education than those who do not. There are, they have agreed, 'elites' and not every one has an equal access to power. However, what is important – so runs the argument – is that there are a number of different, *competing* elites, not only within the political arena (political parties) but within society as a whole. This leads to a healthy plurality of interests, and prevents the domination of a single elite. The political elite is accountable to the electorate and thus must bear the interests of as wide a section of the community as possible in mind, and, when in office, the government is only one among a number of elites who, with competing claims, can provide checks one upon the other.

Critics have pointed out that, if we are talking about relations of power or authority in society, we ought to include in the analysis those other institutions which affect men's lives, their choices, and opportunities (for example, the big corporations, the military) and that these are *not* accountable in any democratic sense to their members or the public; also the fact that there are a number of separate elites does not in itself give us any grounds for asserting that there will be competition or conflict or bargaining between them – there may be or, for example, there may be agreement that each one has a free hand in its own particular sphere or, yet again, they may agree on policies.

It is recognized that barriers do still exist – that wealth, home background, and colour affect the opportunities of those aspiring to reach positions of influence in society – but the suggestion seems to be that within a competitive system where the government has to respond to social pressures these kinds of barriers are likely to come down. The system will be *more* open than others. Unfortunately it seems just as plausible to argue that such competition and accountability will favour the preservation of material and social barriers as that it will tend to remove them. Regardless of this, it remains true that those writing about the democratic process devote time and attention to the question of equality of opportunity.

Those cardinal tenets of the liberal faith – free speech, a free Press, and freedom of organization – and their existence in practice have not claimed as much attention. There is the recognition that some are in a much better position to take advantage of these rights than others. The Civil Rights movement in the United States inevitably brought this to the fore but gave the discussion a rather utilitarian (although nonetheless important) colouring. Freedom is seen as important because it enables individuals and groups to express grievances, to criticize injustices, and to press their own case. This is not the same as arguing that freedom is essential for man to develop as a creative human being. Even more prosaically it has been argued that, without the free exchange of opinions and knowledge, the critical assessment of ideas and proposals, governments are bound to be less capable and efficient policy-makers. This does not sound like the nineteenth-century liberal's passionate advocacy of freedom as man's inalienable right, and indeed it is not. Those who are now writing about liberal democracy have different perspectives and interests. They are aware, in a way that their counterparts of the 1920s were not, that democratic forms are not in themselves enough since they are compatible with a non-democratic content, but they do still think of 'representative democracy' as somehow the ideal. We find them then trying to do two different things: to indicate ways in which the existing political process should be improved in order to make it more 'democratic', and to redefine the concept of democracy in terms of existing characteristics of the American or British system. The result is a confusing justification with little of the moral conviction and certainty that characterized the spokesmen of the twenties.

But if some are still concerned with how to make politics democratic, others have developed a rather different interest. Their involvement with the actual practice of government, the study of how the institutions work, came at a time when there was concern within government circles over the failure of certain policies to produce the intended results. This concern encouraged political scientists to analyse the way governments 'functioned' and their record of success or failure. New criteria to evaluate political systems began to appear: terms such as 'goal attainment', 'effective government', 'stability' and 'flexibility' became popular – terms which sound less emotive and more practical but whose meaning, if one thinks about it, is far from clear. One can see how within this type of approach 'freedom' becomes important because it enables decisions to be taken because they are 'sensible' rather than for any other reason.

Analyses of the Soviet System

Now let us see how these developments affected writing on the Soviet Union. We have to think of a situation in which those who studied the Soviet Union were used to working in isolation, either in separate institutes or in small rooms surrounded by piles of *Pravda*. They wrote about the contrast between a totalitarian state and an idealized American political system. But, in the mid-fifties, government and the Press became less willing to ascribe all virtues to the USA, and the academics (often supported by government money) found themselves having to answer a different set of questions: how did the Soviet Union achieve its economic success? Were there not, after all, perhaps some 'positive' features to the Soviet system? How did the image of the Soviet government set on world domination square with Khrushchev's policy of peaceful coexistence? Blanket condemnation of all things Soviet was no longer required of the Sovietologists. Simultaneously their colleagues with a new interest in the Third World began to seek them out. Maybe, argued those who produced a new subject 'political development', maybe in an underdeveloped country there were special problems which made democracy difficult. (It would at the very least be convenient to be able to explain the non-democratic nature of some of the United States' allies in terms of mitigating circumstances.) Very crudely, it came to be argued that the breakdown of 'traditional' society under the impact of industrialization and urbanization is accompanied by certain tendencies towards centralization, the need to organize political loyalties round a national image – to create a national identity – which in turn produce different political forms from those in advanced western society.[2] But, if this was so, the Soviet experience was clearly relevant and perhaps it too should be explained in these terms rather than by 'ideology'.

Elites and Interest Groups

The response of the Sovietologists, as they emerged blinking from their isolation, has varied. Some simply ignore the new work on American or British politics and continue to write, as before, stressing the differences between the formal mechanisms of constitutional democracy and the iniquitous practice of communist politics.[3] And in general it is true that the Sovietologists paid scant attention to the new 'realistic' accounts of American politics – just as their colleagues who produced them gave little thought to the impact they would have on comparisons between the two systems. But some of those who did were quick to make the point that a crucial difference was that, whereas one could perhaps talk of competing elites in the United States, in the USSR there was one elite, that is the communist party.[4] Since the party sees its task to be one of directing all spheres of social activity, all activity becomes political and one cannot separate out a political sphere in the way that one can in the west. Thus there is no problem in pinpointing where power resides in the Soviet Union: the political elite, the party, is synonymous with the ruling, the power elite. Furthermore, bound as it is into a unity by its ideology, there can be little disagreement within it; if any does arise, such is its organizational structure that opposition or factions can be quickly suppressed; similarly, because of the principles of strict subordination of lower bodies to higher and party control at all levels in society, policy decisions can be implemented without opposition. The rank and file members of the party should be considered part of the elite both because of their vital function in seeing that policy decisions are implemented and because they provide the recruits to the upper ranks.

Central to this view is the assumption that membership of the party is what is important: one is primarily a communist, only secondarily a worker, director, scientist, or peasant. It is because party members share a common 'ideology' and leading officials in all spheres are party members that one can talk of a unified elite and party dominance. Elite theorists, it will be remembered, argued that there is a connection between the political elite and the high socio-economic status groups; the two go together; in part politics is the defence of these privileges. But western commentators who define 'elite' in the USSR in terms of an ideological commitment (party membership) break this connection. Any privileged groups or persons who are non-party are excluded from the elite.

The idea of monolithic unity and control has become increasingly difficult to maintain in its simple form. The discussion of policy alternatives that took place in the USSR following Stalin's death made western commentators aware that, despite being 'communists' or self-appointed, Soviet political leaders could and did disagree over government policy. In the totalitarian model policies were explained in terms of: (a) struggles for power between leading politicians (that is policies were little more than an adjunct, a weapon to be used in the struggle to achieve dominance over colleagues) or (b) Marxist-Leninist ideology or (c) the personal whims of leaders. We leave it to the reader to ask himself whether these 'explanations' are compatible one with another. Suffice it here to point out that the totalitarian approach tends to neglect the actual policy-making process and provides no satisfactory explanation for the adoption of particular policies. By the middle sixties a few daring Sovietologists (influenced by the work on pressure groups in western societies) suggested that the voicing of conflicting opinions by specialist groups within the Soviet Union should be taken to mean that pressure groups could wave their banners, even if rather feebly, under communist rule too. By the end of the decade there were those who argued that although individual political leaders might at times use policy issues in a power struggle there were real disagreements between them over policy, and institutional or specialist groups could and did influence the policy-making process.[5]

Interest group analysis is now an acceptable approach to Soviet politics. In its turn it has necessarily cast doubt on the idea of the party as a wholly united elite After all the majority of the spokesmen for the different 'groups' are party members. But those who talk of interest groups and attempt to define them in the Soviet context usually dodge the question 'where does power reside in the system?' or they retreat to the party apparatus as *the* dominant institution. This becomes the 'real' political elite, a group of ideologists united by Marxism-Leninism, to be contrasted with the pragmatic, rational specialists or purely self-interested groups who are struggling to make their influence felt.[6] But this too has been queried – even within the apparatus one can find evidence of different interests. Not surprisingly the suggestion has recently been made that the Soviet system is best understood within a model of 'institutional pluralism'.[7]

Such a hypothesis is considered unacceptable by most because it 'mistakenly' ascribes pluralist characteristics to Soviet politics. But this is to misunderstand the relationship between a method of analysis and that which is being analysed. If a particular approach 'shows' that both liberal democracy and the Soviet system can be described as 'pluralist', we are quite at liberty to conclude that the *approach* is an inadequate one for analysing political systems – because it does not focus attention on what we consider to be important differences between the two systems. We do not have to conclude, nervously, that therefore the political systems *are* similar – because it is the approach which has influenced our choice of observations. The two systems may be similar in these respects, but they may be trivial ones. What such a 'discovery' should prompt us to ask is whether the pluralist model is of much use in analysing *any* political system. Perhaps the traditional defender of liberal democracy who assumed that the existence of only one party, of State control of the Press, etc. had certain consequences for the policy-making process was right after all? To what extent are differences in the institutional framework (the existence of more than one party, elections, the extent of free speech and opposition) responsible for differences in policies and the way they are made or are other factors (the existence of interest groups or competing elites, for example, or something quite different) the important ones? This is one set of questions to which we shall be addressing ourselves in the following chapters.

This more empirical approach to Soviet politics has been very useful and still is. We now know a great deal more about the way policies are made, about the way the executive machinery works, and about activities at the grass roots. But this type of approach tends to concentrate on *what* happens, *how* things are done, rather than asking, in some broader sense, *why* political activities and relationships take the form that they do. The totalitarian model gave a simple answer; the interest group or 'pluralist' approach does not, in itself, offer one at all. Consequently many leave the question unanswered. But there are a few contenders for the vacant throne.

Industrial Society and Class Approaches

One answer stems from an 'industrial society' approach. If, some began to ask, if there is something in the process of industrialization that affects the political system, what consequences does this have for the Soviet system? Must the Soviet system adapt itself to the 'demands' of a mature industrial society? Some have argued that it must or else in some not very clear sense it will 'fail', cease to function 'effectively'. (We can see the influence of the emphasis on the functioning of political systems here.) Given a much more complex and differentiated society, ideology and authoritarian rule are not merely unnecessary but, it is argued, actually hinder further development. Terror has become an increasingly counter-productive way of achieving goals. This the political leadership has realized, but it, backed by the apparatus, is unwilling to give up the other aspects of a system which has outlived its usefulness. It therefore finds itself in conflict with the technocrats and specialists – the offspring of a modern society – who desire a more open, 'rational' decision-making structure and policies.[8]

The suggestion that the political structures are out of joint with the social environment is not limited to American political scientists. Roy Medvedev, one of the Soviet dissidents who defends a Marxist interpretation of developments, argues that 'the increasingly acute contradiction in the USSR between the requirements of economic, scientific, technical, and cultural development and the bureaucratic caste-oligarchical system of government gives rise to an objective need for reforms directed to the democratization of social life'.[9] The suggestion is that the political system as part of the superstructure is now acting as a brake on further development. As it stands it is not very clear. But the point of interest here is that analyses which differ quite markedly in other respects see the political system as now 'outdated' or 'dysfunctional'. This is a point to come back to in the conclusion, but the reader ought to start asking himself by what criteria one might decide whether a political system was or was not 'out-dated'.

The idea that political structures are related to the base is part of Marxist theory, but this does not provide any ready-made answers to the nature of the relationship at a particular point of time – except in the very broad sense that the political relationships must accord with the class relationships. As we saw in the last chapter the Stalinist argument was that under socialism (that is the social ownership of the means of production), where there are no conflicting interests, the State takes on a guiding role and rules in the interests of everyone. Although the impact of Khrushchev's secret speech on communist parties both in power and in opposition was enormous, it had little effect on official theory within the Soviet Union. In the final chapter we spell out the contemporary Soviet arguments more fully; here it is enough to say that the Stalinist interpretation, in its essentials, still holds good. Politics is still not considered an appropriate subject for study. But since 1956 the Soviet leadership has had to contend with criticisms of its political system and policies from established communist parties such as the Chinese, with alternative proposals and practice in Eastern Europe, and with unwelcome analyses from leading communists such as Togliatti. It was from Eastern Europe, initially from Djilas in Yugoslavia, that criticisms of a 'new class' and class rule in Soviet-type systems began to appear. Of course the splinter groups on the left in the west had never ceased to argue over the class nature of Soviet society – was it a deformed workers' state ruled by a bureaucracy or was it state capitalism – but, with the relaxation following the secret speech and the revival of the left in the sixties, there was an upsurge of Marxist-influenced writing, new analyses of both Soviet and western society, which could not be ignored by party ideologists in the Soviet Union nor by the academic community in the west.

It has seemed clear to many – from Trotsky to Djilas and others – that Soviet society is divided into at the very least a privileged administrative stratum, that acts in many ways like earlier exploiting classes, and an exploited working class and peasantry. However, if this is to be called a 'class society', Marx's definition of class and explanation of the origin of class relationships has to be re-interpreted. Some have been prepared to do this, to argue that a new ruling class has emerged which, although it does not own, controls and manages the means of production and expropriates the product in the same way that a bourgeois ruling class does. It too is driven by a need to accumulate capital in order to develop production and compete within a capitalist world. Supporters of this view differ in their explanations of the origins of this new ruling class and indeed what constitutes it – Djilas, for example, talks at times of the party, at others of privileged office-holders. Some refer to 'the bureaucracy' without being very specific, others seem to have in mind the privileged upper echelons of the party, bureaucracy and intelligentsia – but they all discard the notion that ownership is crucial. In this view then both Soviet and western societies are class societies with an oppressive State structure supporting the ruling class, both impelled forward by the ruling class's attempts to create capital and wealth for themselves and hence by the class conflict this inevitably produces.

In contrast there are those who, from Trotsky on, have argued that for a variety of historical reasons the Workers' State has been deformed by the emergence of a bureaucratic stratum which prevents proper socialist planning, which jealously guards its own privileged position, but which cannot be called a new ruling class.

It does not own the means of production and cannot transfer ownership to its children. Class conflict is not the dynamo of the system, any more than a search for profits is the foundation of the economic mechanism. Instead there is the conflict between the property relationships of *social* ownership and the efforts of the bureaucracy to develop the productive forces in their own interests: this produces some of the same phenomena as in capitalist society – exploitation, inequality, privilege – and could, if the bureaucracy attained a position powerful enough to alter the property relationships, produce a return to capitalism.

In both interpretations it is job or family membership that determines class or elite status, not party membership. In contrast to the other popular analysis, which identifies the party as the political elite and therefore sees party membership as the important characteristic, the Marxist analyses see individuals as primarily workers, peasants, bureaucrats or office-holders – these are the important dividing lines in society – and only secondarily as party members or not. Workers, both party and non-party, have more in common with each other than a worker who is a party member has with his communist enterprise manager. One question then to be asked, particularly when considering the party, is whether it does make sense to talk of it as the political elite or whether the distribution of power within society is such that it is misleading to think of 'the party' as an elite.

Common to all the Marxist-inspired analyses is the tendency to concentrate on social and economic phenomena to the neglect of the political structures themselves. Although they do offer an analysis of what provides the society with its momentum, it is a very general analysis – the conflict between classes or groups – that does not enable one to explain the form the State assumes. The only conclusion we can draw is that the 'rulers' will try to maintain their privileged position. So far very little attention has been paid to the question of whether social ownership affects the relationship of political structures to the base, and if so how; whether the type of political relationships in the USSR are a specifically Soviet product or not. Then what of the relationship between the new 'class' or stratum and the actual political decision-makers? Are those who 'rule' a separate definable group or not? How simple or complex are the social/class/group relationships within this new class or stratum? We shall take these questions up in the final chapter. Here it is sufficient to mention that Marxists have produced little of this kind of analysis. For obvious reasons it is not permitted in the Soviet Union or Eastern Europe, and critical western Marxists have tended to ignore these questions. The more orthodox communist party intellectuals devote their attention to the principles of democratic centralism and the role of the party. It is from those who have recently left Eastern Europe that the first attempts to produce a political sociology of the 'socialist' system have come.[10] This is not surprising if one remembers how pervasive the power of the State is under such a system: its presence cannot be ignored. It demands an explanation, yet the official ideology is silent.

This then forms a background to our account. Much of the time we shall be describing institutions and how they work, or policies themselves in some detail, but certainly implicitly and at times explicitly we shall be asking how useful or enlightening the different approaches are. Then, in the conclusion, we try to 'explain' the system we have described and to suggest its future.

7 The Khrushchev Alternative[1]

Certain important changes have taken place since the dictator's death, changes which, taken together, have resulted in a new structure of power. The following are the most significant: the ending of terror, the replacement of a one-man dictatorship by collective leadership or shifting coalitions, the introduction of new policies accompanied by the existence of public discussion (albeit limited) of policy alternatives, and the re-emergence of the party as the dominant political authority. That these are related one to another can be seen if we look at each in turn, but to do this we must begin by looking at the actions of the top leadership following Stalin's death. The situation which existed was one in which the actions of individuals at the top could have far-reaching consequences, it was one in which initiative for change was going to come from within the leadership. In the post-Stalin environment, control was so tight and any experience of organizing from below so slight that it is hard to see changes being effected from below. The initiative then lay with the new leaders and the question with which they were faced was 'with what shall we replace Stalin?'

We begin by looking at the measures taken to end terror, measures which in turn affected the position of the leadership, the making of policy, and relationships between existing institutions. We then deal briefly with each of these to show how a new *status quo* emerged and what that *status quo* is. This provides the general framework for the subsequent more detailed study of the central authorities, policies, and their execution by the party.

The Ending of Terror; Political Leadership

The party and the secret police were the two obvious contenders for power once Stalin died. Both had branches or members in institutions at all levels; in this sense both were national organizations with a central leadership, although in the party's case this was more apparent than real. The big State ministries did not have these characteristics: they were both specialized and had become separate empires in themselves. The Council of Ministers, where they formally came together at the top, was a huge unwieldy body and even its smaller Praesidium had little, if any, collective force. The other institution, always important where questions of power and control are concerned, was the military. Simply by its control of the use of force the military can impose its solutions on a society's leadership or take over that leadership for itself. But, for this to happen, the military (or at least a section of it) must exist as a united force, strong enough to override opposition, with a reason – usually dissatisfaction with the way government is handling policy – for its extreme action. Neither condition was present in 1953. Stalin had down-graded the military leaders after the war and increased secret police and party supervision in the armed forces, thus preventing the emergence of any potential 'military' group; nor is there any evidence that the military had any particular programme which it felt could be only realized if power lay in its own hands. To take over responsibility for running the whole economy was a task that no military leadership would relish, except in extraordinary circumstances.

In 1952 Stalin had created a party Praesidium or Politburo[2] – officially the leading party organ – of twenty-five leading party and government officials, excluding any military representative. As far as is known this never functioned as a body. On his death in March 1953 the most eminent ten members hastily divided up government responsibilities between themselves and, not surprisingly, retained for themselves the title of leading party organ. After all, this had more of an air of authority or legitimacy than any other because of its history.

They who made up this new government, men who in their previous careers had moved from party affairs to outside posts and back again (or vice versa), now had individual responsibility for major policy fields or institutions: the Council of Ministers – Malenkov, a long-term apparatus official, responsible (it has been alleged) for actively supervising if not instigating a post-war purge in Leningrad, a skilled arm-chair politician, and one of Stalin's closest colleagues; heavy industry – Kaganovich, known as a trouble-shooter because of his ruthless ability to sort out problems (for example, railway transport) by the use of force; foreign affairs – Molotov, the 'honest' Stalinist who moved from an ultra-left position in 1917 to supporting Stalin in the twenties and never wavered; the party apparatus – Khrushchev, the least known and most 'active' of the four with a background which included organizing the construction of the Moscow Metro, running the Ukrainian party, and devising schemes to improve agriculture, etc.[3] They owed their positions to themselves and to their control over institutions, whose members were appointed from above. In addition Beria, head of the secret police, was one of the ten. The existence of this organization with its vast empire, its officials in all organizations, and its unlimited powers of arrest and sentencing made the possibility of any opposition from below remote indeed. But, if the existence of the secret police strengthened the position of the new government, it simultaneously threatened it. If another 'Stalin' were to emerge, Beria – with his control over the police – was the obvious candidate, a threat to all the rest. The continued existence of the secret police in its present form was potentially more dangerous than useful. Very soon the rest of the group moved against Beria. If Khrushchev's memoirs are to be believed, the military leadership was brought into the plot to arrest Beria: the leading generals sat in an adjoining room, armed and ready to rush in to the defence of the Politburo if necessary. Whatever the truth of the matter, it seems plausible that the political leadership would have involved the military in such a move. Any political leadership is anxious to have the backing of the military. A move to reduce the power of the secret police would be only too welcome to the military, who must have objected to the extent of police surveillance within the armed forces, and a diminution of the secret police's power as an institution meant that the military bettered its position as the wielder of force or coercion. Consequently it became even more necessary for the political leadership to retain the loyalty of the military, and, not surprisingly, the next few years saw the political leadership taking up the complaints of the armed forces and, for a short time under Khrushchev, Marshal Zhukov was included in the Politburo.

Although the arrest and subsequent execution of Beria symbolized the decision to remove the secret police as a contender for power, much more than that was necessary if its actual strength was to be reduced. It was its scope as an institution, after all, that gave whoever directed it his enormous power and influence in decision-making. During the next three years the secret police suffered a four-pronged attack. First, the MVD (the Ministry of Internal Affairs or successor to the NKVD) lost much of its economic empire: construction of highways and canals, hydro-electric stations and mining enterprises, were taken from it, and the administration of the labour camps handed over to the Ministry of Justice. Secondly, State security was given to a new body, the KGB or Committee for State Security, a body without ministerial status. Henceforth the head of the KGB has been recruited from the party apparatus, not from within the secret police, and until 1973 excluded from the Politburo. Thirdly leading secret police officials were arrested and accused of staging false confessions, of unwarranted arrests, of using torture, and in general of disregarding the norms of 'socialist legality'. This was part of a campaign to discredit the top secret police stratum, accompanied by a gradual reduction in labour camp detainees. In 1956, with Khrushchev's secret speech, a large-scale review of political prisoners' cases was set in train which continued over the next few years. Those who had survived began to come back; some of those who had died received posthumous rehabilitation. And last, but certainly not least, the police lost their right to judge and sentence those arrested. The Special Boards were abolished; cases had to go before courts; and confession was no longer admitted as evidence of guilt.

This does not mean that the KGB is no longer an important institution. It is still there and it is used by the leadership to suppress potential or actual opposition. In a later chapter we shall try to assess the extent to which the political leadership has used the secret police as an instrument of rule and the extent to which it has used other methods. Here we are concerned with the political consequences of the attack upon the police that took place in the immediate post-Stalin years.

First, the ordinary individual need no longer fear arbitrary arrest and sentencing. Although the political authorities' attitude towards what counts as 'healthy' and 'unhealthy' criticism has differed over the period, the ordinary citizen who limits himself to grumbling at the shortage of goods or bureaucratic behaviour, need not fear arrest. Under Stalin, any behaviour, active or passive, could lead to arrest, which was unpredictable. Since the mid-fifties, the individual or official has had a pretty good idea of the kind of behaviour that is unacceptable. If he is brought in for questioning, it will be for something he is aware of. This is important because it has made dissent take on a meaning. If arrest is indiscriminate, affecting both guilty and innocent, if there are no rules or at least no recognized conventions fixing what is and what is not punishable, it becomes logically impossible to talk of protest or dissent. And in practical terms to have one's protest and an innocent man's behaviour treated indistinguishably reduces the protest to an irrelevance. Unless dissent can be recognized as such by others, it cannot be politically significant.

Secondly, the removal of the secret police as a contender for power, and its subordination to a political leadership which has rejected arbitrary and widespread terror as a method of rule, has altered the rules of the game affecting political succession and policy decisions. In their attempt to rule without Stalin, the new leaders were faced with two separate but related questions: how and by whom is power to be exercised? And what kinds of policies are to be pursued? There could be, and was, disagreement between them on the answers: disagreement between those who wished to preserve existing policies and those who wanted change and, among the latter, dispute over the direction change should take. There may well have been those who were apprehensive of the rapid curtailment of police powers and favoured some kind of collective 'Stalinism' with police controls, but at least there were others who sought an alternative structure of power within which the police should play a subordinate role. Perhaps all that Politburo members did agree on was the liquidation of Beria and the establishment of joint control over the police but, by effecting this, they loosened the strongest thread that bound them together. The way was now open for disputes over policy and the formation of internal coalitions. Since no one individual could win by using the police, both his position and the acceptance of his policy proposals depended on his colleagues' approval. It seems that the leadership thought it could continue in this fashion – determining both its own membership and policies – but, in their disagreement one with another, individual members began to turn to other institutions for support, to initiate press campaigns on their own behalf, or even to turn to the Central Committee. This turning to a wider audience was to affect both the 'rules' governing the leadership and the making of policy.

Let us look at the connection between attempts to produce an alternative to Stalinist policy and the position of the leadership a little more closely. Malenkov began to press for greater expenditure on consumer durables; Khrushchev suggested that, on the contrary, resources ought to be channelled into agriculture: bread and meat should come before shoes and refrigerators. Furthermore Khrushchev pushed for opening up and cultivating the Virgin Lands of Kazakhstan rather than spending money on established agricultural areas. Malenkov argued that peaceful coexistence with the west was possible; Molotov argued against. Khrushchev supported a reconciliation with Tito; Molotov opposed it. According to Khrushchev, there was disagreement over the extent of the revelations in the secret speech. According to Khrushchev again, there was disagreement over whether a more centralized or de-centralized form of industrial administration should be introduced. With the questioning of the old Stalinist policies, the idea of there being one and only one correct and scientific policy died. (And this is an important difference from the Stalin period.) Since no one faction or group controlled the means of coercion or could use it to stifle its opponents' suggestions, the different members of the leadership had to rely upon other means to try and win their case. As we have already mentioned, it was first and foremost essential to get the support of colleagues within the Politburo, but simultaneously individuals began to seek aid outside. But there was after all no mechanism whereby this could be translated into Politburo strength and used to defeat or dislodge opponents. An individual might well be receiving support in the press for his policies from academics, military officials, or enterprise directors, yet there was nothing to prevent his colleagues overruling his suggestions and voting him out of office.

Yet we find individual leaders looking for support and encouraging it. Khrushchev in particular took pains to back up his proposals with evidence of outside support from different sections of the community. To explain these seemingly irrelevant populist tactics, we must remember that previously it had been Stalin who found the 'correct' policy – that which was best and which, therefore, would be accepted by all right-minded people. After his death no one individual had the stature to be able to claim that his policy was the correct one; furthermore conflicting proposals were being put forward. In this situation it was desirable to produce evidence for the correctness of one's proposals and evidence, naturally, consisted in the support verbal and otherwise of as many influential people as possible and of a sprinkling of the 'masses'. By influential is meant those who occupied leading positions within their own hierarchies – ministers, party officials, academics, specialists. This is not to suggest that suddenly there was a free for all in the discussion of policy proposals; on the contrary some policies – notably those relating to the curbing of the secret police – were taken without wider discussion, and the securing of alliances within the Politburo was still undoubtedly the major preoccupation of individual members. However, what is true is that a new element had been introduced. An individual who could claim and produce support for his proposals was, *ceteris paribus*, in a stronger position than his colleague who had none. It was Khrushchev, possibly the least eminent of the members, whose voice had none of Malenkov's or Molotov's authority, who played this card most successfully – notably in his Virgin Lands campaign in 1954 when he argued against Malenkov for opening up the Virgin Lands of Kazakhstan rather than investing resources in the already established agricultural regions. Again this is not to suggest that Khrushchev relied on this alone or even saw it as his major weapon. He also paid considerable attention to forming alliances within the Politburo and to promoting his supporters to positions in the party apparatus and hence to the Central Committee.

When in 1955 Malenkov was deprived of his Chairmanship of the Council of Ministers but not membership of the Politburo by his Politburo colleagues (ostensibly for mismanaging agriculture but probably over his sponsoring of light industry), the Central Committee was not involved. But in other respects it was beginning to stir slightly. Molotov voiced his disagreement over a policy of reconciliation with Tito at a meeting of the Committee and, after discussion, received a minority vote. And in 1957 the Central Committee intervened in a dramatic fashion. In June of that year Malenkov, Molotov, Kaganovich, and other Politburo members, concerned at Khrushchev's policy of decentralization in industry and his rise in stature, obtained a Politburo majority in favour of his resignation as First Secretary of the party. This they assumed was all that was necessary to unseat him. But Khrushchev insisted that the matter be referred to the Central Committee which in theory (that is according to the party statutes) had elected him. It is indicative of the changed climate that, when faced with such a demand, his opponents felt obliged to agree. And it was at this point that Khrushchev's policy of promoting supporters to positions on the Central Committee and advocating policies which were attractive to a sufficient number of the members bore fruit. After lengthy dispute and the hasty summoning of supporters from the provinces, Khrushchev received the support of the majority and his opponents (henceforth known as the anti-party group) were voted off the Politburo.[4] Since 1957 all three factors – careful attention to colleagues' views, promotion of supporters to key positions, and the gaining of support from influential organizations or spokesmen – have been important in deciding both specific policy issues and the question of the leadership. We take up this theme in the next chapter where the central authorities are described in some detail; it is sufficient here to mention it as an important element in the system that has replaced Stalinism.

A New Party in a New Political Order

But, if the actions of the new leaders altered the 'rules' governing the leadership and ended the use of the secret police as a major executive organ, they left a number of questions unanswered. That policy matters could again be discussed, different proposals canvassed, and conflicting opinions voiced – so much seemed accepted. But how far was the discussion to go, who was to participate in discussing policy changes, and by whom was policy actually to be decided? Then what of the execution of policy? How were the ministries, the Soviets, the party apparatus, and party committees to function? What were their responsibilities to be?

At the beginning of the chapter we suggested that the party again holds pride of place as the dominant political authority. This implies a return to pre-Stalinist methods of rule, and indeed Khrushchev in his secret speech emphasized the need to return to 'Leninist democracy' with a proper functioning Central Committee and inner-party democracy. It is true that today, compared with the Stalin period when party organs, secret police, the military, and the ministries jostled uneasily together each claiming Stalin's attention, one institution – the party – stands pre-eminent. The top party bodies – the Politburo and Central Committee – provide the political leadership and the major forum for discussion of policy; the party apparatus controls appointments and acts as the main executive branch; a network of party groups, covering all types of institutions, provides the organization with its base of political activists. But we must be careful not to be misled by institutional forms. An institution may 'look' the same, have the same structure, and even be the dominant authority in two different periods, yet the nature of its authority, its scope, and the relationship between it and other institutions may be considerably different in the two periods. Enough has been written on 'the changing nature' of the Presidency or of cabinet rule to make the point. We should not start by assuming that an institution which preserves the same name and some organizational characteristics is in any important respects the 'same' institution. Whether we should want to say that it is will depend upon which 'respects' or characteristics we consider important.

In the years following the revolution the party managed to retain power both because it could command the loyalty of the soldiers and because it responded to spontaneous movements from below. Furthermore it pursued a policy of non-interference in important spheres of social activity while attempting to change others, often cautiously. Lines of authority between the centre and the local organizations were still unclear; and, within the organization, the Central Committee and to some extent the annual Congress played a part in determining policy. By 1934 the nature of the party both as an institution and as the political authority had changed. The General Secretary and Secretariat with the power of appointment and control over a hierarchic, coordinated party apparatus now dominated the organization to a much greater extent than the original Politburo or Central Committee had ever done; the Politburo was still the chief decision-maker, but the Central Committee and the Congress (in particular) had become extensions of a leadership which adopted a policy of transforming social relationships by active interference in or control of all aspects of social activity, and it was the party apparatus, backed by the local party organizations, which directed the process. The composition of the party had changed, as had the tasks its members were called upon to do. In both periods the 'party' was the dominant political authority, but this meant quite different things at the different times.

Under Stalin the party became merely one of the elements in a structure of power dominated by Stalin; after his death the organization forged in the Stalinist environment became the nucleus of a new type of political authority. There is after all no straightforward answer to the question: what do party leadership and party control mean, what should they consist of? They can and have taken many different forms. In the period since Stalin's death individuals in the leadership have given different answers, and disagreements have occurred in the lower ranks over what the role of the party should be, over the kind of party democracy that is right or desirable, over the appropriate type of party official and the nature of his job. It fell to Khrushchev to create a new type of party and a new political order to replace Stalinism. Essentially it is his scheme that exists today. This is not to say that Khrushchev succeeded in his objectives nor that the present leadership is satisfied with the arrangement. Indeed we shall try to show, in the course of the following chapters, that the political relationships which emerged were not those envisaged by Khrushchev, that certain of his aims and plans were unrealistic, and that his successors seem unable to find solutions to the problems they have inherited.

To understand Khrushchev's scheme we have to look at his objectives and the environment inherited from Stalin. What then were Khrushchev's objectives? To put it crudely, he wanted to maintain (or rather improve) the Soviet Union's defensive capacity and to raise the standard of living. He wanted to end the waste of resources, the bureaucracy, apathy, and discontent; to harness the potential for improvement and initiative in a grand concerted effort by a united people, yet simultaneously to maintain control over the situation and the direction of change. To achieve these objectives, he envisaged a new political order. What was needed was, first, a new vigorous leadership (*his* leadership, it goes without saying) with the 'right' popular policies, a leadership drawing on technical expertise, consulting with and listening to experts and officials. Secondly, the leadership needed the backing of a loyal and efficient executive machine, one strong enough to effect changes, to ensure that decisions from above were carried out, to maintain the leadership's position and to provide one clear line of authority. Thirdly, what was required was an active, popular, national organization with which people could identify and through which they could combine their efforts. Thus Khrushchev was aiming at a strong national leadership, backed by an efficient executive machine, in turn flanked by a popular national organization of enthusiastic citizens.

In his attempt to achieve this Khrushchev re-fashioned the old party and its relationship to other institutions and to society in general. In 1957 the party was not the authority in society; indeed there was no single clear line of command from the centre to the grass roots. There were a number of different institutions vying with one another; a bureaucratic tangle at top and bottom. The party itself was heavily white-collar, poorly represented among the industrial workers, and very weak in the agricultural sector.

The party apparatus, composed largely of those who had stepped into dead colleagues' shoes in the late thirties, sat in offices, engaged in paper-work, fearful of their superiors, and abrupt with their subordinates. Among ordinary party members there was apathy, generated in part by the humdrum routine nature of party meetings, in part by the general atmosphere of fear. As for the rest of 'Soviet' democracy, it was dead. The Soviet and social organizations did not function. Under the new arrangement the Politburo at the top, headed by Khrushchev, should produce policies with the support and expertise of an enlarged Central Committee – a body containing high-ranking representatives of the different political, social, and economic institutions. This brought the different institutions together into a prestigious 'party' body and provided a forum for the discussion of policy. The huge and unwieldy Council of Ministers, with its conservative bureaucratic apparatus which, in Khrushchev's view, was hindering the more efficient use of economic resources, was broken up: the industrial ministries were replaced by regional economic councils (or *sovnarkhozy*) to be supervised by the corresponding party bodies. The party apparatus, itself 'modernized' by the influx of specialists, would provide a centralized chain of command running from the top, down through the republic, regional, and district bodies, to the grass roots where the party was to be expanded, local Soviets revived, and voluntary social organizations encouraged.

Image and Reality

It is worth dwelling, for a moment, on Khrushchev's conceptual framework, on the image of the party and society entailed in such a scheme. When, in his secret speech, Khrushchev called for a return to Leninist and Soviet democracy, he was referring to the period pre-1934 and, if we think of his image of a desirable political organization of society, we can see that it does contain certain features that remind one of the early thirties. Then there was a strong leadership, backed by a party apparatus which was its executive arm, directing the industrialization campaigns. It was a period before the growth of the big industrial ministries, before the entrenchment of the huge cumbersome bureaucratic structures – which Khrushchev hates – instead there was a relatively simple authority structure. And this Khrushchev harks back to, this he wants to bring back, to re-create but with one important difference. *Then* the party was embarking upon the building of socialism, it was operating in an environment which was still largely hostile; *now* the socialist base is there, firm – workers and peasants accustomed to a system of public ownership, and a new loyal Soviet intelligentsia. Now there are no contradictions in the social relationships; nothing is *basically* wrong with the structure of society and hence all can identify with Soviet power, with a national government; the party can be a national popular institution, not simply a small party representing the working class. (At the same time Khrushchev and other political leaders could be plagued by fears that really they lacked the support of the people. This contradictory attitude was particularly marked in the case of Khrushchev – or perhaps he expressed it more openly – and we shall refer to it again.)

In 1961, in the new Party Programme announced with much pomp and ceremony at the Twenty-second Congress, Khrushchev spelt out these ideas a little more explicitly. The State was now an 'all-people's State' (no longer the tool of a class) and would gradually wither away, leaving the business of administration to the party – which would grow stronger – and to purely social organizations – youth, trade-union, and citizens' organizations. What he was referring to here as the State are those 'bureaucratic institutions' such as the ministries. The party and the social institutions remain. The picture is one of harmony, of social unity with the party representing the interests of all.

Yet in 1961, at the same Congress, there were clear indications that somewhere the picture was wrong. In the fifties, both agriculture and industry advanced fast; by the early sixties not only had overall growth rates slowed down but – despite policy directives – agriculture and light industry, those two sectors which symbolized the leadership's commitment to higher living standards, were lagging behind targets. At the Congress Khrushchev attacked the 'steel-eaters' (heavy industry) for consuming resources intended for other sectors. Clearly the executive machinery was not working as intended – or was it that there was no agreement on policy at the top? But the topic which overshadowed all others at the Congress was a renewed attack on Stalin and on members of the 1957 anti-party group. Here there was obvious disagreement among leading politicians and in subsequent months the debate spilt over into the ranks of the artistic intelligentsia. There was a period of bitter public debate over the interpretation of the past and permissible behaviour at present. The new policies were not working nor were all united in pursuit of a common aim. Frustrated by the failure of the new political structure to realize its tasks, Khrushchev introduced a few changes. State committees were created at the centre to provide some coordination within the same branch of industry; agricultural administration was reorganized at the centre and in the localities; and, in 1962, the party was divided into industrial and agricultural sections, with two committees at both district and regional levels. Khrushchev was a great believer in the efficacy of administrative rearrangement: if something was not working well, he sought an administrative solution and, towards the end of his period of office, his solutions had a desperate air about them.

After his ouster in 1964 his successors abolished these recent innovations and then made one change to the original Khrushchev scheme. In 1965 the regional economic councils were abolished and industrial ministries re-established as part of an expanded Council of Ministers but one clearly subordinate to the central party authorities. As the collective leadership has continued, the central bodies have grown in size and number and this has had an effect upon the Politburo – something we look at in more detail in the next chapter – but the grouping together of the different institutions under a party umbrella continues as under Khrushchev. However, and this is the point here, the new leadership also has difficulty in achieving its objectives, the executive machine does not seem to work as it should, nor is party work at the grass roots marked by enthusiastic participation.

Even from the very brief preceding account we can begin to see where problems might arise. We know that the planning and incentive system, and the institutional and hierarchical framework, was relatively well suited to achieving quite simple goals:

for example, increasing the output of heavy industry. But was it suited to achieving a much more complex set of goals – growth of heavy industry plus agriculture plus housing or, for example, quantity plus quality and lowered costs? Khrushchev's scheme merely simplified the executive structure; it did not alter the planning and incentive system. To what extent then were the new policy directives consistent with the rules governing the activities of the enterprises and institutions?

Rather differently, there is the more general question of the type of relationship that existed between different organizations, institutions, and social groups. Khrushchev seems to have envisaged that bringing them together within the party would forge a unity between them, but a number of different institutions included in one organization do not in themselves create an organization with a common purpose, one in which the separate parts will combine to work together. If society is fractionalized, made up of competing units which to maintain or improve their position must fight with others – and this was what each institution had to do in the Stalinist framework – no amount of 'uniting' them under one organization is going to produce unity of purpose or action. Their differences will simply re-emerge within the party. Somewhat similarly the drawing of a wider circle of officials and specialists into the discussion of and participation in policy-making is going to produce conflicting proposals. Following the thaw of 1953–6, when it became possible to discuss some mistakes of Stalinist policy and to suggest alternatives, some specialist groups began to proffer opinions and, as was suggested earlier, their opinions were used by politicians to support their proposals. Since it was no longer heresy and a passport to the camps to support a proposal that was not accepted, many specialists were anxious, now at last, to have their professional voices heard. This professional expertise the politicians were anxious to use. And indeed where specialists were slow to offer useful advice, as for example were the economists initially, the leadership suggested in no uncertain terms that they should make use of their training. By the early sixties, faced with the realization that the economy was in trouble, the leadership was prepared to allow a fairly wide-ranging debate on the problems and possible solutions. In other words the leadership called in the specialists and asked for solutions. This was particularly marked in the debate over economic reform (because of the gravity of the situation) but has also occurred in other fields (e.g. law, military affairs, and education). After all, one does expect a return on the money spent in educating and training the new professional intelligentsia. But the trouble is that the Stalinist system created an intelligentsia which was fractionalized, and narrowly specialist.

From a number of studies that have been done either of a particular professional group or of the discussion surrounding a policy proposal, the extent of the divisions within the groups is striking. Be they lawyers, economists, writers, or scientists, within each group there are the divisions between older and younger generation (or more properly between the different intellectual generations, trained in contrasting periods): between old *praktiki* (those without professional training who learnt their skills on the job) and newly trained; conflicts between those threatened by the de-Stalinization campaign, those anxious for some reform, and those who suffered under the Purges in one way or another; there are the conflicts between the specialists of different institutions, each defending his own institutional interests. Furthermore, because the specialists so long were denied the opportunity to engage in intellectual debate within their own fields, the tendency to engage in specialist infighting and to concentrate on the group's 'special' problems is very strong. The whole economic reform debate was marked by this kind of specialist infighting, and by the tendency to suggest remedies for little bits of the problem, without much interest in other problems which these remedies would create (for example, efficient use of labour but neglect of the unemployment which might be caused). In stressing these characteristics of the professional-specialist groups, it would be wrong to ignore the fact that the political leadership, by setting the limits on what can be discussed, discourages connections being made or attempts at more comprehensive solutions. It must limit discussion in order to prevent its own authority being questioned, but this, in turn, makes it difficult for it to obtain advice on the problems it does wish to solve and conceals the possible consequences of proposed solutions.

The encouragement of local initiative, criticism, and discussion – following a period of repression and social and economic differentiation – is likely to produce disagreement, discord, and even conflict. The post-Stalin situation was one of suppressed demands, one in which dissatisfaction and criticism had been forced underground. It was into such a situation that Khrushchev injected his secret speech and the attack upon the police, releasing both the long-suppressed criticism *and* optimism that now things would improve. But only if everyone is satisfied with their present position and willing to accept the leadership's view of the changes that are necessary is the granting of initiative at local level going to be a 'harmonious' process. To prevent the emergence of such conflict – be it at local or national level – the leadership has to retain control over the amount of discussion and criticism and to limit initiative, which in turn is unlikely to produce enthusiasm and vitality. Furthermore, in order to safeguard its own position and to control the executive machine, the leadership must rely on the appointment of officials from above and demand the execution of orders by subordinates – to prevent their acting in a way which furthers their own but not necessarily the leadership's or anyone else's interests. But again this rigid system of control works against initiative and the encouragement of party democracy.

This is not to imply that Khrushchev or the present leadership has either a naive belief in or a cynical view of Soviet society and political organization. The appointment of officials from above and censorship of the media are accepted as the right and proper way to maintain the leadership's position, provide a body of reliable officials, and encourage support for the present system. Yet Khrushchev certainly seems to have believed that it was possible to combine this with the existence of a new 'representative' and popular organization which would find support from an active population willing to work together to build a better society. The present leadership appears, in part as a result of the Khrushchev experiment, less optimistic but it has not produced an alternative.

These are some of the problems the Khrushchev 'solution' raises. We shall come back to them and others in the chapters that follow, but first let us look at the new central government created by Khrushchev and see how it has developed under his successors.

8 The Central Authorities

Under Khrushchev the Politburo became the undisputed chief executive and policy-maker. This, a small body of leading party and Soviet officials, largely chosen and led by the indomitable First Secretary himself, was to be the new vigorous government. It was to be the linchpin in a set of central authorities which together should be responsible for policy-decisions and implementation. Under his successors the Politburo has retained its dominant position, although its character has changed slightly, particularly since the early seventies, as has that of some of the other central institutions. In this chapter we attempt to spell out for the reader the functions, both theoretical and actual, performed by these institutions and the relationships between them. First a word of warning. Formally there exist two separate structures, each with its own central leading organs: party and Soviet. Some writers prefer to reserve the terms 'State' or 'government' for the Soviet institutions – the Supreme Soviet, Council of Ministers, etc. Although this is formally correct – in the sense that they are described as such in the Constitution – it tends to confuse the reader. When we talk of the 'government' of a country, still more when we refer to the 'State', we mean those central authorities which make policy, which 'rule', that is which pass laws and can enforce them by their control over the means of coercion. In the Soviet context this means the conjoined forces of party and Soviet institutions – or, to put it another way, the 'State' or 'government' in the USSR is a set of interconnected party and Soviet institutions. Hence when we use the words 'State' or 'government' we embrace under them both party and Soviet and, in describing the central authorities, we deal with both.

The Politburo

Let us look first at the Politburo and its relationship to the other institutions. By the late fifties there was no disputing the dominant role of the Politburo or that of Khrushchev within it. In 1957 the Council of Ministers had been cut right down with the abolition of almost all the industrial ministries and before long Khrushchev took on the Chairmanship himself. He was not only First Secretary of the party and Chairman of the Council of Ministers but also responsible for a new bureau for the party in the RSFSR. Much of the strength of Khrushchev's position, and indeed that of the Politburo as a whole, lay in his command over appointments. As First Secretary of the party, he was responsible for a wide range of leading party appointments and, as Chairman of the Council of Ministers, formally responsible for appointments in ministerial and military sectors – powers which he freely exercised.

Yet he never achieved anything approaching Stalin's position. In 1959 at a special Party Congress called to launch a new seven-year plan and in 1961, with the publication of a new party programme, he was being treated with fulsome adulation – reminiscent of the Stalin period – yet, simultaneously, he was unable to get his educational reform through, he was unable to prevent the 'steel-eaters' (or heavy industry) consuming resources intended for agriculture, and he failed to get support at the 1961 Congress to make old political opponents responsible for their activities under Stalin. Then in 1964 his erstwhile supporters, men whom he had promoted to the Politburo, joined with the few remaining old members (notably Suslov and Mikoyan) to vote him out of office and this time *they* had called the Central Committee and made sure of majority support.

The repudiation of terror, once the appropriate means of silencing opponents, and the doubts about Stalinist policies resulted in the re-emergence of factions within the leadership; in turn bringing in the Central Committee as a decisive body in 1957 ended the certainty that final decisions could be confined to the narrow oligarchy of the Politburo. What this means in effect is that neither the First Secretary nor a group within the Politburo nor even a 'united' Politburo is in an impregnable position. A First Secretary (or General Secretary as he has been called since 1966) may promote his supporters but their continued support, in the absence of terror, is something that cannot be guaranteed. Any of the leading individuals, or indeed any of the members, has to retain the support of his colleagues, has to take care that he has support on the Central Committee and must attempt not to antagonize too many influential interests. The failure to observe these 'rules of self-preservation' will threaten an individual or a collective leadership. Perhaps the surest way to lose support or to turn erstwhile supporters into opponents is to produce policy failures. Khrushchev went because his policies were failing and because he was antagonizing his colleagues by his increasingly high-handed methods of rule. Since 1964 the Soviet Union had had a collective leadership within which Brezhnev has gradually emerged as the dominant figure, but the position of this leadership (and Brezhnev's position within it) – that on which it depends for its continued existence – is the same as under Khrushchev. It would be unlikely to survive if major policy differences split the members; even less likely to survive a disastrous policy failure that could be attributed to a group or individual within it. Nor need a policy be disastrous. Some commentators were suggesting in 1975 that opposition from a hard-line group to Brezhnev's detente policies and dissatisfaction with the poor showing of agriculture – a sphere Brezhnev has identified himself with – might produce a majority faction in favour of his resignation. But at the Twenty-fifth Congress in February 1976 he dominated the proceedings much more obviously than at the previous Congress. This could be interpreted as his having weathered a storm and emerged even stronger *or* that the Politburo as a whole agreed to his assuming public dominance in order to end the speculation about his health and impending retirement. But, whatever the nature of Brezhnev's position at present, it is unlikely that the 1976 leadership (whose average age is sixty-six) can stay in power for more than another few years. And, as the collective leadership begins to crumble, younger politicians will begin to compete for the leadership, relying on the same methods – alignments with other leading officials, promoting supporters to positions which give them places on the Central Committee, and new programmes – to try to achieve a Politburo majority that has Central Committee backing.

The Politburo elected at the Twenty-fifth Congress had sixteen full members and six candidates (candidates have no voting rights). The composition of the Politburo has remained remarkably stable under the present leadership: new members have been coopted accompanied by few resignations. Fourteen of the present members were on the Politburo in 1966. But here we are interested not so much in individuals as in the posts whose incumbents are included. As of March 1976 the Politburo was as follows:

Full Members

L. I. Brezhnev	General Secretary
A. P. Kirilenko	Party Secretariat
F. D. Kulakov	Party Secretariat
M. A. Suslov	Party Secretariat
D. F. Ustinov	Party Secretariat
P. Ya. Pelshe	Chairman of Party Control Commission
V. V. Grishin	First Secretary, Moscow City Party
D. A. Kunayev	First Secretary, Kazakhstan Party
G. V. Romanov	First Secretary, Leningrad Oblast Party
V. V. Shcherbitsky	First Secretary, Ukraine Party
A. N. Kosygin	Chairman, Council of Ministers
K. T. Mazurov	First Deputy Chairman, Council of Ministers
A. A. Grechko	Minister of Defence
A. A. Gromyko	Minister of Foreign Affairs
Ya. A. Andropov	Chairman of KGB
N. V. Podgorny	President of the Supreme Soviet USSR

Candidate Members

B. N. Ponomarev	Party Secretariat
G. A. Aliyev	First Secretary, Azerbaijan Party
P. M. Masherov	First Secretary, Belorussian Party
Sh. P. Rashidov	First Secretary, Uzbekistan Party
M. S. Solomentsev	Chairman of RSFSR* Council of Ministers
P. N. Demichev	

* RSFSR = Russian Republic

This Politburo has much more of a 'representative' or 'corporate' flavour about it than any of its predecessors. In the twenties and early thirties members were elected or coopted on the basis of their individual merits or services to the party: there was no thought of including the holders of particular posts. In the Stalin period the Politburo barely functioned. Under Khrushchev it was a body dominated by the First Secretary who grouped around himself individuals whom he hoped would support him with his policy package. Since Khrushchev, although the change is not dramatic, the Politburo has become more of what one might call a 'national government' with the holders of leading party and ministerial posts making up its membership. This practice was furthered by the changes made in 1973. Before then the Minister of Defence, the Minister of Foreign Affairs, the head of the KGB and the first secretary of the Leningrad region were not included. Their promotion emphasizes the development of the Politburo into a body including – as of right – leading central and republican party officials (and from the two major cities), ministers responsible for the most important branches of government policy, and the chairmen of a few other key institutions.

In a sense this is a development along Khrushchevian lines – the idea of incorporating leading officials from all sectors in 'the government' – but Khrushchev did not extend this principle to the Politburo itself. It was the Central Committee which was expanded to include representatives of all different institutions while the Politburo remained a smaller Khrushchev-dominated cabinet which put ideas on policy to the Central Committee. Some have argued that the collective leadership of Brezhnev, Kosygin, and Podgorny has made the Politburo less effective as a policy-making body – that the necessary compromises have resulted in a lack of clear-cut policies. In theory the suggestion seems plausible: a smaller body, dominated by one man, is more likely to produce definite policies than a larger 'coalition' cabinet. It is tempting to imagine that Khrushchev purposely kept the Politburo small and select. But, unfortunately, there is little evidence that policy under the collective leadership for the period since 1964 has been more marked by compromise or any less 'definite' than under Khrushchev. The early years in particular saw policy change and initiative. Since the beginning of the seventies the leadership has produced little that is new, little evidence of vigorous ideas, and in part but only in part this may be attributable to the expansion of the Politburo. The larger and more corporate an institution the Politburo becomes – regardless of whether it is led by one man or by a collective leadership – the greater the likelihood of disagreement and hence inability to agree on policy changes among its members. But, as we shall argue later, more important reasons lie behind the recent more conservative and cautious line.

In describing the change in the Politburo, we have not explained it. Some have suggested that under the collective leadership of Brezhnev, Kosygin, and Podgorny there has been a conscious policy of sharing out the places between party, ministerial, and Soviet officials in part at least to prevent any one 'faction' dominating the rest. This could explain its more catholic composition, but the 1973 changes suggest that there is more to it than that: that its leading members do see it as a body composed of incumbents of certain posts. Also we must be careful with the argument which relates 'posts' and factions. Knowledge of the posts which are represented does not in itself tell us anything about 'factions' or 'groups' within the Politburo. For a start, 'present post' may not be related to past experience or previous career. A Soviet post may be occupied by someone who has previously been a party official; high-ranking party or Soviet officials may be given jobs as heads of other institutions. For example, Solomentsev, originally a member of the party Secretariat, took over the Chairmanship of the RSFSR Council of Ministers; Grishin, now head of the Moscow party, earlier had responsibility for the trade unions. It is true that certain individuals (for instance, Gromyko in Foreign Affairs, Suslov in ideology) have identified themselves with particular policy areas over a long period and do not shift around, but others are politicians of a more 'generalist' kind. As happens in British politics, sometimes cabinet posts go to candidates with particular expertise in the area, sometimes leading politicians with no experience in that field are appointed, just as there are individuals who stick to one area (Douglas-Home) and others (Maudling) who go from one to another. The analogy should not be pushed too far. It remains true that the present generation of Soviet ministers tends to be those who have acquired specialist knowledge from long association with a particular industry, and it is the high-flying party apparatus men who are given a variety of different jobs. But there is some evidence that future ministers may well be drawn from among the ranks of Secretariat officials who have specialized in the problems of particular industrial branches or some other sphere of government policy. What this means, in effect, is that it is perfectly possible, despite a balancing of posts, for the Politburo to be dominated by a majority of 'apparatus' men, men whose previous careers have been primarily in party work. But this in turn need not imply an 'apparatus' faction or one loyal to the General Secretary. It is after all only an assumption (and not a very good assumption at that) that we can predict future behaviour from or relate present behaviour to past career patterns. The existence of such a group or faction – or indeed of any such factions – will depend among other things on the types of policy advocated by the General Secretary or other leading members, and on relationships with other colleagues. The actual splits that occur may well not be related to the distribution of places between party and Soviet posts, nor to the past careers of the individuals.

In emphasizing the development of the Politburo as a body composed of certain posts, we are not implying that the 'individual' factor is no longer relevant. After all posts have to be filled by individuals. In 1973 the first secretary of the Ukrainian party, Shelest, and the first secretary of the Georgian party, Mzhavanadze, lost their jobs and their full and candidate memberships of the Politburo respectively. Shelest's replacement in the Ukraine, Shcherbitsky, received full Politburo membership; Mzhavanadze's successor – not even candidate membership. Now one could suggest that it was Shcherbitsky, the individual, who got the Politburo place in preference to his less well-known Georgian colleague. In some sense of course this is true, but to express it in that way is misleading. Given that the Ukrainian party is the largest republican party in the USSR and given the present policy of including the heads of leading institutions on the Politburo, it is true that whoever was given the first secretary-ship was going to be given a Politburo place and that an experienced individual was going to be appointed. The Georgian party is not as large and its first secretary does not therefore automatically qualify for membership. But, had there been an eminent party figure whom the leadership thought desirable to send to Georgia as first secretary to clear up the corruption uncovered in high places, the individual in question would probably have received or retained Politburo membership. It is also possible that Mzhavanadze himself owed his Politburo place to his own long-term experience as first secretary in Georgia. In general then the post and the individual complement one another; in particular instances the experience of the individual, his potential, or his usefulness to the General Secretary may earn him a place.

Politicians and their Backgrounds

There was a period when western students of Soviet politics made the individual composition of the top leadership their major concern. Some even argued that in the Soviet Union politics only existed in the Kremlin – in the infighting and bargaining that took place between leading individuals. This kind of approach (known at the time and afterwards as Kremlinology) came under attack as others argued that (a) this was a very narrow definition of 'the political' and (b) there were other processes at work which influenced decision-making, notably the emergence of groups with different views and objectives. The reader will be aware that our concept of politics extends far wider than that of the Kremlinologists yet, at the same time, in the preceding chapter we devoted considerable attention to relationships within the leading group of individuals and to their actions. We justified this on the grounds that the political situation following Stalin's death was one in which initiative for action was concentrated in the hands of those who made up the new leadership. In other words this was a situation in which the actions of individuals could and did have far-reaching consequences. What we now have to ask ourselves is whether the same kind of situation exists today. Is the political system one in which much or little seems to hinge upon who occupies the leading post or posts? After all there is little point in devoting time and attention to personalities if they are of minor importance.

As a preliminary answer we can suggest that the fewer the 'checks' upon the actions of the individual, the more important the 'individual factor'. A leader who is continually responsible for his actions to a wider group or faced by institutions which he does not control has much less scope for action than one unrestricted in this sense. Given this, we would argue that the personal composition of the Soviet leadership was important during the post-Stalin period (both because of the autonomous position of the leadership and because of the scope for change following the dictator's death), but it is of less importance today because of the cumbersome institutional structure erected by and around the leadership. Whether today the individual composition of the Soviet leadership is of more significance than that of the British cabinet or, indeed, than the character of the President of the United States is debatable. We would suggest that there is not much in it.

But supposing we agree that the individual factor is of *some* importance. What is it then that we might want to know about the individuals concerned? What can we say of the present leadership? It is composed of men, almost all of whom are in their fifties and sixties and started their party or state careers in the 1930s and 1940s; indeed three of the most eminent – Brezhnev, Kosygin, and Suslov – were candidate or full members of the Politburo created by Stalin in 1952. They were beneficiaries of the educational opportunities and social mobility that accompanied the industrialization campaigns, and have a wide range of administrative experience of one kind and another; they are men who survived the excesses of the Stalin period and then adjusted to the changes under Khrushchev. But does this kind of information tell us any more than we knew already, that is that a certain toughness, resilience, and administrative ability characterize the present incumbents? It tells us that we will not find a Che Guevara among the present leadership (but that we could have guessed already) but it will not tell us how 'hard' or 'soft', how innovative or conservative the individuals are. Let us think back for a moment to the immediate post-Stalin leadership. Here was a group of men all of whom could be thought of as loyal Stalin men: products of the Stalinist regime. Molotov, the most revolutionary of them all in his youth, remained true to Stalinist principles while Khrushchev, with an impeccable Stalinist past, emerged as a more 'liberal' leader than any before or since. Just as we could not have predicted this from looking at their past careers or behaviour, neither can we relate the 'line' adopted by present individuals to differences in past careers. And incidentally, in the Soviet context and particularly under the present leadership which has striven hard to maintain its 'collective personality', information on the line adopted by particular individuals is often hard to come by. There are few personal statements by politicians (Khrushchev was an exception) and no *Sunday Times* Insight Reports or 'revealing' biographies. All that one has are snippets of information of ranging reliability: Brezhnev took a tough line in arguing with the Czech leaders in 1968 while Kosygin remained glumly silent; rumour has it that Semichastny, a 'real Stalinist', asked for permission at a Politburo meeting to shoot 1,200 dissidents and thus end the protest movement; Shelest was soft on Ukrainian nationalism, etc. But this is peripheral to the main point: *probably* the kind of information which would be most useful in helping us to predict how up-and-coming politicians might behave as leaders is of a very 'personal' kind – known by those who have worked with them and their political colleagues but not by western observers – but even this kind of information may be a poor guide to future action. Let us think of Khrushchev for a moment. According to an ex-chauffeur to some of the top political elite under Stalin, it was only in the Khrushchev household that family and servants ate together.[1] This fits with Khrushchev the political leader preoccupied with the standard of living, with his populist, anti-status leanings which distinguish him from many of his colleagues. But, by way of counter-example, it is doubtful that any of his subordinates at the time of the purge in the Ukraine ever imagined he would lead a de-Stalinization campaign. In other words, it is not at all clear how useful even this kind of background information is.

But to turn from the individual to the group. In recent years political scientists have invested an enormous amount of time and energy in studying the backgrounds and career patterns of countless 'elite' groups in different countries, including those of the Soviet elite. We now have a considerable body of information on origins, educational achievements, and career patterns.[2] What is less clear is what conclusions or predictions – if any – we draw from this. We know that those younger men (and they are men) who are moving up in the party hierarchy tend to be Russian, from a variety of social backgrounds, that they have received a higher education (often technical and sometimes combined with a degree from a party high school), some have combined more specialist careers in a particular branch of the economy with party work, others have been involved only in party administration of one kind or another. In very general terms, and they are very general, we can talk of a 'type' but this does not help us to predict what the future political leadership of the USSR will or will not do. The 'type' is general enough to include advocates of a greater or smaller use of secret police powers, more or less critical discussion and participation in policy-making, aggression against or agreement with China, the introduction of a more flexible economic mechanism or more central control, etc., etc. The type certainly excludes any 'radical' politicians (although even here caution is necessary given the swiftness with which certain East-European party men have 'changed' in response to new situations), but that is something we know not from looking at backgrounds and careers but from our knowledge of the policies pursued by the leadership, of the roles played by subordinates, and the system of appointment from above.

It is interesting but not very helpful to know that some Soviet citizens think of the present incumbents of positions of authority as the men of the forties, still imbued with Stalinist principles and attitudes, a fairly tight-knit group with personal and political ties, served by – and this is the point – a stratum of younger, 'totally unprincipled', 'time-serving' careerists who lack even Stalinist principles. It is as difficult to accept that the aspiring politicians have 'no views of their own' as it is to agree with one western view that the present system produces 'clerks' for its politicians.[3] But perhaps these two views tell us something rather different – perhaps it is precisely when observers are unable to produce any particular distinguishing characteristics of the 're-placement' group that we should recognize the relative unim-portance of such factors. To return to an earlier point: there are times of change and uncertainty when the nature of the elite or elites may be of crucial importance. The uncertainty and change may be caused by the death of a dictator. In this case both the individual leaders and the type of existing elite will be important: *Khrushchev*'s victory was significant as was the existence of a Stalinist-trained political elite which effectively braked the de-Stalinization process. Alternatively the uncertainty and change may be caused by the emergence of a new type of elite which, if successful, can fashion roles in its own image. In either of these situations the analysis of the backgrounds and attributes of the elite may help us to foretell future developments. But there are also periods when roles and institutions are well established, tend-ing to dominate the new incumbents, and when the replacement group lacks any marks of a 'new' elite. We would suggest that Khrushchev's substitute for Stalinism resulted in the emergence of a fairly well-established and rigid structure of authority, one in which the institutions themselves circumscribe the scope for manoeuvre and change. This is not to say no change is possible; it is to say that change is not going to come from the present or up-and-coming political elite. What this means then is that the study of the backgrounds and career patterns of present or aspir-ing politicians in itself will be of little use in predicting the future. Instead we want to look at the present structure of power, recog-nizing that it is the leadership's maintenance of its position by a fairly tight control over a number of cumbersome and integrated institutions that circumscribes the scope for action.

The Council of Ministers

If the Politburo is chief executive and policy-maker, it is aided and supported in both functions by the Council of Ministers and the party Secretariat (see Figure 1). Let us look briefly at each and at the relationship between them.

Formally the members of the Council of Ministers are appointed by the Supreme Soviet or, when that body is not in session, by the Praesidium of the Supreme Soviet. As of 1973 the Council of Ministers had 106 members whom we can think of as the heads of the different branches or departments of the civil service. These ranged from Kosygin (Chairman of the Council) and his deputies with overall responsibilities to ministers of Foreign Affairs, Defence, Culture, or of particular industries – Oil, Machine-Construction, Aviation – to the chairmen of committees or other institutions subordinate to the Council of Ministers – the KGB, the State Bank, the Committee on Prices, etc. Not surprisingly this huge body has a smaller Praesidium composed of some of the leading ministers and the chairmen of the fifteen republican Councils of Ministers. In theory the Council of Ministers acts in accordance with the instructions of the Supreme Soviet: clarifying existing legislation and executing policy decisions via its individual ministries. It has the right both to make policy suggestions and to issue decrees. As Soviet authors recognize, its decrees (often issued jointly with the Central Committee of the party) are frequently much broader than mere 'details' within existing legislation: in many cases they establish important principles and have the force of law. But knowledge that decrees are issued in the name of the Council of Ministers does not tell us how this body operates. We do not know how often it meets, whether a decree is only published after a full meeting or whether the smaller Praesidium takes a decision, or whether a decree is only published after Politburo approval. We are told that the Supreme Soviet delegates responsibility for particular matters to the appropriate ministries and we know that individual ministries are consulted on certain issues. Until we have more concrete information, all we can offer is a tentative account based on snippets of information and common-sense.

It is unlikely (given its size and the commitments of its members) that the Council meets as a body perhaps more than twice a year and extremely unlikely that it in fact discusses and 'passes' all the decrees issued in its name. It is much more probable that the smaller Praesidium is responsible for these and acts in conjunction with those ministries involved in a particular piece of legislation. Certainly we would expect the individual ministries

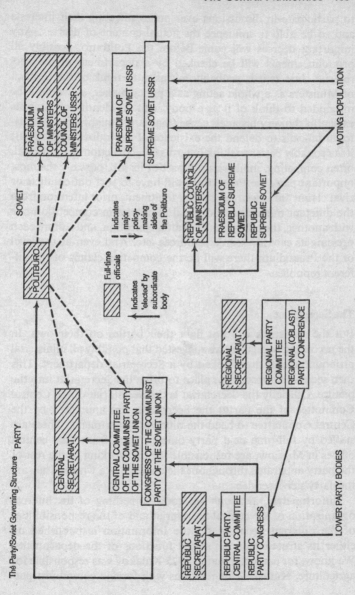

The Party/Soviet Governing Structure

PARTY

SOVIET

Indicates major policy-making aides of the Politburo

Full-time officials

Indicates 'elected' by subordinate body

VOTING POPULATION

PRAESIDIUM OF COUNCIL OF MINISTERS / COUNCIL OF MINISTERS USSR

PRAESIDIUM OF SUPREME SOVIET USSR / SUPREME SOVIET USSR

REPUBLIC COUNCIL OF MINISTERS

PRAESIDIUM OF REPUBLIC SUPREME SOVIET / REPUBLIC SUPREME SOVIET

POLITBURO

CENTRAL SECRETARIAT

CENTRAL COMMITTEE OF THE COMMUNIST PARTY OF THE SOVIET UNION / CONGRESS OF THE COMMUNIST PARTY OF THE SOVIET UNION

REGIONAL SECRETARIAT

REGIONAL PARTY COMMITTEE / REGIONAL (OBLAST) PARTY CONFERENCE

REPUBLIC SECRETARIAT

REPUBLIC PARTY CENTRAL COMMITTEE / REPUBLIC PARTY CONGRESS

LOWER PARTY BODIES

to participate in discussions over policy affecting their interests and to be able to influence the actual content of decrees. Any important decrees will come before the Politburo, possibly all pronouncements will be checked by a department of the Secretariat. Just as it is probably mistaken to think of the Council of Ministers as a whole acting as a policy-maker, so would it be misguided to think of it as a body with an identity of interests except in the very broadest sense (that is, we might expect ministerial officials to defend the existence of centralized ministries); it is probably better to think in terms of a collection of individual, often competing, ministries. As part of its job, possibly the most important part, the Praesidium will have to sort out conflicts or rival claims for resources, special treatment, prior attention from the different ministries: industrial ministries in competition one with another, the ministries of health, education, and culture each pressing its case for scarce resources, etc. And even at the level of the Praesidium there will be the competing claims of the different republics.

The Secretariat

But the ministries will not fight their battles on their own. In the preceding paragraph we suggested that possibly all ministerial pronouncements are checked by a Secretariat department. This then seems an appropriate place to bring the Secretariat into the picture. Officially the Secretariat is the Secretariat of the Central Committee of the party; the Secretaries are appointed by the Central Committee to head the different departments. These are staffed by full-time paid party officials who, from their central offices in Moscow, are responsible for the working of the rest of the party apparatus throughout the country as a whole. They are the party's civil service.

Unfortunately, although we know something of the internal organization of the central Secretariat and of the responsibilities of the different Secretaries, little information is published on either its structure or the actual functions of the departments. We know, for example, that in 1975 Kulakov was responsible for agriculture, Katushev for relations with foreign communist par-

ties, Dolgikh for heavy industry. Within these general policy areas
are a number of departments, each with its departmental head,
deputies, and officials. Thus, for example, under heavy industry
there are departments for different industrial branches; within
the cultural field there are departments for the press, radio and
television, cinema, etc. Rather differently there are departments
(under Kapitonov's general supervision) responsible for purely
party matters – the organization, personnel, and working of the
lower party bodies.

Here we are concerned with particular departments and their
relationship with the ministries. We do not know quite how
closely the Secretariat department responsible for the Chemical
Industry and the Ministry for the Chemical Industry will work
together but we can suggest the following. The ministry is responsible for the everyday running of the industry; the Secretariat
department is responsible for seeing that the ministry is doing its
job – if anything goes 'wrong' in the industry (poor results, waste
of resources) the Secretariat department will be held responsible
for not chivvying the ministry or bringing the matter to the attention of the higher authorities. We can expect that the minister
will be asked to report periodically to the head of the department
and we know that, when the industrial ministries were brought
back in 1965, high-ranking Secretariat officials were appointed as
deputy-ministers. The Secretariat department then has a general
supervisory role but, in turn, its performance will be judged by
the performance of the ministry. What this means, we suggest,
is that Secretariat department and ministry will try to work together. When it comes to making policy proposals, the ministry
will be in a stronger position if it has its Secretariat department's
backing – and indeed we might expect that the Praesidium of the
Council of Ministers will want the appropriate Secretariat views
on any proposed pieces of legislation – and a minister will attempt to back any claims for resources with Secretariat support.
Thus the original picture of policy-making within the Council of
Ministers is too simple – we find ministries plus their Secretariat
departments in competition with other ministries plus *their*
Secretariat departments. It is up to the 'overlords' of the Secretariat – the Secretaries – and the Praesidium of the Council of

Ministers to resolve differences and make the final decisions – and, if need be, to take them to the Politburo.

In addition to its supervisory role, the party Secretariat has other functions which give it an important place within the policy-making framework. It is after all the *Secretariat*, serving the Central Committee and thence Politburo. In this capacity, it will be responsible for preparing drafts, providing the Politburo and Central Committee with information, preparing and checking pieces of legislation. Whatever the policy issue, the appropriate Secretariat department view will be requested. Furthermore as head of the party apparatus it is responsible for sending instructions to lower party bodies, instructions which although they are not 'decrees' or 'legislative acts' are certainly policy statements. These may vary from instructions on the appropriate interpretation of the Czech crisis of 1968 to the banning of exhibitions of abstract or religious art. In this capacity too it acts as a court of appeal or decision-maker on countless matters which are not of sufficient importance to reach the Politburo itself. These may range from decisions on whether particular types of literature should be published or sociology taught as a degree scheme to whether or not to grant an exit visa, sack a corrupt official or rehabilitate a general. For all but the most important decisions, the buck stops at the Secretariat: that is where an individual or organization has to win its case.

Finally the Secretariat can exert an important indirect influence on policy-making by its control over appointments. It is responsible for appointing the secretaries of the republican and oblast party organizations, secretaries of party organizations within the ministries and armed forces, editors of party journals and newspapers. It will also propose names (and probably veto other suggestions if it thinks necessary) for ministerial appointments, heads of state committees, ambassadors, chairmen and secretaries of the Komsomol, trade unions, and other professional organizations such as the Writers Union, editors of other national newspapers, chairmen of the Republic Council of Ministers, top armed service appointments, directorships of the most important industrial enterprises, the top appointments in the academic world, etc.

The Supreme Soviet

The Politburo, Secretariat, and Council of Ministers are the bodies most intimately connected with the making of policy and directing its implementation, but those larger 'elected' bodies which appoint them also play a part, even if only a minor one. Let us take the Supreme Soviet first. The Soviet Union is made up of fifteen republics of which the largest is the RSFSR or Russian republic. In the Soviet structure each republic has its own Supreme Soviet – to be distinguished from the Supreme Soviet for the USSR as a whole, or the All-Union Supreme Soviet as it is sometimes called (see Figure 1). The two-chamber All-Union Supreme Soviet is directly elected every four years and, as a non-party body, contains both party and non-party members as delegates. It meets for a few days twice a year to pass important pieces of legislation and has its own commissions which study draft proposals. It elects a Praesidium to which is delegated responsibility for acting when the Supreme Soviet itself is not in session. The Praesidium is composed of a Chairman (at present Podgorny), the chairmen of the fifteen republic Supreme Soviets, and a sprinkling of party and Soviet officials from different levels in the two hierarchies. Although the population votes separately for its delegates to the All-Union Supreme Soviet and its own republican (for example, Russian, Georgian, Ukrainian) Supreme Soviet, one individual can simultaneously be a member of both. As just mentioned, the chairmen of the republic Supreme Soviets sit on the Praesidium of the All-Union Supreme Soviet (and similarly, the reader will remember, the chairmen of the republic Council of Ministers – on the Praesidium of the All-Union Council of Ministers). Thus there is an overlap of personnel between the republic and all-union bodies.

In theory the Supreme Soviet is the chief legislative authority in the political system, but in practice it merely 'passes' the laws presented to it. There is some evidence that in recent years its commissions (or sub-committees) have played a part in suggesting minor amendments to proposed legislation. If this practice is extended, we should probably want to include these commissions among the policy-makers, but at present the Supreme Soviet is the least important of the central institutions. Its power of appointment too is nominal rather than real. At present its elections and meetings do little more than emphasize the unity of party and non-party citizens and provide an opportunity for re-affirming support for the leadership.

The Central Committee and Party Congress

In some ways the leading party organs parallel those in the Soviet structure. The All-Union Party Congress (which now meets once every five years) is officially the supreme party body and it elects a Central Committee to act in its absence. But these two bodies, in particular the Central Committee, are much more interesting and influential assemblies than their counterparts in the Soviet structure.

If the Politburo is the place where the most important policy decisions are made, the Central Committee provides a forum where a much larger group of representatives from the different institutions hear and discuss policy proposals and decisions. It has grown steadily in size over recent years. In 1961 it had 175 members, in 1966 195, in 1971 241, and at the recent Congress in 1976 287 were elected. These are the figures for full members. Just as the Politburo is composed of full members and candidates without voting rights, so has the Central Committee its candidates – 139 at the last election. One factor to be borne in mind when thinking of the role of the Central Committee is its increase in size. With its 400 odd members and candidate members, and meeting as it does only twice a year, it is no longer a compact body the members of which can all know each other and quickly sense shifts in opinion and calculate possible allies and opponents. Simply because of its size it must have become more of a blind gathering, less of a body which could establish a corporate personality during its elected period of office. (The Politburo in turn is getting bigger – as large as the original Leninist Central Committee – and here, we have been told, an inner grouping of the most senior members sometimes meets. As it is one wonders whether Rashidov, first secretary of Uzbekistan, really manages to make the meeting each week.)

As was the Politburo in the days until Stalin killed it, the Central Committee used to be a body composed of party men of some standing. But, when Khrushchev brought the Central Committee back as the highest consultative body in the land, it came back as a kind of grand council with places on it reserved for leading officials from different institutions. Certain posts seem to carry automatic membership status with them: (a) from the party apparatus: the eight to ten secretaries in charge of the Secretariat, the fourteen first secretaries of the republican parties, the first secretaries of the Moscow and Leningrad party organizations, and roughly thirty-five of the first secretaries of the biggest obkomy or regional party committees (b) from the Council of Ministers: the Chairman and two deputy chairmen, the Ministers of Defence and Foreign Affairs, the chairmen of the Councils of Ministers of the larger republics (c) from other organizations: the Secretary of the Komsomol organization, the Chairman of the trade unions. The military always has some representatives, as does the KGB (apart from a short period after 1956). A rough breakdown of the occupations of the members at the time of election gives us some indication of the changing composition of the body:

Table I Occupation of Central Committee Members at Time Elected

	1952	1956	1961	1966	1971
Total number of full members	125	133	175	195	241
Occupation: % of total					
Party and related*	63·2	54·9	48·8	43·2	40·7
State and related (incl. police)	28·3	38·3	32·2	39·5	39·8
Military	4·8	4·5	8·0	7·2	7·9
Other	3·2	2·3	10·9	10·3	11·9

* Includes party posts in mass media.
Source: R. Donaldson, 'The 1971 Soviet Central Committee', *World Politics*, April 1972, p. 398.

We can see the decline in the percentage of posts held by the party apparatus and the substitution of Soviet representatives and others. But not only has the Committee become more representative of the major institutions, it has also become more 'representative' in other ways. On the one hand officials from different *levels* in their respective hierarchies (central, republic, regional, and even district) are given places and the smaller nationalities have been rewarded with seats for the first secretaries of the party organizations in their regions. On the other hand the practice of including representatives from the scientific, academic, and literary professions, the occasional enterprise manager and collective-farm chairman, trade union and komsomol officials, and a few rank-and-file party activists from among the industrial or collective-farm workers has been widened and accounts for the relative increase in the 'other' category. Thus Khrushchev brought back a new type of Central Committee, one which his successors have not altered.

What then is the role of this grand 'representative' council? According to the party statutes, in between Congresses it 'directs all the activities of the party, and of the local party bodies, selects and distributes leading officials, directs the work of the central government bodies and social organizations of the working people through the party groups in them, sets up various party organs, institutions and enterprises and directs their activity, appoints the editors of the central newspapers and. journals operating under its control, and distributes the funds of the party budget and controls its expenditure' (Clause 35).[4] As is often the case with a set description of an institution's functions, this leaves much to be desired. It is true that formally the Central Committee is responsible for electing the Politburo, appointing the Secretaries and other leading party officials, and ratifying certain government appointments; it is also true that the Committee will hear and pass reports on party funds or on the educational institutions under its jurisdiction. Furthermore any major decisions on party work will only be issued after a meeting of the Committee. But in practice the Committee usually merely ratifies or approves proposals of this kind in much the same way that a university Senate 'passes' the suggested list of appointments that comes to it from lower bodies or sub-committees. In the Soviet case it is the Politburo or Secretariat that puts 'decisions' before the Central Committee for ratification. However, given what happened in 1957, the Politburo cannot discount the Central Committee as a potential force in any disputes over the leadership. No one faction or group within the Politburo will want to see a Central Committee heavily dominated by supporters of another faction. It is possible that following Khrushchev's ouster, the senior members of the Politburo (Brezhnev, Kosygin, and Podgorny) came to some tacit agreement on this score and a good deal of hard bargaining took place in 1966 and 1971.

The Central Committee then cannot be discounted as a 'creator of governments' but where it has been more important, or perhaps more continuously active, has been as a forum for the discussion of policy. A meeting of the Committee should be called every six months and under Khrushchev these meetings were usually devoted to a particular topic – agriculture, the economy, foreign affairs. These were occasions when Khrushchev would put new proposals up for discussion (sometimes expanding the size of the meeting by inviting outside specialists to attend) with two aims in mind: first, to gain publicity for his proposals and, secondly, to find out what the responses of this influential gathering would be. He did not always get the response he wanted and certain proposals were dropped or modified as a result. The Brezhnev and Kosygin leadership has not used Central Committee meetings in quite the same way. They have still been called to discuss particular topics: agricultural policy or economic reform, but there has been less discussion of alternatives, less participation by all and sundry and, since the late sixties, reports of the meetings have not been made public. This makes it difficult to judge their present function. It could be that discussion is, as a result, freer and that the Committee does play a greater part in decision-making. On the other hand, during the first few years after 1964 the reports of the meetings suggested that Brezhnev seemed to see the Central Committee less as a discussion or consultative forum, more as a select gathering to which he reports results and new policy.

In so far as this is true the Central Committee is becoming more like a Party Congress. The Congress had ceased to be a decision-maker by the late twenties. It gradually became a gathering for the faithful to hear the reports of the party leaders, to receive encouragement and a sense of belonging to a victorious army before going back to carry on with party work. No Congress met between 1939 and 1952. After Stalin's death, as part of the return to Leninist principles, it was decided that a Party Congress should meet every four years. In 1971, after a year's delay, it was announced that henceforth the Congress should convene once every five years to coincide with the beginning of a new five-year plan for the economy. Delegates are sent by the republic and regional party congresses or conferences. (As in the Soviet structure each republic party has its own party congress and organization – with the exception of the Russian republic whose regional party bodies are directly subordinate to the central party authorities. And again, as in the Soviet structure, leading republican officials serve simultaneously at republic and central level.) The Congress – which meets only once, for perhaps two weeks – is now a huge affair: 4,998 delegates attended the one in 1976. Preparations are made and meetings held for months beforehand to organize the election of delegates; special work targets are set by enterprises, farms, and institutions; meetings are held by every party organization to discuss the importance of the forthcoming Congress. And afterwards – although everyone is somewhat exhausted by then – meetings are held again to discuss the new directives. The Congress itself – which brings together delegates from all over the USSR and from foreign communist parties – is in its composition similar to a magnified Central Committee, although it has a greater proportion of rank-and-file delegates. Apart from one occasion, the Twenty-second Congress in 1961 when Khrushchev tried to obtain support for more far-reaching de-Stalinization measures and failed, the Congress has not in any sense influenced decision-making. It has listened to reports on past achievements and accepted the tasks for the future. It has provided a forum for the party leaders to appear before a cross-section of the party, an occasion for a few of the rank and file to mingle with the mighty, for old acquaintances to renew their ties and aspiring younger men to make new connections.

A Unified Structure

We suggested initially that, although formally separate, it makes better sense to think of party and Soviet as forming one State structure. It is a structure within which the separate parts do different things and one in which the party bodies dominate or, in Soviet terminology, 'lead' or 'direct' the others. This is achieved in a number of ways. First, although the Soviet bodies are 'elected', their composition – whether in terms of individuals or the balance between social and occupational groups – is monitored by the appropriate party bodies at all levels. What this means at central level is that a department of the Secretariat will be responsible for seeing that the Supreme Soviet contains an appropriate 'mixture' of party and Soviet officials and 'ordinary' delegates from different levels in the hierarchies and different parts of the country. Secondly, party bodies are responsible for appointing, suggesting, and/or vetting candidates for a wide range of posts. We mentioned, when describing the Secretariat's functions in an earlier section, that one of its departments will be responsible for seeing that appropriate individuals occupy the posts of chairmen of the republic Supreme Soviets and Councils of Ministers; probably ministerial appointments at All-Union level are a matter for the Politburo itself with Secretariat advice. It is the Praesidium of the Supreme Soviet which, the reader will remember, formally appoints individual ministers between sessions of the Supreme Soviet itself. But the Praesidium too is a strongly party-dominated body, containing among its members several important party officials from the Secretariat and republic party organizations, including Brezhnev himself.

This brings us to another, perhaps the most important, point. The Soviet and party organs are not composed of two separate or distinct sets of officials or delegates. Brezhnev and other leading party officials are members of the Praesidium of the Supreme Soviet. Kosygin and some other ministers are members of the Politburo, as is Podgorny, President of the Supreme Soviet. All are members of the Central Committee. Several are deputies to the Supreme Soviet. In other words, in terms of personnel, the party and Soviet structures are interlocking. Many individuals will be members of both the Supreme Soviet and the Party Congress; some of these will then be elected to both the Praesidium and the Central Committee, and a few of these occupy even higher posts. Brezhnev, for example, is a delegate to the Supreme Soviet, a member of its Praesidium, a delegate to the Party Congress, member of the Central Committee, General Secretary (in charge of the Secretariat), and member of the Politburo. Masherov, first secretary of the Belorussian republican party, a delegate to the All-Union Party Congress, is a member of the Central Committee, candidate member of the Politburo, and simultaneously a delegate to the Supreme Soviet and member of its Praesidium. Solomentsev, chairman of the Council of Ministers of the RSFSR and a member of the Praesidium of the Council of Ministers of the USSR, is simultaneously a delegate to the Party Congress, a member of the Central Committee and of the Politburo. The examples of Masherov and Solomentsev show how, in terms of personnel, the two structures come together vertically and horizontally. Republican ministers will sit on the Central Committee and republican party secretaries find a place on the Praesidium of the Supreme Soviet. Secretariat officials may be elected to republic Supreme Soviets. The only bodies between which this kind of overlap does not occur are the Praesidium of the Supreme Soviet and the Council of Ministers on the one hand, and the Secretariat and Council of Ministers on the other. In the latter case the reason is obvious: no one individual could simultaneously work as a full-time minister and as a party official, but why no ministers should sit on the Praesidium of the Supreme Soviet is not so apparent.

In effect there is an 'inner core' of personnel who weld party and Soviet institutions together: a group of politicians who change hats as they go from a meeting of one body to the next. At the centre is the small group of leading officials who make up the Politburo; in their capacities as members of other bodies they are surrounded by groups of lesser personnel, some of whom also sit on more than one body. And it is when they meet as party bodies that they are responsible for taking decisions – decisions which are then 'shared' with Soviet institutions, to be put into practice by the Council of Ministers and Secretariat, whose most important members sit on the Politburo and Central Committee. Taken together the party and Soviet institutions comprise a centralized State structure that is integrated both vertically and horizontally.

In the preceding account we have attempted to describe the complex relationships between a set of central authorities. As we have shown, these overlap one with another in terms of personnel and functions. The result is a cumbersome structure of interlocking institutions: an unchallengeable authority which dominates all others. But while this conjoining of the different institutions at the top creates a Leviathan, it simultaneously makes for a Leviathan that has difficulty in acting. The Politburo, compared with many other chief executives, is clearly in a very powerful position – exempt from regular elections, in control of appointments, of the judiciary and civil service – yet by virtue of combining in itself the spokesmen for quite a wide range of institutions and attempting to rule through a cumbersome set of institutions (which combine in themselves an even wider range of organizations) it embodies their different aspirations and has to try to rule through them.

Although Khrushchev welded the different institutions together, he kept the Politburo separate as a small cabinet and, until the early sixties, reduced the size of the ministerial civil service to a minimum. But since his departure the gradual development of the Politburo into a corporate cabinet of all has been accompanied by the expansion of the central institutions into an enormously complex and bureaucratic structure. Certainly, on the face of it, the present institutional structure at the top would appear better suited to maintaining the *status quo* than effecting change. But enough of the structure of institutions; let us now look at them in action.

9 Policies and Policy-making

Traditionally the accountability of the leadership, the extent of participation in policy-making, the degree of freedom of discussion, criticism, and opposition have been held to be important determinants of the way in which a political leadership 'behaves'. We want to see whether they are. To do this properly would entail looking at a wide range of policy areas in a number of different political systems. It might well be, for example, that foreign policy is made in a remarkably similar fashion by governments operating within very different political systems but that differences in the treatment of domestic issues can be traced to differences in the systems themselves. Be that as it may, the aim here is more modest: to look at a few policy areas in one political system to see what conclusions (or perhaps, rather, what hypotheses) can be drawn.

We have chosen agriculture and industry because of their intrinsic importance. They are obvious candidates for inclusion. Policy towards culture provides a good contrast of a very different policy field and leads naturally into the wider question of freedom of speech, criticism, and dissent. But, it may be objected, to discuss industrial or agricultural policy without reference to the Soviet Union's international position, to defence commitments in particular and foreign policy in general, is to distort the framework before one begins. This is certainly true in the following sense. The Soviet leadership's intention of maintaining defence parity with the United States means the continual and, compared with the US, greater drain on resources. Defence expenditure continually takes resources from areas where they are badly needed and slows down the development of other sectors. Hence the attempts by the Soviet leadership, from Khrushchev on, to come to agreement with the Americans on different forms of arms expenditure are not surprising. The political struggles over the distribution of resources between the different civilian sectors of the economy always take place against a background of prior struggles over defence versus civilian expenditure. All this is true but it is not the case that the level of defence expenditure either precludes the expansion and development of the civilian economy or determines the distribution of resources between the different civilian sectors nor that changes in the level of defence expenditure 'explain' changes in industrial and agricultural policy. For example, changes in the volume of investment devoted to agriculture cannot be related to changes in defence expenditure. Hence, as long as we bear the general constraints of defence in mind (and at times they will be mentioned more specifically), we can look at domestic policy without its foreign counterpart

(i) Agriculture

Khrushchev's Remedies

It's time for us to realize that the teaching of Marx, Engels, and Lenin cannot be hammered into people's heads only in the classroom and newspapers and at political rallies; agitation and propaganda on behalf of Soviet power must also be carried on in our restaurants and cafeterias. Our people must be able to use their wages to buy high-quality products manufactured under socialism if they are ultimately to accept our system and reject capitalism.[1]

Throughout his period of office Khrushchev continually stressed the importance of agriculture if the standard of living were to rise. Although one of the reasons he was ousted in 1964 was agriculture's poor performance, it was he who brought the agricultural problem out into the open and produced new policies to cope with it. But Khrushchev was not simply interested in agriculture as part of his general aim of improving living standards. Agriculture was a topic that particularly interested him and one about which he prided himself that he knew. Even under Stalin he had made a vain attempt to suggest that changes were necessary and, after the dictator's death, he began almost immediately to advance concrete proposals.

One of Stalin's bequests to his heirs was a backward and un-productive agricultural sector. Agriculture never received the necessary investment in machinery, buildings, fertilizer, transport, storage facilities, and skilled personnel which could have pro-duced large-scale, modern, and efficient farms. Given the large size of the labour force, even though productivity per man was very low, the agricultural sector produced enough to feed the towns and itself (although badly) without taking the scarce re-sources that were needed for industry. Given the collective- and State-farm system, the State could control the percentage of total output that it took from the peasants. This then was what Stalinist agricultural policy amounted to – ensuring that the State received a steady supply of grain for the towns while ignoring the question of raising total agricultural output. But, towards the end of the period, the consequences of such a policy were beginning to make themselves felt. As the agricultural labour force shrank, so too did its ability to maintain even *existing* levels of output. And this was at a time when total population was increasing and when the ever-growing urban population required more food. Khrushchev later stated that during the period 1948–53 both total output of grain and deliveries to the State remained static; milk output failed to increase and meat production was below the pre-war level.

In 1953 collective farms far outnumbered State farms. Often the form that a collective farm took was that of an existing village or two or three villages grouped together with little new except an office and house for the collective-farm chairman. Each house-hold retained its small private plot of land and a few animals (a cow, a goat, and a few hens), which its members cared for when not working for the collective farm, and the produce of which they consumed or sold on the open market, often trudging many miles to the nearest town. The farms were subject to two masters: the regional or district party committees and the machine-tractor stations. (There were three different agricultural ministries but they were far away in Moscow and, unlike their industrial counterparts, not directly responsible for the primary units in their sector.) It was upon the shoulders of the regional party organizations (and their subordinate district organizations) that responsibility lay for setting output targets, seeing that they were met, and appointing new chairmen. And it was to the local machine-tractor station (or MTS), which kept the mechanical equipment and operators necessary to serve all the farms in the district, that the collective-farm chairman had to turn to get his land ploughed and sown and his crop harvested. This then had to be 'paid' for with produce which went straight to the State.

Faced with unsatisfactory output figures, Stalin's solution was simple. Quotas for the farms should be raised and the peasant's activities on his private plot restricted. Cut down the size of the plot, tax the peasant who owned a cow or an apple-orchard, and he would put in more work on the collective farm. The trouble with this was that it reduced the supply of milk, eggs, vegetables, and fruit reaching the towns from the private sector (peasants gave up their cows and cut down the apple-trees) and still gave the peasant no incentive to work for the collective farm. With the State taking almost all the farm produced (as it did in one form or another), there was often little or nothing to distribute to the members by way of payment. The local party authorities were aware of the anomalous situation but there was little they could do: they received their orders from above and were judged by how well they carried them out. To be a collective-farm chairman, caught between the demands or orders of the party authorities and a labour force which saw no point in even turning up for work, was indeed a thankless occupation. Party membership was thin on the ground in the collective farms. The chairmen might be party members but one fifth of all collective farms had no party cells in 1953 and, of the little more than a million party members in agriculture, few actually worked in the field.

Table II

	Population			
	Total (millions)	Urban (millions)	Rural (millions)	Urban as % of total
1953	188·0	80·2	107·8	43
1972	246·3	142·5	103·8	58

Sources: 1953: R. Clarke, *Soviet Economic Facts 1917–1970*, Macmillan, 1972, p. 4; 1972: *Narodnoye khozyaistvo 1922–72*, Moscow, 1972, p. 9.

Khrushchev took it for granted that if output on the existing farms were to increase some kind of an incentive system and substantially more investment were needed. After all the rural labour force was shrinking and an ever-growing urban population would need more food simply to maintain the existing standard of living.

At first sight the rural–urban shift appears to be reflected in figures on the changing social composition of the population but here we must be wary.

Table III Social Composition of the Population

	1955	1959	1972
Total	100	100	100
Workers and white-collar workers	58·3	68·3	80·7
of which: workers	—	48·2	59·8
white-collar	—	20·1	20·9
Collective farmers (kolkhozniki)	41·2	31·4	19·3
Others	0·5	0·3	—

Sources: *Nar. khoz. SSSR*, Moscow, 1956, p. 19; *Itogi vsesoyuznoi perepisi naseleniya, 1959 g.*, USSR vol., Moscow, 1962, p. 90; *Nar khoz. 1922–72*, p. 35.

According to Soviet usage the category 'workers' includes those employed in State farms and their families. Thus the drop in the proportion of collective farmers (or kolkhozniki) is not synony-

Table IV Distribution of Employed Population by Sector (%)

	1950	1971
Total	100	100
Industry and construction	27	37
Agriculture and forestry	48	26
Transport and communications	5	8
Trade, supply, etc.	5	7
Health, education, science, culture	8	16
Government, social organizations	3	2
Communal services	4	4

Source: *Nar. khoz. 1922–72*, p. 343. Excludes armed services, students.

mous with a decline in the rural population. During the period the transformation of collective farms into State farms was responsible for at least part of the shrinkage of the kolkhoz sector. A better indication of the changing structure of the economy and hence the way of life of the population is given in Table IV.

What such a table does not show (or at least one assumes that it does not) is the number 'employed' in the labour camps. In 1953 this accounted for perhaps eight million men and women engaged in construction, mining, transport, and lumbering under the jurisdiction of the NKVD; by the 1970s the figure was probably in the hundreds of thousands. We notice that the sector which improves its position most over the period is health, education, etc. This suggests a relative increase in white-collar personnel in the economy as a whole – a shift towards the 'post-industrial society' as it has been called – and the latest census figures indicate that the white-collar group accounted for slightly more than a quarter of the employed population in 1970 compared with slightly less than a fifth in 1959.[2] But this is still a far cry from a 'post-industrial' society. However, it remains true that employment in science, health, education, trade, and communal services (in that order) grew relatively faster than total employment between 1950 and 1971,[3] and that educational standards of the population as a whole and of the employed population rose significantly over the period.

Although the decline of the agricultural labour force was to be expected and, in the long term, desirable, the existing conditions in the countryside drove the young men to the towns leaving a labour force dominated by women and children. This was hardly likely to meet the demands of the growing urban sector. It was hoped that a better incentive system would both stimulate higher productivity and, in turn, make life in the countryside more attractive. Prices paid to collective farms for their products were raised while output quotas were initially held steady and limitations on the private plot relaxed. Simultaneously investment in agriculture was increased and then a chemicals programme with a strong emphasis on mineral fertilizers pushed very forcibly. But incentives and investment are expensive and do not produce dramatic results. Hence it is not surprising that Khrushchev sought other remedies too.

In 1954 he drew attention to the unploughed lands of Kazakhstan which, if brought under cultivation, could – he argued – produce grain in abundance. Such a suggestion was not new, but Khrushchev turned it into a 'practical proposal': it appeared in the press as a topic for discussion with influential backers, meetings of agricultural and party officials were organized to work out its implications, and Khrushchev carefully canvassed Kazakh officials and made efforts to appoint those who supported him to responsible positions. The campaign resulted in the proposal being accepted by the Politburo.

Two other measures were of this kind, that is chosen by Khrushchev from among a number of possible measures regardless of the amount of institutional support for them. They were not necessarily his ideas but they were ideas that he took up and personally championed. The first was a move to abolish the machine-tractor stations, the MTS, and to turn their agricultural equipment over to the collective farms. The MTS were financed directly out of the State budget: if the collective farms took over the equipment (furthermore if they paid for it) and were responsible for new purchases, central expenditure would be reduced. Although this surely influenced Khrushchev's thinking, his argument naturally enough was rather different: there was now enough equipment for each farm to have its own and the new system would be more efficient than the present dependence upon the MTS. As can be imagined this was the kind of proposal that touched several different interests and on which there was room for real disagreement over the probable consequences. Collective-farm chairmen (depending upon whether they thought they could afford the machinery), agricultural officials and party secretaries (depending upon their assessment of the farms' ability to cope and the efficiency of the MTS), and MTS officials themselves were divided. Again there was a press campaign and this time (1958) the proposals were put to the Central Committee. Khrushchev's committed position was enough to ensure that supporters of the reform got a better press and that, albeit with some modifications, the Central Committee accepted the proposals. Even more 'personal' was Khrushchev's conviction that the cultivation of maize would solve all kinds of problems (animal feed among others) or that a particular rotation of grasses was the best technique. These became unquestionable tenets of agricultural policy.

We can think of decision-making on agriculture as taking two different forms under Khrushchev. First, as in the case of the Virgin Lands or the MTS, he employed the tactic of whipping up outside support as one way of exerting pressure on reluctant colleagues or overriding opposition. He would throw matters open for discussion, reckoning that he could control and divert the discussion into the direction he wished. He used to win – his position, his power over appointments, and the attitude towards 'the leader' ensured that – but opponents could and did win concessions on timing, modifications of one sort or another that were not insignificant. Although the extended meetings of the Central Committee or the press debates served a straight political purpose, they were also part of Khrushchev's whole style of rule. He liked discussion (provided it ended up by his winning), he liked to feel that he had support from a range of different sectional interests and that he was in touch with 'the masses' – both 'ordinary people' and specialists could have ideas that were worth listening to. But, simultaneously and this is where we see another side to Khrushchev and to decision-making, he could be utterly stubborn in the defence of his views and expect subordinates to accept them as right without questioning. The maize campaign was an example of this type of approach and, as Khrushchev's agricultural policy ran into difficulties, this arbitrary decision-making from above became more pronounced.

Initially everything went well: the Virgin Lands of Kazakhstan produced bumper harvests, productivity and output rose on the established farms. But by the end of the fifties progress had slowed right down, and in 1963 the government had to resort to buying wheat from Canada and raising the prices of meat and dairy products which were in short supply in the shops. The causes were several and tell us something of the factors that influence policy-making. First, although investment in agriculture did increase and increase substantially, the demands of industry and defence began to eat away at the gains – particularly as agriculture did well. Planners and others were willing to listen more sympathetically to supplicants from other, traditionally more important, sectors, as the Virgin Lands seemed to be 'solving' the grain problem. But, by the end of the fifties, output from the Virgin Lands was well down on the first years' harvests. The pressure for instant success (from the top) meant that the land was ploughed up, sown and reaped, then again the following year with scant regard to soil preservation. Consequently, as had happened in earlier days in America when the settlers took the goodness from the soil and then moved on to new land, the soil became less and less fertile until in places it was little more than a dust bowl. Added investment was then necessary to reclaim it. In turn the incentives introduced to boost output on the existing collective farms suffered: as the Virgin Lands' harvests looked less good, farm quotas in the established areas were raised (and, as the situation looked worse, raised even more in desperation) and restrictions re-imposed on the private plots. Furthermore the machinery the farms had acquired from the MTS had to be paid for and this, at least in the short run, was a drain on resources that could otherwise have gone to paying their members. Too many collective farmers still had no incentive to work for the farm.

Faced with grain and livestock shortages at the beginning of the sixties, Khrushchev convinced himself that the answer lay in 'administrative re-organization' (and the continuation of the maize campaign). The Ministry of Agriculture (whose original minister had been dismissed for lack of support over earlier policy) was limited to responsibility for research and techniques; a State Procurement Committee was set up (an earlier ministry had been abolished) and a new organization – Selkhoztekhnika – created with responsibility for agricultural equipment and its distribution. At regional and district level the party committees were split into two – an industrial committee and an agricultural committee – but then a wholly new administrative agency – the territorial production agency or TPA – whose jurisdiction coincided neither with the region nor district, was formed to oversee the farms. This upset the long-established relationship between party committees and 'their' subordinate farms. These changes were suggested and introduced with little discussion and still less criticism. In 1964 Khrushchev had a new idea – the creation of State Committees (under the Council of Ministers) for different agricultural products – and it is said that one of his last proposals, and one that was instrumental in persuading his colleagues he must go, was that individual Politburo members should take responsibility for particular agricultural products or types of livestock.[4]

Brezhnev's Policy

In March 1965 Brezhnev called a plenum of the Central Committee to hear his agricultural policy and, ever since, he has been the major spokesman on agriculture. His proposals were not radically new, rather they were a re-affirmation of Khrushchev's original arguments that what agriculture needed was investment and a better incentive system. But first he abolished the administrative tangles of the previous few years by restoring the Ministry of Agriculture to its original position as the central agricultural authority, and by making the regional and district party committees (no longer sub-divided into industrial and agricultural) responsible for the farms again. As an incentive, prices for agricultural products were raised (and those for above-quota sales raised substantially) and the farms were assured that their quotas would remain unchanged for five years. This was important, because it is clearly not in the farm's interest to overfulfil its quota in a particular year (and gain the extra income) if its quota is correspondingly raised the following year. Simultaneously restrictions on the private plots were again eased. More interesting was the announcement that from 1966 onwards collective-farm workers were to receive the wage rates paid on State farms for the equivalent jobs. Unlike all State employees (that is the rest of the labour force) collective farmers had never been entitled to set wage rates or to social security benefits (and only in 1964 had they received a right to a pension). All that they had been entitled to was payment for work done in the course of the year if, after meeting all its other commitments, the farm had anything left. The new wages scheme did not guarantee the peasant a minimum monthly wage but it did make payment for jobs done, on a monthly basis, the first charge on a farm's income. The scheme was introduced in the great majority of the collective farms during 1966.

Increased investment was the other major plank in Brezhnev's agricultural programme. Machinery, fertilizers, irrigation systems all received a powerful boost. There were signs towards the end of the sixties, that, with good harvests and pressure from other commitments, the rate of investment was going to suffer as it had done under Khrushchev but there has been a renewed spurt in the seventies. The following figures show the relative and absolute improvement since 1953.

Table V

		Industry	Agriculture
		Investment (milliard new roubles at constant 1955 prices)	
1953	approx.	6·0	1·9
1970		29·6	14·2

Source: Clarke, *Soviet Economic Facts*, p. 13.

In certain other respects the Khrushchev policy has continued. Over the period as a whole collective farms have been amalgamated into larger units and some converted into State farms. (A State farm is nationalized property; all employees receive regular monthly wages and investment is provided by the State.) And where new territories have been opened up – as in Kazakhstan for example – State rather than collective farms have been introduced.

Brezhnev stressed, as did Khrushchev, the need for more agricultural specialists, for raising skill and educational qualifications in the countryside, and increasing the number and spread of party members. In certain respects these demands have been met. Each farm now has its party cell (of course there are now far fewer farms) and party membership, including manual workers, has risen sharply. The educational qualifications of collective-farm chairmen have greatly improved, and the number of 'specialists' employed in agriculture increased. But the number employed still falls short of demand and of the number trained, and there is little evidence that agricultural institutes of one kind or another have received special government support and encouragement. It is clearly easier to enrol party members than it is to persuade specialists to take up jobs or to remain in the countryside – given the paucity of material and social amenities. Neither have the improvements in living conditions been enough to stop the inevitable drift of the young men to the towns.

In general we can characterize agricultural policy since Khrushchev as the continuation of his general line but without his dramatic solutions or hasty panaceas. Although Brezhnev made himself responsible for agriculture, he has not attempted to take sole responsibility the way Khrushchev did. Matskevich, the deposed minister, came back to head the Ministry of Agriculture; important secretariat officials responsible for agriculture have been included in the Politburo; and, for a time at least, the RSFSR Council of Ministers under the chairmanship of Voronov successfully advocated agricultural policies that ran counter to Secretariat views. In particular Voronov was far less enthusiastic about reclaiming the non-black-earth lands of the RSFSR and the emphasis on investment in fertilizers and equipment than was the General Secretary. In 1971 Voronov lost his job and in 1973 the hapless Matskevich was replaced by Polyansky, one of the leading Secretariat experts on agriculture. This gave the smaller inner policy-making group, consisting of party and ministerial leaders involved in agriculture, more of a unity about it. Under both Khrushchev and Brezhnev we see the sacking of ministers or other important figures if they fail to agree with a policy to which the General Secretary has committed himself. This is hardly surprising; nor is the impression that the more 'collective' nature of the present leadership may make it more difficult for the General Secretary to dislodge an opponent if he has support within the Politburo. Perhaps more interesting is the observation that a minister or the chairman of a republic Council of Ministers does, while he remains in office, wield sufficient independent authority to be able to pursue his own policies.

Under Brezhnev there have been no extended public Central Committee meetings, no noisy debates, instead the sober announcement of policy within established guidelines. But is this at least in part because the Brezhnev leadership, by consolidating the advances made under Khrushchev and building upon them, has solved the agricultural problem? The overall increase in output and improvement in productivity since 1953 has been substantial.

Table VI

| | Gross Agricultural Production | | |
	Total	Crops	Livestock
1940	100	100	100
1953	104	96	124
1970	221	204	265

Source: Clarke, *Soviet Economic Facts*, p. 11.

Table VII

| | | Grain | |
| | Harvest | Procurements | Yields |
	mill. tons	mill. tons	cn/ha*
1935	75·0	27·5+	7·1+
1953	82·5	31·1	7·8
1970	186·8	73·3	15·6
1972	168·2	—	14·0
1973	222·5	—	17·6

+Average for period 1933–7.
* cn/ha = centner per hectare.
Source: Clarke, *Soviet Economic Facts*, pp. 111–15;
Nove in Brown, A., and Kaser, M., (eds.) *The Soviet Union since the Fall of Khrushchev*, Macmillan 1975, p. 2.

Certainly the new policies have had results and must account in part for the rise in the standard of living over the period. But, impressive though the gains are, it is still the case that agricultural produce is in short supply, poor quality, and relatively expensive. Khrushchev's boasts of catching up with the standard of living in America by 1980 seem quite unrealistic. Furthermore the supply of agricultural output – to the consumer or to industry – is unreliable. In a bad year such as 1972–3, when lack of snow and then rain ruined many basic crops, or again in 1975–6, food runs short in the towns and industry suffers. The government once more has to purchase large quantities of grain abroad. Figures on the overall improvement mask the following problems: the inability of the agricultural sector to meet consumer demands; its unreliable performance; the high cost of the sector in terms of investment, subsidies on meat products to keep prices down in the shops, or purchases abroad; the low productivity despite more expensive incentive schemes.

But, some have argued, because of the climate and the terrain (most of the USSR's vast territory is unsuitable for agriculture) one year out of three can be expected to be bad: the shortage of food in bad years must be attributed to the weather rather than to man; if anything, the Soviet leadership should invest less and import more. Others argue quite differently: productivity in those parts of Canada which experience similar soil and climatic conditions is considerably higher than in the Soviet Union; the difference lies in the different systems of ownership and incentives – if the Soviet government was prepared to return to private farming it would have a more efficient agriculture.

There is some sense, but only some, in both these arguments. It is true that Soviet agriculture suffers from serious natural handicaps but it is also true that their effects could be mitigated. If, for example, productivity was higher, a bad harvest would not produce such poor results in absolute terms; if storage facilities, canning and freezing stations, and a good transport network existed, much more could be salvaged and reach the towns. If a better incentive system existed, more would be produced in good and bad years. But this is a long way from arguing that the answer lies in private peasant farming. Advocates of this view emphasize the contribution made by the private plots to the population's supply of eggs, milk, vegetables and fruit – which is certainly significant – but to imagine that this should be taken as an example for the whole of agriculture is misguided. The Soviet Union is not Canada or the United States with a tiny proportion of its labour force working on large, highly mechanized farms, served by a good transport network; it still has more than a third of its population, more than 100 million people, living on the land. A return to private ownership (and the mind boggles at the thought of how the actual transfer would take place) would mean either small farms (not necessarily productive) or some process of pushing the less able off the land – never a smooth process – to add to the pressure on urban facilities. It is hard to imagine the leadership contemplating private farming, quite regardless of any commitment to cooperative or social ownership, because of the problems it would produce.

This in turn does not mean that the present collective-farm system 'works': it clearly does not. It provides the peasant with little incentive, and the collective with little autonomy of decision-making. This is important because agricultural performance is affected immediately and visibly by decisions on what, when, and how to produce; if these are made from above, the collective is already deprived of an incentive – the ability to make the best use of its resources. The obligation to carry out orders which seem unsuitable and which bring little material benefit produces poor results, waste of resources, and neglect of machinery.

In the attempt to give the collective farmer more of a stake in the land, an experiment called the 'link' system has been tried in a few areas. A section of the collective-farm land is handed over to a small group to farm as the members think fit and they are rewarded according to results. The experiment has taken slightly different forms in different places, and the reports tend to be written by enthusiastic supporters of the idea. Hence it is difficult to assess the results. The leadership appears to have remained unimpressed in the sense that it has not publicly urged the wider application of the scheme. This, in the Soviet context, is sufficient to limit its introduction: it is easier to prevent change than it is to effect it, a point we shall return to later. It is the kind of proposal that Khrushchev might have taken up and pushed – or again he might have come out strongly against it, which would have killed it quickly. The Brezhnev leadership has a more cautious, less optimistic approach. Its lack of enthusiasm for 'new' measures suggests that it sees the main advances in productivity coming from mechanization, the use of fertilizers, storage facilities, etc. – from technical change in a broad sense – rather than from tinkering with the collective-farm system.

Policy-making and Implementation

The range of agricultural policies adopted over the period is wide. In certain respects agriculture is the sector which has seen most change. It has leapt from being a neglected sector to one which consumes a substantial part of total investment and is personally supervised by the party leader. Its labour force, although still the worst paid, has seen the greatest relative improvement in its income. Institutionally the MTS have gone, State farms are replacing collective farms, and enormous new tracts of land brought under cultivation. Where there has been no change is in the relationship of the State to the producing units. The collective- and State-farm system, operating under orders from the regional authorities, in their turn subordinate to the centre, remains untouched: the nature of the hierarchical central control has not altered. Nor does it seem that relationships at the centre have changed very much. Let us look at this a little more closely.

The extent to which the First Secretary or the First Secretary plus his advisers has been responsible for initiating policy is marked. In thinking of agricultural policy, it is difficult to see the leadership being pushed this way and that by powerful interests or responding to a barrage of suggestions from agricultural specialists. It is rather that the leadership has acted in the absence of either strong institutional or specialist pressures. Agriculture as a sector has few organized institutions. The agricultural ministries inherited from Stalin were few in number and the neglect of agriculture had made them institutions of secondary importance. The Ministry of Agriculture does seem to have exerted a 'negative' influence more than once, but each time this has resulted in the fall of the minister and his replacement by more pliable officials. In addition the relegation of agriculture to 'poor neighbour' status meant that as a profession it attracted neither able personnel nor resources. It was not the case that the opening of the debate on agriculture released strong and coherent opinions. It is true that in the more liberal publishing climate a few writers began to offer 'realistic' accounts of life in the countryside, but this did not have an impact upon policy.[5] The only institutional change, compared with the Stalin period, is the emergence of the Central Committee as a discussion forum and restraining influence. Under Khrushchev, at the plenary sessions called to discuss particular agricultural issues and attended by agricultural experts and collective-farm chairmen, participation in policy-making was extended slightly, but his successors have halted the practice. There was the suggestion that the Collective-Farm Federation might be re-born and organized on a national basis, but little came of it. Agriculture remains a sector with few organized lobbies or institutions of any kind.

Policy proposals then have come from a relatively autonomous or independent leadership which has met with little opposition. This in turn accounts for the nature of the policies. In such a situation the leaders' perception of the situation is important. Khrushchev's fairly drastic measures (investment, chemicals, maize, the Virgin Lands, etc.) reflect his perception of the situation as serious *and* his ability to push his 'solutions' through. But, if the policy-making situation is of this kind, it is hardly surprising that there has been no change in the relationship between the centre and the subordinate units. A political leadership will not spontaneously and unprompted divest itself of its powers of control. To do so would be to decrease its authority, alter the basis of its political power and, in its eyes, work against the introduction of a successful agricultural policy.

But what of the success of the policies? A political leadership may be able to initiate a policy with ease but unable to get it implemented. Here we notice a number of things. First, the absence of strong agricultural institutions at the centre makes it easy for the leadership to get its policies through but difficult to ensure continued support for them. The existence of institutions representing other interests, for example heavy industry, means that agricultural interests are constantly under threat. Deprived of leadership intervention and support, agriculture loses out. This is best seen in terms of the distribution of resources: when the leadership relaxes the pressure, resources intended for agriculture are diverted to those sectors whose institutions can pull more weight. The leadership has then to intervene constantly, reiterate its commitment to agriculture, if its policies are to be carried out. It is different when we think of policies which only affect the sector itself. Here we note two different phenomena. Certain policies are executed very speedily: the Virgin Lands, the planting of maize, the setting up of the TPAs. In these cases the executive machinery clicks into action very effectively and here surely the relatively simple lines of authority – from the Secretariat down through the regional party bodies to the farms – are a relevant factor. But we should also note that this kind of policy decision is sometimes executed 'too well', in the sense that overzealous officials carry the campaign to absurd lengths – which suggests that a certain unthinking execution of commands characterizes the work of the executive machine and that those employed in agriculture have either no influence or no inclination to prevent such absurdities. However, simultaneously we have to account for the failure of certain policies: the continued waste of fertilizers and neglect of machinery or the inability of the sector to recruit and maintain its quota of specialists. This implies that perhaps we ought to think in terms of an executive machine suited to implementing a particular type of policy directive and unable to cope with others.

We leave a discussion of this until the next chapter, but one point which emerges and which is relevant to the present analysis of policy-making is that, if we are to talk of group influence in agriculture, we shall find it at the implementation rather than at the policy-making stage. Party secretaries, planning officials, collective-farm chairmen, and peasants all influence the outcome of policies but play little, if any, part in actually deciding them. Some argue that, since their behaviour must have an indirect effect upon the policy-makers' decisions, we should consider even the peasants as constituting an 'influence' or a 'latent interest group'. This extension of the term 'interest group' to include everybody is not very useful. We do want to be able to distinguish those who are directly and actively involved in making decisions from the rest. But this in turn does not mean that an analysis of policy-making need ignore peasant behaviour. Under the collective-farm system the peasant can withhold his labour (because of the existence of the private plot) in contrast to the situation in industry. This does not *in itself* give the peasant a greater bargaining power. After all the peasantry had the same 'weapon' under Stalin and what did it achieve for them then? But, given a shortage of labour on the land and the leadership's desire to raise the overall standard of living, peasant labour does become more 'valuable' in the eyes of the leadership and it is willing to pay a higher price for it. As we already mentioned the collective-farm worker sees a marked relative improvement in his income.

Table VIII

| | Average Monthly Wages (roubles) | | | |
	1950	1960	1970	1971 (plan)
Collective-farm workers*	17	28	75	77
State-farm workers	36	52		104
Industrial workers	69	90		135

* Includes payments in kind.
Source: *Nar. khoz. 1922–72*, pp. 350–51; and *Soviet Economic Prospects for the Seventies*, Joint Economic Committee, US Congress, Washington, 1973, p. 513.

This suggests that, whereas institutional strength influences the distribution of resources between different branches of the economy, it does not affect the distribution of income. Again this is something to come back to.

We have noted several different aspects to policy-making on agriculture. We now have to ask whether the picture is similar when we take a different policy area. In the USSR ultimate decisions lie in the hands of a small, self-recruiting group, uncontrolled by elections but aware of the dangers of antagonizing leading officials of the major institutions. Through its control of appointments and a censorship network the leadership can influence the composition of the subordinate political elite and set the limits on discussion and criticism. Do these factors, which remain constant whatever the policy area, seem to have a substantial or a marginal effect upon policy-making? If we compare different policy fields do we find the same characteristics reappearing or are the differences such that we must conclude that the factors mentioned above are not crucial?

(ii) Industry

Is industrial policy made in the same way as agricultural policy? Although politicians and others criticized the inadequacies of the industrial sector in the post-Stalin period, the leadership's actions suggest that it at least thought in terms of problems that could be solved without too much difficulty. By the early seventies the situation looked different. Those shortcomings, visible in the fifties, proved more enduring than imagined and, what was more worrying, growth rates had slowed down. Despite a number of changes, industry refused to respond as had been hoped. At present the leadership appears less optimistic; indeed it seems uncertain how to proceed. For a start then the leadership's attitude towards the two sectors has differed.

Although growing at an impressive rate, the industrial sector in 1953 was still trapped in the mould of the thirties, and the new leadership knew it. Iron, steel, coke, and coal forged ahead while the level of consumer goods remained pitiably low. New branches of industry such as plastics or chemicals had not been developed; equipment in general was relatively old or old-fashioned, technology stood still and western innovations were ignored. While the mal-distribution of resources and the lack of encouragement for new industries could be blamed on the chief architect of the plan (that is, Stalin), the industrial ministries came under attack for their inefficient use of resources, wastefulness, and conservatism. Ministries had attempted to make themselves self-sufficient with their own transport systems, and factories producing common components; they showed no interest in promoting greater efficiency, or innovation in their subordinate enterprises. Instead they deluged the enterprise with plans (often late), counter-plans, and instructions throughout the course of the year.

The labour force of the early fifties, composed of recruits from the countryside and the sons and daughters of an earlier wave of peasant labour, had been turned into an industrial work force in very hard conditions. Women, who accounted for nearly half the labour force, shared the most arduous jobs with men; compulsory overtime, strict penalties for absenteeism and drunkenness remained in force after the end of the war and a law of 1941 which tied workers to their jobs was still operating. Trade-union rights or workers' rights of appeal against management were negligible. The managerial stratum was composed of those who had acquired engineering qualifications in the drive of the thirties and the *praktiki*, men of little formal qualification who had worked themselves up from the bench. To survive as top management officials they had to push their labour force, fight with the ministry in Moscow for resources, hide their shortcomings, try to get as easy a plan as possible, and enlist the help of the district or regional party secretary in obtaining extra or even planned resources and personnel. It was a tough and hazardous job for which the material rewards were great and the penalties for failure severe: demotion, transfer to a less well paid and responsible job in a less attractive region.

The post-Stalin leadership seems to have thought as follows. The impressive growth rate, perhaps 10 per cent per annum, was a consequence of central direction of the economy: the planned distribution of resources, consumption, and investment, and the ministerial–enterprise relationship. Within this framework slight changes were desirable: (a) a somewhat different distribution of resources in order to achieve improvements in the standard of living and (b) a greater emphasis on technological change, a reduction in waste, and better working conditions in order to raise productivity and perhaps even improve on the growth rates.

The Distribution of Resources

It was Malenkov who first queried the existing distribution of resources and opened a debate that has continued ever since. Soviet economists make a distinction within industry between sector A (producer goods) and sector B (consumer goods). Sometimes these are translated as heavy and light industry respectively. Unfortunately it is not quite as simple as that. Sector A includes producer goods for the producer sectors (for example, machinery for a blast furnace) and producer goods for the consumer sector (e.g. a lathe for a textile mill); B refers simply to consumer goods, e.g. the textiles themselves, but this in turn is not synonymous with light industry. (Certain sections of light industry do not produce consumer goods.) It was a law of Stalinist economics that sector A should not only account for a greater share of industrial output than sector B but that it should also grow at a faster rate. In practical terms this meant giving priority to heavy industry and neglecting the consumer although, as we can see from the above, one could operate the law in such a way that the share of goods for making consumer goods (in sector A) increased fastest of all.

Malenkov argued in favour of increasing the share of investment of sector B; he did *not* argue that the *absolute* amount of resources devoted to B should be larger than that granted to A nor that B should grow *faster* than A but he did argue that B's growth should be speeded up. His opponents, including Khrushchev at the time (and supporters of the heavy-industry lobby ever since), raised the cry that the sanctity of the principle of priority of heavy industry was in danger. It was not. What happened was that first under Malenkov, then under Khrushchev, the share of resources allocated to the B sector increased and then, later under Kosygin in the 1971–5 plan, sector B was given a slightly faster growth rate than sector A. This, however, hardly affects their respective shares of gross industrial output: sector A continues to account for nearly 75 per cent of the total.

The A/B debate has at times occupied the centre of the stage, at others been pushed into the background by more pressing problems, but the topic has always been treated cautiously. As we mentioned, Malenkov never openly attacked the Stalinist principle and even when Khrushchev was pushing for an expansion of consumer goods he continued to emphasize, even if rather vaguely, the 'priority of heavy industry'. Kosygin in his turn, announcing the new growth rates for the 1971 plan, did it casually and reiterated the importance of sector A. It is an issue which arouses strong feelings – not only among officials in charge of heavy industry or representatives of the military and defence establishment who have a personal interest in the outcome, but also among some party officials, planners, and academics for whom the priority of sector A symbolizes the proper (Stalinist) approach to the economy and to planning. Consumer goods, the poor relative, can marshal far fewer influential supporters. In this respect the consumer goods' industry is similar to agriculture and it too, despite the leadership's commitment, began to lag badly behind planned targets by the early sixties. It clearly is not enough for the plan to award more to consumer goods production. Something goes wrong in the execution of the plan.

Before we look at what this is, we should note the other ways in which the distribution of resources was altered. Now that war between capitalism and socialism was no longer considered inevitable, socialism would triumph by the superiority of its economic system, a system that would provide for people's wants without the waste, inequality, and hardship that accompany capitalism. This meant that although defence remained important, as did steel production, so now were housing, consumer goods, and new branches of industry such as chemicals and plastics. Both under Khrushchev and since there have been injections of investment into housing or, for example, chemicals and the development of different sources of power – a move away from the traditional concentration on coal, steel, and iron. Khrushchev, in his usual fashion, tended to overdo it – in particular with regard to the chemical industry which he began to see as another panacea – but at least he emphasized the importance of new industrial developments.

This does not mean that there has been a dramatic change in the composition of Gross National Product.

Table IX Expenditure Composition of Soviet GNP (%s)

Use	1952	1960	1969
Private consumption	55·2	51·2	50·9
Public consumption	5·2	5·2	7·1
Capital investment	22·4	33·1	29·5
Defence	13·3	8·4*	10·1
Administration	3·9	2·1	2·4
GNP	100·0	100·0	100·0

* Represents the all-time low of the post-Stalin period.
Source: *Soviet Economic Prospects*, p. 151.

As we can see, the proportions devoted to defence and capital investment have wobbled over the period, and the proportion devoted to consumption has decreased. But, given the overall increase in GNP, this is compatible with substantial improvements in consumer welfare.

Table X Per Capita Real Disposable Income

	1950	1955	1960	1972
Roubles	224·4	367·8	492·0	989·0
Index of (1950 = 100)	100·0	163·9	219·3	440·7

Source: *Soviet Economic Prospects*, p. 393.

It was not only the Stalinist profile of industry that Khrushchev attempted to alter. Questions of tapping new sources of energy inevitably raised questions of industrial location – the development of the North and Far East or the Central Asian republics versus continued concentration on existing sources in the western regions. We argued earlier that the Stalinist system produced sectional interests, which in the industrial sphere meant branch ranged against branch. In the post-Stalin period this acquired new dimensions. Whereas previously there had been an accepted order, a ranking of importance of the different branches, now it was not so clear and this gave more scope for disagreement over resource allocation. (Some established branches, coal, for example, were actually threatened by the newcomers.) Furthermore the move to re-emphasize the importance of the republics and to 'improve' relationships with the smaller nationalities provided a setting within which republic or national claims for resources were more legitimate. And the attempt to open up Siberia and the Far East produced another set of conflicting claims. In the preceding chapter we suggested that Secretariat and ministerial officials responsible for a particular branch work together to defend their interests. Similarly it is noticeable that Far Eastern spokesmen, for example, whatever the post – party secretary, enterprise director, economist – will argue their case against a common enemy, the central authorities.

The Sovnarkhoz *Reform*

From 1957 until 1965 of course most of the industrial ministries did not exist. They were replaced by the *sovnarkhozy* or regional economic councils. This was Khrushchev's solution to the problem of ministerial conservatism and waste of resources. Hopefully the regional authorities would be interested in the whole of industry, and actively promote technological change and the careful use of resources. The *sovnarkhoz* proposal was a sudden and drastic suggestion pushed hurriedly by Khrushchev, perhaps for two reasons: first, a longer campaign would give ministerial and planning officials (of whom there were plenty) time to form a more coherent opposition and, secondly, his insecure position in the Politburo needed bolstering by a quick success. The attempt was risky and, as we know, culminated in his colleagues' move to unseat him, but his victory over them ensured the acceptance of his *sovnarkhoz* proposals. If ministerial and planning staff were sceptical (to put it mildly), regional party secretaries must have seen the decision to make the *sovnarkhoz* boundaries coincide with their regions as an indication of their importance in the industrial structure. And Khrushchev surely hoped that they, perhaps the most important link in the party structure, would guide industry along the new lines laid down at the centre.

Unfortunately, but not surprisingly, the *sovnarkhozy* turned out to be as unsatisfactory as the ministries. They too built their empires – only this time it was the region – and ignored the needs of other parts of the country. Given that party secretary and economic officials were rewarded for the performance of their region, they put 'local interests' first. Coordination of production and supplies within a single region improved but at the expense of national or inter-regional coordination. And, disappointingly, the *sovnarkhozy* failed to encourage the introduction of new technology, improvement in quality, or the more efficient use of resources. Khrushchev's response was to amalgamate them into bigger units, to create State Committees at central level to coordinate research developments within a particular branch of industry (these quickly took over the old ministerial buildings in Moscow), and to fashion and re-fashion the central planning bodies. This was typical of his approach to industry. He took it for granted, as did the majority of those responsible for planning or administering industry, that the system was basically sound – the setting of targets from above, the central distribution of supplies and fixing of prices, the system of rewards based on centrally established indicators. Hence, if things went wrong, the fault lay in administrative arrangements or in incompetence and mismanagement.

Khrushchev might dismiss the Minister of Agriculture and then abolish the Ministry. He could appoint men with some agricultural expertise as first secretaries of the important agricultural regions, but he could not dispose of the army of industrial administrators, officials and their institutions in the same way. As far as we know, there was an influx of younger people into enterprise management posts and from industry into the party apparatus, but that higher stratum of industrial officials inherited from Stalin remained remarkably constant. With the abolition of the ministries, many of them went to *sovnarkhoz* or republican posts but, by the early sixties, they began to come back to staff the new central institutions and indeed, when the industrial ministries were re-established in 1965, many ex-ministers took up their old posts. And of course certain institutions – the State Bank, the Ministry of Finance (known for their conservatism), and a few key industrial ministries – remained throughout. In thinking of industrial policy we must remember this phalanx of officials, trained within the Stalinist economic framework, conscious of its successes, and sceptical of innovation.

The *sovnarkhozy* were the only major industrial innovation of the Khrushchev period. Other measures aimed at improving industry's performance were half-hearted. The incentives offered to encourage innovation were too small to make it worth the risk of disrupting existing production processes; despite repeated criticisms of poor quality production, gross output remained the chief criterion of success. In 1959 managerial bonuses were tied to the wages fund – in an attempt to make management more careful of wage costs – but, since the director could lose more than his bonus if the enterprise failed to meet the output targets, the wages fund continued to be overspent. The conservatism of the policies was surely a combination of Khrushchev's 'understanding' of the problems and the unwillingness of the leading stratum of officialdom to recognize that any change was necessary. No new ideas were going to come from discussions with these industrial administrators. And so, one feels, matters might have continued – given the size and strength of this part of officialdom – had it not been for a series of shocks in the early sixties.

Falling Growth Rates and Economic Reform

It was not simply that defence requirements and heavy industry absorbed resources intended for consumer goods or housing but rather that these sectors hardly grew at all. The 10-per-cent growth rate for industry as a whole fell to perhaps 6 per cent and this was not for lack of resources: the same amount of inputs was producing a smaller return. There is little agreement among either Soviet or western economists on the reason for the slackening off – whether it was somehow to be expected at that 'stage' of industrial development or whether particular administrative arrangements, investment decisions, or incentive schemes were responsible. However, it does seem that the Stalinist planning and incentive system, with its emphasis on orders from above and gross output, while reasonably well suited to the achievement of relatively simple goals (steel, and then more steel), was less well suited to the more complex tasks Khrushchev demanded of it: steel *and* chemicals *and* consumer durables *and* agriculture; quality as well as quantity; cost-consciousness as well as output.

The leadership was worried and Khrushchev baffled. He did not hesitate to rail against the production of enormous armchairs, light fittings so heavy that they brought ceilings down, the waste of expensive machinery brought from abroad, and the greed of the 'steel eaters'. From the mid-fifties the political leadership had been asking of the economists that they turn their attention away from abstract laws of political economy and concentrate on actual problems of the Soviet economy. Faced with the poor growth figures (although we should remember they were still very respectable by West European or US standards) Khrushchev sanctioned the opening of a far-reaching debate in the press. No longer was the issue that of a slight change in the proportions of A and B but it was rather the whole nature of Stalinist planning and inter-enterprise relationships. It was not only economists who argued in favour of or against more enterprise autonomy, a more flexible price system, the computerization of planning. Planners, enterprise managers, research workers, and party officials all entered the debate. Unlike any of the agricultural debates, it was one in which the leadership took no active part; rather it stood on the sidelines and observed. This does not mean that *anything* could be said. Compared with the situation in Eastern Europe, the published debate was more limited, more directed to piece-meal reforms than to basic restructuring, but it is difficult to judge to what extent this was the view of the participants themselves and how far they were constrained by the political setting. As we mentioned earlier the specialists in the post-Stalin period tend to indulge in narrow factional infighting anyway. What emerged from the debate were the sharp disagreements within the econ-omist camp over both the failings and the remedies and, to a lesser extent, among enterprise directors or party officials who included both reformers and conservatives in their ranks.

The debate continued after Khrushchev's fall until in the autumn of 1965 Kosygin announced the outline of an economic reform to a meeting of the Central Committee. This was not a proposal for discussion but rather the conclusions drawn by the leadership from the debate. Its major elements were as follows. The industrial ministries came back, but some of the State com-mittees were retained. What was to be new was the ministry–enterprise relationship and the enterprise's objectives. Far fewer planned indicators were to come down to the enterprise; it was to control more of its own activity. It was no longer to be con-cerned with gross output but with sales and 'profits' – its income compared with its expenditure – and henceforth a charge would be levied on capital. The enterprise would retain a proportion of its profits to put into a socio-cultural fund, a production fund, and an incentive fund for distribution in the form of bonuses to employees. The aim was to make enterprises interested both in producing what was 'wanted' rather than in simply fulfilling orders from above and in economizing on labour, capital, and raw materials. The reform, to be introduced gradually over the next few years under the guidance of a commission staffed by senior planning, industrial, and party officials, was hailed by some as introducing an entirely new economic era. 'Administrative regulation' had been replaced by 'economic levers' – rationality and efficiency would triumph; the consumer would at last receive a variety of good-quality products.

Yet by 1969, at a closed Central Committee meeting, Brezhnev was attacking every facet of industrial activity and at the Congress in 1971 the whole tenor of the speeches was sober. Growth rates were only marginally better and it was clear that the reform had produced no startling gains for the consumer. Kosygin talked bravely if glumly about perfecting existing arrangements and the reluctance of some to abandon administrative methods, but Brezhnev emphasized the improvement in welfare payments of one kind or another as though that were the direction improvements in the standard of living were expected to be taking. And by 1973 attention had shifted away from 'economic levers' to other methods of improving industrial performance.

So here we have a reform – the result of a wide-ranging discussion, produced after consultation with leading officials and directed by an impressive body of planners, politicians, and industrialists – a reform which fails. Why should this be? Let us think again of the reform itself. We note (a) the return of the ministries (plus the old ministers) and the traditional planning and supply agencies (b) the creation of a wide range of republic bodies – ministries and agencies (c) the introduction of new enterprise rights but the continued dependence of the enterprise on the central authorities for its suppliers and centrally determined prices. All the major participants in the debate have been given something. It is a compromise reform but one whose provisions are sufficiently vague to allow for different interpretations, and in such a situation those with the most authority or control over resources will determine the interpretations. And these, the ministries and planning officials, had never been ardent advocates for reform in the first place. The new Statute on the Enterprise was published in 1965, but not until 1967 was one produced for the ministries. Even then it left a number of points vague, most notably those on central versus republican powers. If this was not clear, neither was the relationship between enterprise and ministry and, not surprisingly, very soon the ministries were issuing enterprises with more detailed plans. 'Economic levers', given centrally determined prices and detailed instructions from above, did not mean very much.

New Measures

We would suggest that the post-Khrushchev practice of consulting with a wide range of officials and specialists in the hope of finding a 'satisfactory' solution is doomed to failure because of the opposing interests of the participants. Here then is a situation in which discussion and participation will produce muddled policies. As an example we can mention the policy on 'associations', one of several recent attempts to tackle poor industrial performance by other means. This is a policy of amalgamating or linking enterprises in 'associations' in order to cut out duplication, allow for greater specialization, and reduce administrative personnel; and of linking the ministry with its enterprises (or an association) via as few intermediary organizations as possible. Despite the leadership's talking of the value of the new arrangements, official directives on how the different levels should operate have been far from clear. New rulings were issued in 1973 and 1974, but neither the 1965 Enterprise Statute nor that on the ministries has been officially amended or repealed. From official documents it is impossible to tell who is empowered to do what. There seems to be no clear direction from above and no unity of action below. One can readily see that ministerial officials and enterprise directors may well be slow to implement such a scheme, but the confusion or disagreement among those responsible for drafting policy surely makes their opposition easier.

By and large then traditional methods triumph. But something needs to be done to raise productivity, and the leadership has supported two, very different, methods. The first is the time-honoured method of socialist competition: an organized campaign of friendly competition between enterprises to produce the best year's indices, or between shops or brigades within an enterprise on a monthly basis. Small money prizes or gifts are the reward. Its effectiveness is impossible to assess, but it is easy to organize (the party and trade unions are responsible) and always produces 'positive' results, that is a winner. The renewed emphasis on socialist competition accords with the leadership's frustration with the failure of more sophisticated methods, and signifies that failure. The reform was intended to provide the enterprise's employees with an incentive system that in itself would encourage productivity and efficiency.

Very different and more interesting is the Shchekino experiment. Soviet industry suffers from a labour shortage, but this is accompanied by the phenomenon of enterprise management hoarding surplus labour where possible and using it inefficiently. Under a scheme worked out by the State Committee on Labour and Wages, the Ministry, and enterprise party committee, the Shchekino chemical plant in 1969 carried out a number of measures to raise labour productivity and, as part of this, reduced its labour force while retaining the wages saved to distribute in one form or another to the remaining employees. The scheme was then approved by a meeting of the Central Committee, to be applied carefully where appropriate. It is interesting because of its implications. Some economic reformers in the early sixties did argue that enterprise management should be able to distribute the wages fund as thought fit, but it was clear all along that the political authorities would not abandon the idea of a central wages policy. The problem of the inefficient use of labour, redundancy, and hence possibly unemployment was left largely alone – although all must have been well aware of it. Job security is well established in Soviet industry. To threaten this, in the absence of any proper mechanisms for supplying alternative employment let alone unemployment benefit, at a time when improvements in the standard of living were slowing down, was hardly desirable. (There is no unemployment benefit in the USSR: it was abolished at the end of the twenties when unemployment officially ceased to exist.)

Yet by 1969 the leadership was supporting the Shchekino experiment. The scheme has spread since but not as fast nor as far as its advocates would like. By its advocates we mean the occasional economic journalist, enterprise director, or party official who complains in the pages of *Pravda* of the lack of enthusiasm for it shown by some ministries, managers, and local authorities. It does seem clear that it has its critics among enterprise managers unwilling to lose their labour 'reserve'; and it is difficult to imagine management, party committee, and union welcoming the task of dismissing substantial numbers of management personnel and production workers and then attempting to find them alternative employment. Unfortunately it is impossible to tell whether the slow pace of the experiment is because of opposition from those who are intended to organize it or because signs of discontent from the labour force have persuaded the leadership to go slow *or* because the leadership, although sceptical of its success from the start, thought it worth supporting if only to try to get rid of some of the surplus labour in the chemical industry and as a means of indicating to industrial administrators that something was going to have to be done to cope with the labour shortage.

A Comparison with Agriculture Policy-making

What then of industrial policy as a whole and the similarities to and differences from agriculture? We suggested that the relatively autonomous position of the leadership in agriculture explained both the wide range of policies adopted and the preservation of the existing lines of authority. In industry too the initial attempt to alter the distribution of resources, the *sovnarkhoz* reform, and certain 'worker' and trade-union reforms (on which more detail in a moment) seem to have originated from within the leadership. At that time the leadership appeared to propose and pass its policies in an unchallenged fashion, although we should remember that there was opposition to Malenkov's mild A and B proposals right from the start. But from 1958 onwards it is difficult to see the leadership as standing 'above', pursuing its own policies unchecked and unhindered. Far more 'institutions' and 'interests' are associated both with the making and implementing of industrial policy than with agricultural.

Let us take resource allocation first – between the different industrial branches, republics, and regions. We do not know how much consultation takes place with representatives of the different institutions in the early planning stages and we have no way of knowing whether the plan which finally emerges (be it under Malenkov, Khrushchev, or Kosygin) already represents a concession to the '*status quo*' lobbies or whether it represents the leadership's original preferred resource allocation. What we can say though is that spokesmen for the different interests certainly consider it appropriate to state their claims publicly and that it would be odd if (a) they made no attempt to lobby either politicians or planning officials and if (b) the political leadership made no attempt to listen. We can go on to say that those institutions whose interests are best served by maintaining the *status quo* (heavy industry, the military) are a bigger lobby in terms of resources and personnel. The caution of the leadership in trying to effect changes and its defensive public stand on the A/B issue suggests that the 'heavy boys' do place a constraint upon the leadership's plans.

It is true that the *sovnarkhoz* reform, a sweeping measure which must have antagonized a wide range of leading industrial officials, suggests a leadership strong enough to act arbitrarily. But this was not typical of industrial policy over the period and, as we suggested, was part of a gamble by Khrushchev to improve his weak position by a drastic move. Since then all has been caution and compromise. The discussion before the economic reform of 1965 suggested that far-reaching changes might occur, but, as we saw, the reform itself turned out to be very much of a compromise. Whether we are thinking of measures to speed the introduction of new technology, the formation of associations, or changes in resource allocation, of policies under Khrushchev or Brezhnev, the degree of change implied by them has been small. And this is because of the number and nature of the institutions or interests involved in the process. There are ministerial and planning officials, republic and regional spokesmen, technical specialists, economists, enterprise directors, party and trade-union officials who – particularly since the early sixties – engage in discussions on policy alternatives and advance proposals. And the most important of these, given the scope and complexity of the sector, are involved in the actual devising of the policies.

There are then far more interested parties 'legitimately' besieging the leadership and participating in producing policy. Whereas in agriculture group influence, where it existed, tended to operate at the implementation stage, in industry it is there at the policy-making stage as well.

This in turn affects the nature of the policies. First, given the greater institutional strength of the *status quo* supporters at the centre (from planning officials to military spokesmen), policy will naturally tend to be of a conservative kind; the leadership will have to push hard to get any changes. Secondly, the conflicting interests of those involved means that, if the leadership attempts to listen to all, to cater for all, it will produce unworkable compromises. Khrushchev did not try to do this and he fell; the Brezhnev-Kosygin leadership has been far more 'responsive' and 'representative' but, if anything, that has only hindered the discovery of a successful industrial policy. (Of course this is not to imply that Khrushchev's policy was successful; it is to imply that, if the different interests conflict, 'accommodating' them all will produce stalemate.)

Whereas in agriculture we noticed differences in the way different types of policy were implemented or not, in industry there is more consistency. With the exception of purely administrative changes – the *sovnarkhozy*, the re-instatement of the ministries – changes which either go into effect or do not, industrial policy is very poorly implemented. The executive machinery does not seem to respond kindly to the demands made on it by the leadership. In part we would argue that this is because it is not geared to dealing with the more complicated demands made on it, but that is something to return to in the next chapter.

The Industrial Labour Force

In describing industrial policy and those participating in making or implementing it, we have made almost no mention of those directly involved in production, the industrial workers. Their numbers double over the period, increasing from just over twelve million in 1950 to twenty-six million in 1971 and, as one would expect, educational standards and skill qualifications rise as second- or third-generation urban inhabitants enter from school.

In the de-Stalinization drive of the middle fifties the trade unions were once more referred to as defenders of the interests of the workers and white-collar workers and this, together with their other functions of boosting production, improving labour discipline, and administering social security, has since been one of their duties. The trade-union leadership comes nearest to being an official spokesman for the workers on policy discussions at the top. But this is too simple a picture. The trade unions, organized on a branch basis, embrace *all* employees from ministers via managers down to production workers and typists. The workers as such have no separate organization because, it is argued, their

Table XI Average Monthly Pay of Workers and White-collar Workers (roubles)

	1950	1960	1971	
Average	64·2	80·6	125·9	
Science	93·7	105·3	140·9	(3)*
Industry	70·8	91·6	137·9	(4)
Admin.-technical personnel	122·9	135·7	181·6 ⎫	
Workers	69·0	89·9	135·4 ⎬	
Clerical	64·3	73·8	114·4 ⎭	
Transport	70·7	87·0	144·0	(2)
Government, economic admin., social organizations	68·8	86·4	123·8	(5)
Credit and insurance	66·8	70·7	114·6	(6)
Education and culture	66·8	69·9	107·4	(7)
Construction	65·6	93·0	154·4	(1)
Arts	55·9	63·7	96·4	(12)
Communications	52·9	62·7	99·2	(9)
Communal services	49·2	57·7	96·8	(11)
Health, sport, and social security	48·6	58·9	92·9	(13)
Trade, material-technical supplies	47·0	58·9	96·9	(10)
Agriculture	38·3	53·8	106·3	(8)
Admin.-tech. personnel and specialists	84·6	115·5	178·4 ⎫	
Workers	36·2	51·9	103·6 ⎬	
Clerical	51·5	65·7	101·1 ⎭	

* Refers to present position in the rank-ordering.

Source: *Nar. khoz. 1922–72*, pp. 350–51.

interests (which coincide with those of the other classes and social groups) are pursued by all the official organizations – party, Soviet, trade unions etc. Be that as it may, there is no evidence that the trade-union leadership adopts a different attitude on, for example, wage questions from that of the government's State Committee on Labour and Wages or of individual ministries. (And incidentally personnel seem to move between posts in the State Committee and top trade-union jobs quite naturally.)

One of the tasks of the State Committee (set up in 1955) was to produce a simplified wage structure. This it worked on with the trade unions and ministries. The Stalin period had seen increasing wage differentiation both between unskilled and skilled workers and between workers and management, and the wage structure had become hopelessly complex as each ministry produced more and more of its own wage schemes. The wage reform, which began in 1957, did simplify the wage structure and reduce differentials. The above table shows how wages in the economy as a whole (excluding collective farms) have moved over the period.

If we look at either Industry or Agriculture, we can see that the difference between administrative-technical staff's and workers' wages was considerably larger in 1950 than in 1971: management has lost out in relative terms. If we look at the difference between average earnings in the highest- and lowest-paid branches of the economy, we notice that in 1950 it was 93·7r. (science) to 38·3r. (state farms) compared with 154·4r. (construction) to 92·9r. (health, sport, etc.) in 1971. We should add that in 1972 the minimum monthly wage was raised to 70r. and that doctors and teachers (relatively poorly paid professions) received an increase.

The table does not tell us what has happened to earnings in the different branches of industry – coal-mining versus textiles, for example – or to workers' wages within a branch of industry – the ratio between skilled and unskilled. Suffice it to say that by steadily increasing the minimum wage, and as a result of a reform of the wages system in the late fifties, these differentials were reduced. As far as can be told the economic reforms of the late sixties initially enabled administrative personnel and skilled workers to regain some lost ground, but by the seventies they were losing out again.

It could be that in the post-Stalin period of change lower party and trade-union officials emphasized the need to raise the lowest wages and to narrow differentials between management and workers if morale was to improve. We simply do not know. Unfortunately such politically sensitive topics are studiously avoided in the press. But there is no evidence that the trade unions were active in pushing for other reforms which benefited the workers and indeed, throughout the whole period, trade-union spokesmen had very little to suggest publicly on anything. In 1956 the law tying workers to their jobs was officially repealed; in 1957 a new law was passed on arbitration procedures for settling disputes over workers' grievances, and in 1958 the primary trade-union committee acquired new rights. Trade-union spokesmen had little to say on the topic of economic reform either before or after its introduction. On the Shchekino experiment they have been very obviously silent. Is it that the union leadership (composed of officials from party, industrial, and trade-union backgrounds) sees itself responsible for social security, socialist competition, and various 'personnel officer' functions rather than anything more controversial, or is it that a topic such as economic reform or Shchekino raises such awkward problems of reconciling the unions' functions of raising production and defending its members' interests that the leadership does not know what to say? Or is it that the union leadership disapproved of Shchekino for the problems it could cause and refused to support it? Without more evidence it is impossible to tell. But more generally there is no reason to suggest that the improvement, both material and otherwise, in the workers' situation over the period is the result of union pressure. In the normal course of events one would expect to see ministry, trade-union, and Secretariat officials responsible for a particular branch of industry arguing together for a larger wages fund for their branch, and then interested in distributing it in order to retain and attract labour.

In agriculture the relationship between the collective farm and the higher authorities was never openly questioned. In the pre-1965 reform debate on the economy it was suggested that the industrial enterprise be granted much greater autonomy. This suggestion with its political implications of a change in the hierarchical relationship that exists in industry as elsewhere went much further than any proposal in the agricultural sphere. But, as we saw, it never became a reality. It was some 'reformist' economists and enterprise directors who were the loudest advocates of such a change but they held nothing like a strong enough position to persuade the leadership. Indeed it is interesting to note how badly enterprise management has fared over the period. Why should this be? Why should it have lost out financially and, in terms of authority *vis-à-vis* its labour force, find itself subject to new pressures with very little, if any, compensation? We suggested that the gains made by the industrial labour force (and hence the reverses suffered by management) cannot be explained by trade-union pressure. To what extent then can the workers themselves be held responsible and to what extent the higher authorities? We can talk of a labour force taking advantage of a situation where there is both a shortage and mobility of labour in order to push up earnings. In order to attract and then retain labour, management has had to practise a 'soft' wages policy and piece-workers in particular have been able to benefit. Management, on a salary system, is dependent on increases granted from above and on the bonus system, which, as we saw, the authorities used against it. Although the worker is then in a better starting position to influence his wage level than is a salaried employee – and this in part accounts for the relative improvement in wages over the period – it remains true that the political authorities cut top management salaries in the wage reform and have not awarded increases that would maintain the differential between wages and salaries.

We would suggest that the reason management have fared badly is as follows. In the industrial hierarchy the relationships between the different levels are broadly similar to those in the wider political ordering of society. In the Soviet system – be it in the party, trade unions, or industrial ministry – each level is responsible for the activities of the one immediately below it. Each must control, check the activities of the one below and, in doing so, safeguards its own position because the major threat comes from below. In its turn the subordinate institution always looks up and concentrates its attention on its immediate superior, because the latter has most influence over its activity. The Politburo looks to the Central Committee and vice versa. Hence for those planning or administering industry – be they *sovnarkhoz* departments, industrial ministries, state committees, or the trade-union leadership – enterprise management is the institution to be harried, ordered about, held responsible for failure, and penalized for industry's unsatisfactory performance. Their advice to the leadership and their actions are unlikely to be pro-management. Any granting of greater autonomy to the enterprise would weaken the central industrial administration's control and authority. If one is attempting to slow down wage drift, then management is an obvious target. The labour force is already a stage removed: it is management's responsibility, and the central industrial authorities are not particularly concerned if improvements to the worker's position makes management's lot more difficult. They will not object if the fact that the political leadership grants concessions, identifies the central government as being pro-worker and fosters the belief that it is management which is to blame for any shortcomings. This distracts attention from the political authorities themselves who can remain 'above', the well-meaning and responsible leaders, and particularizes discontent, concentrates it on the individual enterprise and individual managers. It is interesting that the one protest document we have from a group of workers, in Kiev, appeals to the Central Committee, to the leaders 'whom we believe', to remedy the situation on the assumption that, if only the leaders knew . . .[6] This is not to imply that the political leadership or the industrial ministers sit down and cynically work out a strategy aimed at setting management against workers. It is rather to suggest that, in a situation where participation in policy-making is dominated by those in charge of the central institutions, and where authority relationships are set within a hierarchy, the central authorities will concentrate efforts on maintaining control over their subordinates. If they produce policies aimed at ameliorating conditions below – and this will seem to them reasonable and possible – this will create greater tension or conflict within the lower levels of the hierarchy. Thus one can argue that the very nature of the political relationships tends to produce a certain type of policy and a certain type of conflict. We will come back to this in the concluding chapter when we try to assess the system as a whole.

(iii) Culture

Sincerity in Literature

In 1953 an article entitled 'Sincerity in Literature', published in the literary monthly *Novy mir*, took up the theme of the dullness of contemporary literature. In an imaginary dialogue between writer and reader, a writer criticized editorial boards, critics, and the Union of Writers for accepting only certain themes and stifling creativity; the reader argued that the writer himself was as much to blame for not following his own heart and instincts, for not being 'true' to himself. The article opened a debate on the role of the artist and his relationship to the political authorities which engaged the artistic community for the rest of the fifties and brought sections of it into conflict with the political leadership. By the early seventies the situation was very different. There was by then a wide range of small 'protest' groups of very different persuasions whose supporters were willing openly to oppose the political leadership, to circulate underground publications, engage in demonstrations, and demand change in a number of different directions. The writers and artists who had played an important part in the early years in raising certain 'delicate' topics were now only one element in a much more active opposition.

If in agriculture the political leadership has been an initiator of policy changes throughout the period, and if in industry it has tempered its own policies with suggestions from outside, its approach to the arts has been very different. Here we are talking about a policy area in which the political authorities had no policy except the maintenance of the *status quo*. In the fifties they produced nothing new; they merely responded defensively to demands from outside. It is a situation in which the leadership at times seemed at a loss to know how to respond and one in which it appears continually to be on the defensive. It has no new cultural policy to offer. What we want to look at is the way the leadership has responded to criticism, the way in which it has attempted to deal with it, and the consequences this has had for future criticism and activities.

The 1953 article inevitably raised the question of the type and extent of controls over the writer. Briefly, the way cultural activities are organized in the Soviet Union is as follows. There is a Ministry of Culture with separate departments for different branches of the arts. These administer the museums, art galleries, theatres, etc., the training schools and institutes, and some publishing houses. Another government agency is Glavlit, the censorship organization, with central and local departments and representatives in the publishing houses, responsible for everything from military secrets to artistic material. It seems that Glavlit is directly subordinate to the party Secretariat. Its status and organization is obscure. The writers and artists themselves have their 'own' institutions – their professional organizations with their journals, publishing houses, newspapers, funds to help members, etc. The Union of Writers, for example, 'elects' a Board, a praesidium, and a secretariat at its four-yearly Congress, and these bodies then run the affairs of the Union. At each level and in each branch there will be a party group of those writers who are party members. But there are no 'private' publishing houses in the USSR and nothing can be published without permission from the censor. Overseeing all cultural activities and organizations is a department of the central party Secretariat with sectors responsible for different aspects. The officials who work in the department will keep in touch with the leading officials in all the cultural institutions – from the Ministry to the Union of Writers to the Academy of Fine Art – and will issue instructions on the appropriate policy to be pursued – for example, no public abstract art exhibitions, no labour-camp literature, more on poets of the Third World and less on West European art.

There is then a powerful organizational network for controlling what is published or publicly produced. Even without Glavlit, which can be thought of as a backstop, editors, theatre directors, and museum curators know what is permissible and their jobs depend on their interpreting policy directives aright. Authors and artists must either meet the requirements or remain unpublished. But, as we can see, the effectiveness of such a system depends upon either (a) the existence of clear, unambiguous pronouncements on what is acceptable and (b) sufficiently severe penalties for 'mistakes' (this crudely was the basis Stalinist policy operated on) *or* (c) an identity of views among those in charge of cultural institutions, publishing houses, etc. on what art is. If either (a) or (b) is lacking, then (c) becomes all important; if that too is missing, then the system breaks down. We shall be arguing that this was what had happened by 1963. Belatedly the leadership realized the dangers and attempted to reassert its control.

In the more 'liberal' atmosphere following Stalin's death some writers and artists seized the opportunity to criticize editors for their conservatism, for their anxiety over anything but stereotyped manuscripts, and to complain about the amount of editing, checking, and altering of an author's work that was usual practice. Accusations were made that those in charge were illiterate, lacking in any understanding of art or talent. Glavlit was not openly mentioned, but it was clear that at times the reference was to the censor; at others it was to 'cultural officialdom' or to those who had risen to greatness in the Stalin period on the basis of some of the worst products of 'socialist realist' art. In 1954 this theme of the creative artist, misunderstood and scorned by the cultural establishment while the hack artist is acclaimed, was a central feature of Ehrenburg's controversial novel *The Thaw*. In these early years we can think of the artistic community – or at least a section of it – as preoccupied with its own suffering, with its own problems. This was not surprising. As was mentioned earlier, the Stalin period was one in which professional groups of all kinds were denied the opportunity to discuss and analyse their own activity, and the artistic world in particular had suffered badly both in the purges and again in 1946–8. After the Zhdanov campaign of the late forties, editors were extremely conservative and critics as bad if not worse; the anonymous censors did often seem illiterate; the artistic establishment – in the unions, academies, and publishing world – was dominated by a generation of artists and writers who, with few exceptions, had produced the dullest art of the Soviet period and were not favourably disposed to talent. It was a stifling atmosphere, one in which almost everything was stacked against an adventurous or new writer. It was not surprising then that those, old and young, who felt themselves oppressed tried to achieve more air for themselves.

The secret speech gave them powerful impetus. There was a renewed attack on 'bureaucratic controls', on the whole system of editing before publication, and demands that literature should be able to portray the negative as well as the positive aspects of Soviet society. Some argued that interference from above and the present interpretation of socialist realism were offshoots of the 'cult of personality' and should therefore disappear together with the Stalinist past. The reply by Serov, a leading conservative artist, was not far wide of the mark: 'The danger is that the mistakes bound up with the cult of the individual leader are being exaggeratedly represented as well nigh the ideological foundations of Soviet art. Persons seeking to pass off the concept of socialist realism as an offspring of the cult of the individual are jostling their way in under the banner of just criticism aimed at eliminating the effect of the cult.'[7] It was a situation in which so much, previously sacred, was being questioned that those who wished could ascribe almost everything to 'the cult'.

We can think of the institutions actually responsible for publishing – the publishing houses, editorial offices – as momentarily insecure after the secret speech. Was there any longer a clear policy on the arts? Neither the Secretariat nor the censorship agencies seemed to know quite what to do in this novel situation when the First Secretary himself had dwelt at such length on the negative aspects of the past twenty years. There were some who held responsible positions who were prepared to publish critical articles, short stories, and poems. Not all were of one mind. But the greater part of the cultural establishment and the political authorities felt threatened by the demands and criticism. The artistic establishment owed its position to its willingness and ability to produce 'socialist realist' art of the late Stalin period, and politically it was associated with the purges of the late thirties and forties. Fadeyev, a leading Stalinist writer, might shoot himself upon hearing the secret speech, but the rest had no intention of adopting the liberals' arguments. The political authorities in turn, particularly after the events in Poland and Hungary, were not prepared to allow even a small section of the intelligentsia to take the matter further than the secret speech and to question the right of the party to control the arts.

By the end of the year instructions were coming down to halt the criticisms and to slow down the publication of 'negative' literature, and the institutions responded accordingly. But this did not mean a return to the *status quo ante*. There was a tacit acceptance that literature could, albeit cautiously, describe certain less positive aspects of life; there were no recriminations and personal attacks on those who had been most outspoken, and there was the rehabilitation of certain authors and their works from the twenties and thirties. This response from the leadership was an attempt to maintain control without resorting to 'Stalinist' means. One consequence was that, by implicitly accepting the existence of 'conservatives' and 'liberals', it legitimized both: there could be different interpretations of art and culture.

Open Politics

By the early sixties the liberals were still pushing for greater freedom of expression (and the form this took was support for abstract art and experimentation in the arts as a whole), but they had also begun to take up political and social issues: life on the collective farms, in the labour camps, the non-heroic side of the Second World War. And in this they were joined by others, by historians or military men anxious to dismantle the Stalinist picture of Soviet history. Khrushchev's public attack on Stalin at the Twenty-second Congress in 1961 (as part of a campaign to oust political opponents and push his reforms more forcefully) gave them the opportunity to move into the attack and this time they made attempts (and succeeded) to get members onto some editorial boards, to displace some of the old Stalinist notables from posts in the cultural unions or academies. The old guard again felt insecure. By now the publishing houses were being inundated with 'purge' literature and it was at this point that Tvardovsky, editor of *Novy mir*, a highly respected author, editor, reformer, and member of the Central Committee, took Solzhenit-syn's *One Day in the Life of Ivan Denisovich* to Khrushchev for permission to publish. Khrushchev, defeated by his colleagues at the Congress in his attempts to rake up the Stalinist past, agreed. Not only had labour-camp literature become acceptable, but Yevtushenko devoted poems to 'Stalin's heirs' and to the German massacre of Jews at Babi Yar in the Ukraine during the war. Other poets were producing more adventurous poetry, and artists were organizing semi-public exhibitions of abstract art. Thus on the one hand there was the attempt to get rid of 'cultural bureau-crats' and to experiment in art forms, on the other the attack on Stalinists in a broader sense and on social and political aspects of the past and present. And because the two often went together, the conservatives could, by attacking one, discredit both simul-taneously.

In December 1962 Khrushchev was taken to an art exhibition which included one room of abstract paintings. This it seems was carefully engineered by a small group of conservatives who ob-tained the desired result. Khrushchev lost his temper, hurled abuse at the artists, and departed in a rage. The evening editions of the newspapers contained articles calling for the amalgamation of all the cultural unions into one. (This is an indication of how quickly the media can react when the First Secretary feels strongly enough and it is also interesting in that we see Khrushchev's penchant for 'administrative' solutions surfacing again.) There was an immediate 'freeze': the exhibition was closed, a contro-versial setting of Yevtushenko's Babi Yar to music by Shostako-vich stopped in rehearsal, and abstract art, formalist poetry roundly criticized. But the reformers did not give in. There were signed letters to the political authorities supporting experimen-tation.

A meeting was organized by the Secretariat between Khrush-chev and a large number of representatives of the artistic community. This was the occasion when Khrushchev introduced Solzhenitsyn, an unknown figure, to the gathering and publicly congratulated him on his writing; he then attacked abstract art. In effect he was attempting to suggest a compromise: a con-tinuation of social and political de-Stalinization along certain lines but not 'way-out art'. But neither side among the artists was prepared to accept this. The conservatives reminded Khrushchev (even though only implicitly) that those who insisted on raking up the Stalinist past should remember that they too had a Stalinist past; Yevtushenko, for the liberals, insisted on bringing the issue of anti-semitism up (something guaranteed to anger Khrushchev) and defending a particular abstract artist. The meeting was not a success. The political leadership then, to all intents and purposes, withdrew from the scene and left the two opposing factions to argue it out in the press which, for the next few months, was what they did. There were liberal journals and conservative journals and hostile exchanges between them. In effect the political leadership had refused to lay down a definite line and this meant uncertainty among the officials administering policy. In such a situation the split in the artistic community could and did become visible.

In March the political leadership intervened. By then Khrushchev had lost his de-Stalinization campaign in the upper circles of the party. The wrangling in the artistic community had revealed two things: first, the conservatives were a force well able to hold their own against the liberals (as in the wider political arena were those in positions of authority); secondly, that the liberals were not willing to accept the First Secretary's views on art nor to keep their attack on the Stalinist past in line with the leadership. Although at times he was defensive about his judgement on artistic subjects, Khrushchev clearly felt that he had a duty to pronounce on what was acceptable if the artistic community was unable to control its own rebels. The events of the past few months had shown that, in the absence of a forceful line from above, the liberals were going to continue their demands. Khrushchev publicly re-stated his views on art, criticized certain poets for their themes and type of poetry, and criticized individuals for their attempts to distort the consequences of the Stalinist past. This was a strong enough message to send the liberals into retreat, but into fairly honourable retreat accompanied by very lukewarm admissions of past errors. One or two journals retained their liberal editors and by the autumn even some of the named individuals were back in print. It looked like a temporary setback in an artistic world that had changed beyond recognition since 1953.

Not only had the artistic world changed. Less obtrusively, but as actively, social scientists, natural scientists, historians, and lawyers had been pressing for change. We have already referred to the debate over economic reform. Sociological research began again at the beginning of the sixties; historians touched upon previously forbidden topics. This does not mean that anything was allowed: far from it. The extent of the discussion was still very limited, criticism of social phenomena was still very mild, and criticism of the political present almost non-existent. The reasons were several and cannot all be attributed to the tight political control maintained over these professions – some had lost the ability to criticize, others had never had it; some had a position to defend, others felt it improper – but, be that as it may, for those who did want change the early sixties were a period of optimism.

The Dissidents Appear

In 1965, with the arrest of Daniel and Sinyavsky and their subsequent sentencing for slandering the Soviet State in works sent abroad under pseudonym, the whole situation changed. It is not clear who instigated such a move, whether it was the KGB, or the result of pressure on the political authorities from members of the artistic establishment, or a decision taken by the political leadership as part of a new offensive against the liberals. Although in the USSR interest in the trial was limited to small circles of the intelligentsia, for them at least it changed attitudes and their actions. It is probably true that the end to de-Stalinization and with it the lost hopes for further reform, together with the voices of the camp returnees who no longer 'feared' the authorities, plus the more permissive atmosphere, would of themselves have produced a more critical opposition than that of the previous period. But the trial was a danger signal and therefore a spur to action: it was evidence that further reform was only going to be won by a fight.

Daniel and Sinyavsky defended themselves; friends and colleagues (despite pressure) came forward as witnesses for the defence; individuals and groups wrote open letters to the press and political leadership demanding a fair trial; and an unofficial transcript of the proceedings was secretly circulated. This type of activity has characterized what can be called 'the protest movement' ever since. First, individuals – some eminent, some unknown – began to write letters, sharply criticizing either particular policies (the invasion of Czechoslovakia, the rehabilitation of Stalin, the persecution of religious or national groups) or aspects of the political system (the denial of legal or constitutional rights, the existence of censorship). These they sent to the political authorities, to the appropriate organizations, and to the press (they were of course never published and usually not even acknowledged). Solzhenitsyn's letter to the Board of the Writers' Union in 1967, demanding an abolition of censorship, and the support for an open discussion of the letter from over seventy members was a far cry from the muted criticism of 'bureaucratic controls' of an earlier period. Secondly, these letters, accounts of meetings or trials, and unpublished literary works began to circulate in an ever-increasing number. Samizdat (the unofficial circulation of typed manuscripts) became a recognized phenomenon. And, in the second half of the sixties and beginning of the seventies, two journals – the *Chronicle of Current Events* and the *Political Diary* containing accounts of trials, persecution, unofficial analyses of domestic and foreign policy – were brought out and circulated successfully and anonymously for a few years. Thirdly, the activities and those involved in the movement for change altered. There were still individual writers criticizing the censorship system and producing works which circulated in Samizdat, but now there was a small civil rights group composed of different members of the intelligentsia, there was direct action by religious groups (delegations sent to the Kremlin) and by national minorities demanding the right to return to their homelands. There were Ukrainians openly prepared to accuse the central authorities of Russification, student protests in Latvia, Jews applying for exit visas for Israel. Among the 'intellectual' dissenters themselves there have been those arguing for a more liberal democratic framework, those demanding a return to

Leninism, and those (such as Solzhenitsyn) calling for an abandonment of Marxist-Leninist ideology and an emphasis on 'traditional' Russian values and interests. Behind these, less well known but surely far greater in number, are the staunch defenders of the Stalinist past and those who, propounding old slavophile ideas, see the Jews and the Chinese as the enemies.

This is not to imply that suddenly a wide-scale protest movement sprang into being. Compared with the liberal democracies of the west or some of the East European societies at particular points in time, the extent of dissent, protest, or opposition has been very small. Those actually prepared to run the risk of losing jobs and suffering imprisonment have been few. There is a much bigger band of intellectuals who write about social and cultural themes in a critical fashion, pushing forward a little but not openly supporting causes that involve a direct clash with the authorities. Many of them probably read Samizdat and sympathize with parts of it, but they do not contribute to it, sign petitions, and protest to the authorities. The range of permissible activity – listening to the BBC, meeting foreigners, reading western materials, painting abstract art and showing it privately, writing about social problems – remains far wider than under Stalin and, indeed, wider than ten years ago. This kind of activity pales by comparison with the activities of the dissidents, and the leadership seems to have realized (even if the KGB sometimes forgets) that they do not pose any real threat.

It is interesting but not surprising that opposition has taken the form that it has. It is not only because under Stalin nationalities, religion, and intellectual freedom were ruthlessly suppressed that opposition has focused around these issues, but also because they are easy to identify with. They are particular issues, the group involved is recognizable, and the fractionalized nature of Soviet society encourages a concern with narrow interests. We shall return to this later. Here we simply point out that the political leadership's control over the media and its prevention of any open discussion of social and political phenomena and issues encourages the tendency for opposition to focus around obvious issues, those with a direct visible impact on a group, and to spring up in an unorganized form (the *Chronicle* attempted, even if only on paper, to put the different activities together). And in turn of course the scattered and unrelated nature of the protest movements makes it easier for the political authorities to suppress them.

By 1973 the leadership used the KGB in a campaign to suppress the dissenters. At least some of those responsible for the journals were arrested and the journals themselves ceased to exist. Several prominent dissenters were either arrested and sentenced to labour camps or certified as insane; some were allowed to emigrate, others, such as Solzhenitsyn, deported. The 'public voice' of the intellectual dissenting movement was largely stopped. This in turn weakens the position of others attempting to criticize and oppose the authorities in that the old channels for publicity no longer exist. It has always been the case that the unknown dissenters have most to lose: they cannot hope for support from abroad, indeed their case may not even reach the ears of sympathizers in Moscow. But the knowledge that even the leaders have been silenced must discourage others. It is less easy to suppress the Jews, the nationalist and religious groups and indeed the policy of discriminating against Jews because of their unreliability can only encourage the desire to emigrate. By 1975 a slight variation to the general policy of actively harassing and suppressing any overt opposition or criticism of official policies appeared. Certain known dissidents have been left at liberty – usually those whose views are sufficiently idiosyncratic to attract little support within the Soviet Union. This makes good political sense: the leadership can appear liberal in the eyes of the outside world while in no way endangering its own position.[8]

We can think of the political leadership maintaining its control over public and printed discussion in the fifties because of the existence of an organizational network geared to support the *status quo* (and when the leadership did intervene it supported the *status quo*) and a conservative artistic establishment anxious to defend its position. By the early sixties the leadership's indecisive, if not contradictory, policy plus the activity of the liberals had thrown the system into disarray. Leadership intervention was sufficient to restore order, but its more conservative attitude plus its hesitancy to use coercive methods to gain conformity prompted a wider and more active opposition. The Daniel-Sinyavsky trial did not herald the immediate return to coercion. Indeed for the next few years the leadership attempted to maintain control by relying on the authorities in their separate institutions (the Writers' Union, Academy of Sciences institutes, universities, etc.) to respond to directives from above and discipline the 'rebels' themselves. But although the institutions responded, often with alacrity, the dissidents remained unrepentant and Samizdat literature increased. By the seventies the leadership stepped in to use its own force.

What is striking is the 'over-reaction' of the bodies responsible for quelling dissent, primarily the KGB. Any minor activity – particularly a sit-down, a tiny demonstration, or the organization of a meeting – is broken up, sometimes with the use of physical violence. This suggests either that the political authorities seriously consider such activities so potentially dangerous, because of widespread, latent discontent, that they must be stamped on hard or that the KGB cannot conceive of any other way of dealing with such activity. It is hard to imagine that the leadership does view the situation in such a light, although their careful handling of a number of issues in the post-Stalin period suggests that they do not feel sure of their constituents' support. This brings us back to a point made earlier – when discussing Khrushchev's image of society – the ambivalent attitude of the leadership, confident one moment, insecure the next. And we can suggest that one of the consequences of being a self-appointed leadership is that it is difficult to assess the degree and nature of support from below. But it is more probable that, after forty years of acquiescence, the secret police, court, and political officials are at a loss to treat what must seem totally unacceptable, 'deviant' behaviour and therefore adopt the crudest methods. It is impossible to know whether KGB officials or conservative members of the political or legal establishment began to push for stronger measures once it was clear that the leadership had called a halt to further de-Stalinization or whether similar calls came from the cultural establishment unable to cope with its dissidents. The Brezhnev-Kosygin leadership did at first appear undecided, but it may have been the increasing activities of the dissidents as much as any conservative lobby that persuaded it to adopt a hard line. All we can say is that it is a line which receives the support of an impressively large lobby.

(iv) Conclusion

From looking at the three policy fields, we can see that Soviet policy-making takes a variety of different forms. At times the leadership acts suddenly, 'arbitrarily', with a minimum of consultation and, in such instances, it is behaving least like an 'accountable' government. But most of the time leading officials and specialists, sometimes more sometimes less, participate in the making of policy. The policies themselves range from clear, sharp pronouncements on a new line to wordy attempts at compromise; we can find evidence of quite drastic reform, cautious conservatism, and the prevention of change. Similarly the record on 'who benefits?' is mixed. Sometimes institutional size and strength seem to determine the outcome but not always.

To some extent the variety is accounted for by differences between the three policy fields. Although the leadership has acted 'arbitrarily' in all three, it has done this least of all in industry. Also the degree of participation in policy-making is greatest on industrial matters. To some extent then 'accountability' and 'participation' are determined by the presence or absence of established 'interested' institutions whose advice and cooperation is needed. But what of the type of policy, the degree of reform versus conservatism? Does this depend on the leadership or does it depend on the alignment of forces within each individual sector? We would argue that both are relevant. There were more reforms and attempts at reform under Khrushchev, which might be taken as evidence that it is the composition of the leadership that matters. But the Brezhnev-Kosygin leadership was also a 'reforming' government in its early days – both in industry and agriculture – and has continued to push for change in the agricultural sphere. Reform has gone furthest in agriculture, the sector with the fewest established institutions at the top. In industry, despite the leadership's obvious anxiety over the performance of the sector and willingness to allow far-reaching debate, the battles over reform have almost always been won by the conservatives. And in the arts, even when Khrushchev was encouraging certain aspects of 'liberalization', the conservatives still dominated the field. All of which suggests that the line-up of forces within a sector does influence the outcome.

We would argue that Khrushchev came to power at a time which favoured reform, a time when a cure for Stalinist inadequacies without radical change seemed feasible to many in leading positions in all sectors. This was the situation which made reform possible – although it did not entail it, nor did it entail 'a reformer' winning the position of First Secretary. However, Khrushchev did win and did push for reform – with some success. But it was not long before his attempts began to bring conflicts to the surface, and those in positions of authority began to ask themselves whether the inadequacies (on which it now appeared there was no agreement) could be cured quite so simply. This did not happen all at once. The search for reform in the industrial field, for example, carried on into the Brezhnev-Kosygin period. But by the end of the sixties the situation was different on all fronts. Even those in favour of reform seemed to doubt that piecemeal measures would have any impact; hence, for want of an alternative, there was a willingness to accept the inadequacies. The leadership, more responsive to its immediate subordinates than Khrushchev had been, in turn adopted a cautious view. This makes the higher ranks of the establishment and the leadership much more in tune with each other: content with minimal change.

Who benefits from this type of policy-making? The leadership's ability (and willingness) to act 'arbitrarily' means that not even the largest institutional lobby is automatically safe (viz. the attack on the secret police, the industrial ministries). But this is much less marked of late. In general we can say that those with control over valuable resources, organized on an institutional basis, manage to maintain or improve their position. But simultaneously certain 'disadvantaged' groups, who lack any organized or institutional strength, have benefited. Leadership sponsorship is sufficient to ensure this. However, their 'benefiting' has not been at the expense of any of the big lobbies nor has it impinged on the material position or authority of the top stratum of administrators. If a particular group or interest is neither a large institutional lobby nor has leadership backing, there is little chance that it can achieve anything (the Jews seem to be an exception, but then their lobby is the US Congress) and, if it actually offends established interests, its treatment will be rough indeed.

But to go back to the more general question of the consequences that the existence of a self-recruiting elite, unhampered by elections, controlling appointments and discussion, has for policy-making. These features of the Soviet system are not of much help in enabling us to predict the form policy-making will take and the type of policies produced. If we had hazarded the suggestion, 'the leadership will act arbitrarily, as it wishes', we would not really have been right; if we had said, 'it will pursue a single, consistent set of policies unchecked', we would have been no more correct. On the contrary the picture is much more muddled – and, apart from the reasons already mentioned, we can think of another more directly related to the self-appointed nature of the leadership. The leadership does not come to power with a coherent, explicit programme, flanked by its 'supporters' who are in favour of the programme, and then set about 'passing' it. On the contrary it has to spend a considerable part of its time creating its 'supporters' by the system of appointments. Since there is no coherent programme (there is merely an individual leader and a number of separate policies), the nature of the 'support' is rather different from that in a system with opposing parties. A minister may be with the First Secretary on issue X and opposed to him on Y. Whoever is appointed obkom secretary in Magadan, or Minister of Chemicals, is going to champion his region or ministry when the occasion arises. Thus, as 'supporters', the leadership has a political and administrative elite that is continually thinking of its individual sectional interests – not a body of men united round a set of policies. Consequently policies are arrived at and 'passed' by a process of bargaining, making new appointments (to change the balance of 'support' although it may upset it for the next issue) – and this has to be done for each policy. At times the Soviet leadership must wish it had an obedient parliamentary party it could call to order with a three-line whip. It must continue with control over appointments to produce a 'party of supporters', because there is nothing else to produce unity.

The lack of freedom of discussion and criticism accentuates this. Without open criticism, no coherent critique – which would compel the leadership to produce and defend a programme – can emerge and provide an alternative. In some sense Khrushchev's de-Stalinization reforms did produce two sides, each with a programme, but they faded with the reforms. Now no one is producing a programme: a specific, detailed programme would split the central authorities a number of ways; a programme that united them would have to unite them *against* somebody. And how could that be compatible with the idea of a government representing everybody's interests?

10 Execution and Participation: The Party

From looking at policies it becomes clear that, although at times a decision is translated quickly and effectively into action, this is by no means the general rule. Instead the implementation of policies often seems to be marked by procrastination, inertia, and sometimes a downright lack of success. If anything this has become more pronounced in recent years. In order to explain these features of the political system, we must look at the party in a little detail because it is the main executive arm of the State.

In outlining Khrushchev's attempts to replace Stalinism with a more coordinated structure of power, we suggested that he thought of the party as an organization that would simultaneously provide the policy-makers with a responsive executive machine and unite and encourage activities at the grass roots. The party committees at each level, composed of full-time party officials and elected activists, should provide a hierarchy of executive authorities, subordinate to the central Secretariat in Moscow. They were to be the dominant authority in each republic, region, or district. As part of this, they were to receive new responsibilities and the apparatus itself was to be 'modernized'. At the bottom, this new, more efficient organization would receive support from a larger rank-and-file membership. The party was to expand – every enterprise, farm, and institution should have a party cell and new members recruited to ensure that new policies were carried out and to rally the population around re-vitalized local groups.

Although some of Khrushchev's organizational innovations were discarded by his successors, and although Brezhnev talks of the party in a slightly different way, the party of today is basically Khrushchev's creation in terms of its membership, structure, and relationship with other institutions. What type of an organization is it? For a start it is one whose membership and internal relationships are controlled from above. Information on its membership and structure will therefore give an indication of the type of organization the leadership thinks appropriate for carrying out the dual tasks of executing policy and rallying popular support. And perhaps it may help to explain why the executive machinery functions as it does. Is it that the leadership has created an unsuitable machine or are matters more complicated than that?

Membership and Organization

Let us begin with a brief description of membership and organization. In 1973 the party had over fourteen million members – approximately 9 per cent of the adult population or one out of every eleven adults of eighteen years and over. As can be seen from Table XII, the party has grown much more rapidly than the population as a whole since 1956.

Table XII

	Population		Party (members and candidates)
		millions	
1940	194·1		(1932) 3·1
1956	197·9		7·1
1959	208·8		8·2
1964			11·0
1970	241·7		14·0
1971	243·9		14·3
1973			14·8

Source: *Nar. khoz. SSSR 1922–72*, Moscow, 1972, p. 9; *Partiinaya zhizn*, no. 14, 1973, p. 10.

It is important to realize how large the party is today. Although in some sense it can still be thought of as a selective organization, it is clearly very different from its forerunner of the twenties and thirties which, with a membership of one to three millions, felt itself isolated and sometimes swamped in an indifferent or hostile environment.

Table XIII provides the official figures on the class composition of the party.

Table XIII Class Composition of the Party

	July 1932 %	January 1956 No. (millions)	%	1964 %	1971 No. (millions)	%	1973 No. (millions)	%
Workers	65·2	2·2	32·0	37·3	5·7	40·1	6·0	40·7
Peasants	26·9	1·2	17·1	16·5	2·1	15·1	2·1	14·7
White-collar	7·9	3·6	50·9	46·2	6·4	44·8	6·6	44·6

Source: 1956, 1971, 1973 from *Part. zhizn*, p. 15; 1932, 1964 from H. Rigby, *Communist Party Membership in the USSR 1917–67*, Princeton, 1968, p. 325.

The table uses the standard class categories employed in the census. (Peasants, it will be remembered, refer to kolkhozniki or collective-farm workers and not to those employed on State farms.) But when applied to party membership the categories refer to the member's class standing at the time when he or she *joined* the party. Thus the majority of the present Politburo would be included as workers or peasants. Over the past fifty years different criteria have been used to classify party membership – occupation at the time of the revolution, occupation on joining the party, present status – and hence one has to be sure when faced with a set of figures that one knows exactly what they refer to. In the twenties it was customary to publish two sets of figures – party membership by occupation on entry into the party, and party membership according to *present* occupation. As can be imagined, the latter made the white-collar category larger because of the movement up to white-collar and administrative positions by worker entrants. Given changing rates of mobility over the period, it is not possible to form a picture of today's party membership in terms of present occupation. All one can really say is that (a) the white-collar group must be larger than in Table XIII, because there must be substantially more of those who entered the party as workers or peasants and since moved into white-collar positions than vice versa and (b) the discrepancy between original and acquired class status – given the higher mobility rates in the earlier periods – would be more marked in 1956 than in 1973.

From Table XIII we notice that, although there has been a shift to increase worker representation since Stalin, the white-collar category still remains the largest. If we compare the party figures with those of the employed population, the 'overrepresentation' of the white-collar group is very marked.

Table XIV Class Composition of Employed Population and Party (%)

	Population 1959	Party 1956	Party as % of population	Population 1970	Party 1973	Party as % of population
Workers	47·9	32·0	4·8	57·6	40·7	9·0
Peasants	33·3	17·1	3·6	15·5	14·7	11·0
White-collar	18·5	50·9	18·0	26·6	44·6	20·1
	100·0	100·0		100·0	100·0	

Source: *Nar. khoz. SSSR, 1922–72*, p. 35; *Itogi vsesoyuznoi perepisi naseleniya 1970 g.*, vol. V, Moscow, 1973, Table 4; *Part. zhizn.*

Given that the population figures refer to *present* status and those on the party to *original* status, the table is not comparing like with like and hence the estimates of party representation in the three social groups can only be treated as very rough indeed. But they do given an indication of the differences in party representation and the changes over the period: whereas approximately one out of every twenty workers was in the party in 1956, by the early seventies it was one out of every ten – but this still lags far behind white-collar representation where roughly one out of every five employees is in the party.

If the party is more white-collar than its parent population it is also, not surprisingly, better educated. The close relationship between the better educated and the party can be seen very clearly if we look at actual numbers with higher or specialized secondary education. In 1970 out of the just under twenty million people with these qualifications, almost six million or 29 per cent were party members. Nearly one in three was in the party compared with one in five ten years earlier.

Table XV Educational Qualifications (%)

	Population 1959 (twenty years+ age group)	Party members and candidates 1962	Population 1970 (twenty years+ age group)	Party members and candidates 1971
Higher	2·9	13·7	5·4	19·6
Incomplete higher	1·2	2·9	1·6	2·4
Secondary	11·5	27·2	20·8	34·3
Incomplete secondary	19·6	28·4	23·5	24·9
Primary or less	64·7	27·8	48·7	18·8
	100·0	100·0	100·0	100·0

Sources: 1959, 1962 from Rigby, *Communist Party Membership*, p. 407; 1970 calculated from *Itogi vsesoiuznoi perepisi naseleniya 1970*, vol. III, Table 1; 1971 from *Part. zhizn*.

We shall discuss causes and consequences of recruitment policies later; here we are merely presenting a brief outline of the party's development over the period. It is more heavily white-collar, better educated and more urban than the population as a whole. The average party member is younger than his average counterpart in the population, and the word 'his' is used advisedly: women accounted for only 22 per cent of party membership in 1971, whereas they made up 61 per cent of the twenty-five-years-plus age group in the population in 1970.[1] In terms of nationality the Russians still dominate the party (as they do the population) but some headway has been made over the past twenty years in making the national composition more representative (for example, reducing the Russian, Georgian, and Armenian overrepresentation) and boosting party membership among the smaller nationalities.

This kind of information does not in itself enable us to make any predictions about the aims of the organization or whose interests it will pursue. The assumption that information on the composition of a political party enables one to say something about its behaviour is a shaky one, even for voluntary associations. We need to know about the relationship between the leadership and the wider membership – the way the party is organized, the methods of choosing and rejecting a leadership, the relationships between the separate parts – before we can say whether membership will tell us something of party policy or behaviour. How then is the party organized? All party members (represented by the large square at the bottom of Figure 2) belong to a primary party organization usually centred on the place of work. Someone wishing to join the party must be sponsored by colleagues and, if successful, is accepted as a member of the primary organization at his work place. An industrial worker will belong to the party organization in his enterprise, the Minister of Foreign Affairs to one in the Ministry, Brezhnev to the one in the central Secretariat. There were 378,740 such primaries in 1973 with a membership ranging from an average of eighty-nine in industrial enterprises to forty-nine on collective farms. As can be imagined they may vary in size from a few communists in a collective farm or retail shop to a huge organization of over 1,000 communists in a large industrial concern. The structure of the primary organization itself differs depending upon its size. If there are fewer than fifteen members, a secretary and deputy-secretary are elected from among the members to serve for one year; a rather larger organization elects a bureau with a secretary in charge, and one with 300 or more members elects a party committee, again with a secretary. In 1973 only 33,279 primaries were large enough to have a committee. The great majority of the committee or bureau members and the secretaries at primary level combine their party work with their full-time jobs but, where the primary has a membership of 150 or more, the secretary is entitled to work full-time for the party and to be paid accordingly. (Whether he is paid by his enterprise or by the party is not clear.) He may be elected from among the work force and give up his original job (perhaps to return to it, perhaps to move on up the party hierarchy) or he may come from outside, a nominee of the district party organization or from even higher up.

All the primary party organizations in a particular district are subordinate to the district party organization. Given the increase in the number of primaries (particularly marked in institutions as opposed to enterprises or farms), the district party committee – the raikom – may be responsible for 150 to 200 primaries. One

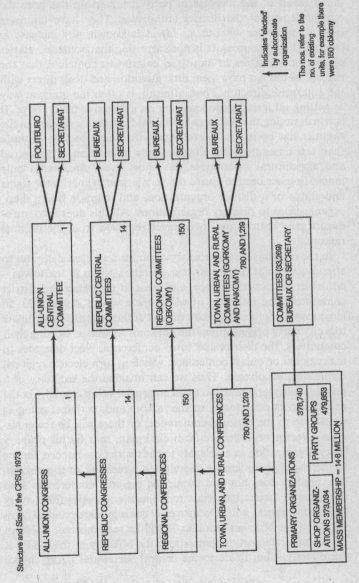

Structure and Size of the CPSU, 1973

← Indicates 'elected'
by subordinate
organization

The nos. refer to the
no. of existing
units, for example there
were 150 obkomy

ALL-UNION CONGRESS	ALL-UNION CENTRAL COMMITTEE	1	POLITBURO
			SECRETARIAT
REPUBLIC CONGRESSES	REPUBLIC CENTRAL COMMITTEES	14	BUREAUX
			SECRETARIAT
REGIONAL CONFERENCES	REGIONAL COMMITTEES (OBKOMY)	150	BUREAUX
			SECRETARIAT
TOWN, URBAN, AND RURAL CONFERENCES 780 AND 1,219	TOWN, URBAN, AND RURAL COMMITTEES (GORKOMY AND RAIKOMY) 780 AND 1,219		BUREAUX
			SECRETARIAT
PRIMARY ORGANIZATIONS 378,740	COMMITTEES (33,269) BUREAUX OR SECRETARY		
SHOP ORGANIZATIONS 373,034	PARTY GROUPS 479,853		
MASS MEMBERSHIP = 14·8 MILLION			

direct result of the increase in party membership has been the overburdening of the district authorities. They have far more units to supervise without, as far as is known, any increase in personnel or resources. It is not surprising that some secretaries of party committees in industrial enterprises complain that the raikom or obkom pays them little attention and deals direct with the enterprise director. That, after all, is often the quickest way of getting information and passing on a directive from above. It is worth noting that the organizational framework devised in the twenties has been retained to cope with a membership of more than ten times the size. Khrushchev's innovation of industrial and agricultural committees was short lived. Brezhnev's only innovation has been to award the very largest primaries the rights and status of a district organization, and upgrade their 'shop' organizations to primary organizations. All this does is to introduce a new bottom tier, two stages removed from the original raikom.

In the countryside the primary organizations elect delegates to attend a biennial rural district conference, those in the towns – an urban district conference, and these in turn elect the district committees, the raikomy, of which there were 1,219 in 1973. In large towns or cities the urban district authorities are subordinate to a city party organization, the gorkom. As well as electing their committees, the district and town conferences elect delegates to the regional or oblast conference, which in turn elects a regional committee, an obkom. Thus we can imagine the secretary of a primary party organization in an enterprise being elected, via the urban district conference, to the raikom and, perhaps, going as a delegate to the regional conference; or there will be the enterprise director or collective-farm chairman, sent by his primary party organization as a delegate to the district conference, thence to the regional conference and elected a member of the obkom. The process does not end there: the regional conferences send delegates to their appropriate republican congresses (held every four or five years), which in turn elect the republican central committees. (The Russian republic, it will be remembered, does not have a separate party organization: the obkomy in the RSFSR are directly subordinate to the central Secretariat.) And thence one moves up to the All-Union or central party bodies. Thus officials of lower organizations or party activists from a variety of backgrounds can sit simultaneously on a number of different bodies within the party hierarchy, culminating in the All-Union Central Committee.

As can be seen from Figure 2, each committee from the district level upwards elects a bureau (or smaller inner body) to direct party affairs. The full committee may number fifty members at raikom level and as many as a hundred at obkom level. Whereas in British local government, for example, a county council or town council will have a number of different committees to deal with specific areas (planning, education, etc.) and often one 'key' committee, the party committees merely elect a smaller bureau of perhaps seven to eleven members to direct all party activities. At obkom level and above, the majority of the places on the bureaux are held by full-time party officials.

Just as the primary organizations have a secretary, so do the higher party committees, but they have more than one, all of whom are full-time party officials. At obkom level, for example, there are usually five – a first secretary with overall responsibilities, a second and third secretary with responsibility for particular areas – industry, agriculture, or ideological work, etc. And, as can be seen from the diagram, each committee has its secretariat of full-time officials – party workers and instructors specializing in different areas – who, grouped in departments, work under the guidance of the secretaries. Members of the secretariat, and indeed the secretaries themselves, may be former secretaries of lower organizations, enterprising party activists, industrial or Soviet officials who have since moved into the party apparatus.

In outlining the relationship between the different tiers in the hierarchy we have used the words 'elect' and 'subordinate to'. According to official theory intra-party relationships are governed by the principle of 'democratic centralism': lower bodies 'elect' higher ones but must in turn obey decisions of those higher bodies. Obviously a principle such as this can be interpreted in different ways (and has been at different periods in the history of the party), but the current interpretation in practice is as follows. Each party body in the hierarchy is responsible for the working of any lower party organizations in its area – the regional party committee is responsible for the activities of all the district committees of the region, the district committee for all the primaries in its district – and the form this takes is not only requests for information on performance or the issuing of directives on a new line but also the vetting of personnnel or the appointment of officials to serve on the lower committees. Thus, although the appropriate party body at whatever level (from primary to republican congress) 'elects' its secretary or secretaries and committee, the outcome of such an election is supervised by the higher party body. The reader will remember the 'appointments' role of the central Secretariat. Each secretariat from district level upwards has similar responsibilities. It will keep a number of lists: (a) a list of full-time party posts which it is responsible for filling, (b) a list of non-party posts (for example, chairman of Soviet executive committee, enterprise director, head of technical college) whose occupants it does not necessarily nominate but whose appointment it must ratify, and (c) a list of individuals who, living and working in the region or district, are potential candidates for any job that may need to be filled. Aided by these lists, a department of the obkom secretariat will suggest candidates for the secretaryships of the district committees and probably some other suitable members too; similarly a department of the secretariat of the raikom may nominate full-time secretaries of the primary organizations and will vet all candidates proposed from below. The higher up the hierarchy one goes, the more obvious the system of appointment becomes: the central Secretariat openly sends or appoints individuals to be obkom or republican secretaries. This system of appointing or vetting personnel is known as the *nomenklatura*.

The degree of supervision over the activities of lower party bodies varies from place to place and probably from one level to the next but, at whatever level, an instruction from a higher party body is meant to be carried out by its subordinates. Whether this is always done is another matter, but it is clear that any open flouting of instructions from above is considered as 'breaking the rules' of party discipline.

The Executive in Action

Let us now think how well such an organization might operate as an executive machine. The first point that comes to mind is that Khrushchev's scheme of a central Secretariat, served by republic and regional bodies and a minimum of central ministerial bodies, is far less cumbersome than the present one which includes a large and growing Council of Ministers. Khrushchev's original scheme became increasingly complicated as time went on, but the Brezhnev-Kosygin alternative has not improved matters. The number of central and republican institutions issuing orders of one kind or another steadily increases; the central party apparatus has continually to try to embrace them all, coordinate activities, and maintain clear lines of command down to the primary institutions. But it is not simply that the party apparatus at the top has more to control: life too – as we saw – has become more difficult for the district organizations. Thinking purely in administrative terms, the growing size of the party must make it a less efficient vehicle for command than the party of twenty years ago.

But, one might argue, although it is true that the more stages there are in a chain of command the slower and less effectively it operates, there are certain traditional features of the party that encourage speedy implementation. The system of appointment from above is an important means of ensuring that politically reliable and loyal persons occupy the executive positions and they act in the knowledge that their promotion, or even their job, depends upon the faithful execution of orders from above. We are then dealing with a 'civil service' of unquestioned political loyalty and zeal, where material and moral incentives combine to influence behaviour, and obedience to orders from above is a long-established principle. If an instruction comes down from the central Secretariat or the Politburo on any topic – the rate of recruitment of new members, the undesirability of publishing labour-camp reminiscences or articles on traditional Russian art, measures to improve productivity in industrial enterprises or grain output on the farms – it will reach the appropriate organizations and they will react accordingly. But, if we think for a moment, we see that it is not as simple as that. Even the most centralized and streamlined organization will not in itself guarantee the implementation of directives.

If it were the case that policy directives were always clear, straightforward, and unambiguous (so that subordinates knew what to do without questioning), then we could expect prompt implementation. And indeed presented with this type of instruction (105 *sovnarkhozy* are to coincide with oblast boundaries, change the names of *all* streets and institutions named after contemporary Soviet leaders, stop *all* Jewish recruitment into the party), the party machine does operate very effectively. But the majority of directives inevitably allow for different interpretations and may not be consistent. Where this is so, a number of different factors will affect the outcome: the rules and traditions of the executive machine itself, the officials' perceptions of the leadership's priorities, the interests of those implementing the decisions, and hence the extent of agreement within the executive machine on the appropriate course of action.

One might argue that there are certain traditional features of the party that encourage a particular type of behaviour. The party organization, at whatever level, is considered to be the vanguard, responsible for guiding and controlling the activities of others or its own parent institution. Under Stalin any unsolicited spontaneous activity was seen as a threat, an indication that the party was not in control. Any such activity was illegitimate and should therefore be suppressed. Hence, the argument might run, the party will tend to act as a conservative force, defending the *status quo*, opposing innovation and change from below. Now it may well be that the party does act as a conservative force, but it is difficult to see that the roots of this lie in the hierarchical-vanguard tradition. It is more probable that attitudes encouraged in the Stalinist era and still held by the leading stratum of Stalinist officials are responsible. We will come back to this and to other possible explanations later. Here we are more interested in possible consequences of the intra-party relationships, and in this connection a quite different argument can be advanced. Because of the traditional stress on obedience to orders from above, plus the emphasis on 'overfulfilment' rather than 'fulfilment', the party has a 'natural' tendency to overimplement policy decisions. The maize campaign, for example, shows overzealous officials blindly overreacting to orders.

But this will not really do. We only have to think of a few policies to see that if there is a natural tendency to overreact it is usually suppressed. The maize campaign was overimplemented, but when Khrushchev permitted the publication of labour-camp literature it was *not* the case that nothing but purge literature filled the journals. It is true that it only needs a favourable mention of socialist competition from on high for every worker in the land to find himself participating, but, despite the leadership's public backing, the Shchekino experiment spread at a snail's pace.

How then do we explain the very different fate of these policies? It is clear that subordinates' perception of the leadership's priorities does not by itself determine the outcome: in the Shchekino case and in the publishing world subordinates were prepared to act in opposition to fairly clear signals from above. Why? We argued earlier that the dominant stratum in the cultural world was opposed to the liberal movement supporting abstract art and purge literature because it threatened its position and authority. Here then the leadership's proposal for change impinged directly on the position of those responsible for implementing it. And, by virtue of their position as cultural arbiters, they were able to wage a campaign against 'an excessive concern with the past'. Regional party authorities and ministries were the bodies which were meant to push the Shchekino experiment, yet they did little about it. This time it was not that their position was threatened but that to do so was to raise a hornets' nest of problems. An obkom which sent out instructions to enterprises would have been besieged by enterprise directors, backed by their party committees, complaining that it would entail a disruption of the production process and a drop in output, that their labour situation was a peculiar one, that it would be impossible to find alternative employment for redundant employees, etc., etc. Should the obkom insist, it might well find that output targets were not met (which would be ill received above), and that it was held to blame by disgruntled management and party officials who, in turn, had to face a discontented labour force. Here then the implementation of the policy would bring the party body (or the ministry) into conflict with other organizations and might well make another task – that of maintaining output – difficult. Socialist competition and the maize campaign are different. A socialist competition campaign does not conflict with any other aims and produces little opposition because it makes no real difference to activities or rewards at the grass roots. The pressure for maize was objected to by some collective-farm chairmen, but the party authorities could brush this aside: if maize targets were met, they were going to be rewarded, and it was not as though this would cause peasant discontent – the peasants had so little interest in what it was they planted and reaped. Socialist competition and maize clashed with no other objectives or interests.

We can agree then that, where policies allow of interpretation or where they contradict one another, officials will try to implement them as suits them best. The more general or the more contradictory they are, the more room for disagreement. Policy-making under Khrushchev was particularly marked by its contra-dictory nature – *everything* became a priority (steel *and* housing *and* agriculture, etc.); liberalization was accompanied by sudden clamp-downs – and this in large part allowed those who staffed the executive machine to implement it in 'their' way. Policy under Brezhnev has been more consistent but, in industry at least, far from clear. Here too then the executive machine can influence the outcome. But, if this is so, we need to know a little more about the machine itself in order to understand how it will behave. Whose interests will it advance?

An immediate answer is 'the interests of those who make it up'. In the case of the arts, the interests of the dominant cultural officials, in that of agriculture, those of the regional party officials. But who does staff the relevant organizations? Is it the case that those who make up the committees and bureaux agree on what their interests are or is it that within the party different interests jostle with each other? The controversy over the arts was fought out within the ranks of the party just as much as without. Perhaps we should look at the relevant party bodies to see who does sit on them. But first a word of warning. Just as we cannot assume any necessary connection between the composition of the party as a whole and the types of policy pursued, neither should we think that information on the composition of party committees will in itself tell us whose interests the party committees further. To a large extent this depends on the scope the committee has to act autonomously. And here we ought to distinguish between different levels in the hierarchy. The obkom, for example, as the most important executive authority in a region, responsible for dealing with all aspects of policy, can exert considerable influence on the way decisions are executed. Hence here one would expect the composition of its membership to give an indication of the line adopted. The primary party committee, on the other hand, is much more restricted in its activities. Here composition would be much less relevant.

The Primary Organization

Let us look first at the primary party committee and see what it is meant to do.[2] It recruits new members, checks the credentials of those applying for further education, organizes meetings on current affairs, or runs a campaign against drunkenness. In industry it should encourage the rest of the work force to meet new targets and to reduce waste; it should check that management is organizing production efficiently and observing the safety and labour legislation. It should, in general, respond enthusiastically to any instruction from above and see that it is implemented, explaining the importance of the measure to the non-party population. Its function, then, is primarily one of control, of seeing that the enterprise or institution is running 'properly', and encouraging participation by all and sundry.

Now let us suppose that an instruction comes down that productivity must be raised by weeding out surplus labour or that illegal overtime must stop. In theory the party committee should throw its weight behind the instruction. In practice it may well back the director in pleading extenuating circumstances and turn a blind eye to infringements of overtime legislation. Suppose an obkom issues collective farms with new, higher output targets – party secretaries and kolkhoz chairmen will argue that their targets are already higher than those of neighbouring farms, that they have specific problems to cope with and cannot take on the extra burden at the moment. If they do otherwise, they will find themselves with targets they probably cannot meet and the unwelcome task of chivvying an even more disgruntled labour force; if by chance they meet the targets, the 'reward' will be an even higher target the following year. In industry, as we saw, a campaign to economize on labour raises a number of problems   r the enterprise, not least the danger that it will affect the success of output targets; similarly a strict observance of the overtime laws would probably result in a drop in output, for which the party secretary would be called to account.

In such a situation the primary party organization has to weigh up the relative advantages and disadvantages of pursuing one objective rather than another. In theory there is scope for choice, but how wide is this in practice? The primary party organizations are engaged in the day-to-day business of production, on the receiving end of orders from above. Given the control over the enterprise's or farm's activities from above, the party organizations are operating in a restricted environment. There is little scope for independent activity. Somehow they have to satisfy their superiors, their immediate superiors. Given that a party secretary who took each clarion call from the leadership literally would find life impossible, the primaries must fall back on the existing incentive system, the penalties and rewards, as their guideline for action. If the penalties for not meeting output targets are greater than those for breaking overtime legislation, one meets the targets. If the ministry repeatedly changes the enterprise plan in the course of the year, and the supply system is inefficient, it is only sensible to try to get an easy plan in the first place. If an obkom suggests reducing the labour force, but the party secretary knows that, come the summer, the same obkom will be demanding the release of workers to help with the harvest, he will resist such a suggestion.

When a directive is straightforward, clear, and has no 'negative' effect upon activities, it will be carried out. When directives do allow of interpretation, or when they clash, it is the existing incentive system that determines the line adopted by the party body. This, however, does not mean that the composition of the party committees tells us nothing interesting. While it may be true that, where scope for action is so limited and where the incentive system determines 'rational' choice, it will make little difference whether the committee is worker or management dominated, the composition of the committee will at the very least tell us what it is that the leadership thinks appropriate.

In 1973 approximately two million (or 12 per cent of the total membership) were serving on the committees or bureaux at primary level. One of Khrushchev's innovations was to limit the number of consecutive terms of office for secretaries and to lay down rulings on the proportion of committee members who had to be 'newly' elected each time. His successors abolished these rules although they have not denied that the intent – to break down local cliques and to bring as much of the membership as possible into active party work – was right, and they continue to report the figures on those newly elected. We really do not know what proportion of the total party membership does, at one time or another, serve on the committees nor whether, despite a high turnover, there is a fairly constant inner core. But even at primary level a core of 'permanent activists' probably exists. As in almost any organization there are those individuals who – for whatever reason – are anxious or willing to be the committee men, taking on duties and participating in decisions. But perhaps more important than this is something else: the committee is expected to concern itself with all aspects of its parent institution's work – the state of production, next year's plans, introduction of new technology, worker morale – and to act with authority. Consequently it makes sense to include on the committee those in responsible positions who have both information and authority – the director, the chief engineer and one of his deputies, the trade-union chairman, party organizers or shop superintendents from the most important shops. Where details are given on the composition of individual committees, in industry at least, it is customary to find the director as a member and several other important management officials as well. This tends of itself to provide at least some continuity of membership.

The official report on party statistics with its statement 'More than one million workers and collective-farm workers were elected to the bureaux and party committees of the primary and shop organizations'[3] is not helpful, because we do not have the figures for total membership of the bureaux and party committees at this level. But, even if we did, we would be little better off. Any figure on all the primaries includes those in industry and agriculture where worker membership is high and those in institutions (schools, scientific institutions, government departments, etc.) where it is necessarily low, and this makes it pointless to work out what proportion of the 'average' primary committee is composed of workers. However, a detailed study of one particular region – Moscow oblast – does, by distinguishing between the primaries in different areas of employment, give some idea of the background of party 'activists' at this level.

Table XVI Moscow Oblast* Primary Party Organizations 1970

| Primaries with bureau or committee | No. of elected members | Of Which | |
		Workers	Collective farmers
Total	4,119 29,912	8,402	382
No. in industry, transport, communication, construction	1,729 13,972	6,662	—
No. in State farms	346 3,307	1,363	—
No. in collective farms	63 502	8	382
Remainder †	1,981 12,131	369	—

* Moscow oblast excludes Moscow city. † Calculated.

Source: *Moskovskaya gorodskaya i moskovskaya oblastnaya organizatsii KPSS v tsifrakh*, Moscow, 1972, p. 178.

We notice the variation between 48-per-cent worker membership in industry, etc. (and 76 per cent farm workers on the collective farms) and 3 per cent in the 'remainder', who must be those from the white-collar institutions. All we can say is that even in industry those holding white-collar jobs account for just over half the bureau or committee members.

But what of the secretaries themselves?

Table XVII Occupations of Secretaries of Primaries in Moscow Oblast 1970

Secretaries		Workers	Kolkhoz-niki	Agri-cultural specialists	ITR*	Other†
Total	6,196	383	18	91	1,508	4,196
No. in industry, transport, etc.	2,055	235	—	2	1,016	802
No. in State farms	351	5	—	36	17	293
No. in collective farms	64	—	18	8	5	33
Remainder†	3,726	143	—	45	470	3,068

* Admin.–Technical Personnel. † Calculated – original table confusing.
Source: *Moskovskaya gorodskaya*, p. 177.

'Other' occupations must refer to other white-collar jobs and will include those full-time party officials who are appointed to secretaryships in large enterprises and institutions. If one made a single white-collar category (agricultural specialists, ITR, and 'other'), it would be even clearer how, in industry and related branches, a very small proportion of the secretaryships are held by workers. Whereas workers make up perhaps 60 per cent of party membership in industry in the country as a whole (and there is no reason to suppose Moscow oblast is unusual in this respect), only 6 per cent of the secretaries are workers.

In reporting information on the primaries, Soviet commentators tend to stress the rise in the secretaries' educational qualifications over the period.

Table XVIII Educational Background of Secretaries of Primary Party Organizations

	Higher	Incomplete higher	Secondary	Incomplete secondary	Primary	Total
1956	11·4	7·9	29·5	30·6	20·6	100
1973	42·1	4·7	44·4	8·2	0·6	100

Source: *Part. zhizn*, pp. 25–6.

Can we simply assume that a new type of better-educated party secretary is replacing the old? Since the table does not tell us how many secretaries there were in the two periods and where their primaries were situated, we cannot. Another table tells us that primaries in institutions accounted for 24 per cent of the total in 1973 compared with only 14 per cent twenty years earlier. We would expect the larger the percentage of 'white-collar' institutions, the higher the educational qualifications of the secretaries. And indeed, in Moscow oblast, although 40 per cent of the secretaries had higher education, the figure masks the difference between 22 per cent in industry and 50 per cent in the 'remainder' category of institutions. Hence at least part of the rise in educational qualifications is accounted for by the rapid growth of 'white-collar' primaries.

The picture which emerges of the committee at the bottom of the party hierarchy is that of a body which (in industry at least) contains both worker activists and administrative and white-collar personnel (and usually more of the latter) and whose secretaries tend to come from white-collar backgrounds. We have already mentioned that the inclusion of senior personnel on the committee makes sense (from the point of view of those in authority) in view of the committee's management or executive role, and the 'white-collar' emphasis in its composition must make it difficult for the committee not to be seen as an adjunct of management by the rest. But, one might argue, since it is meant to be responsive to its wider membership, and since worker recruitment has increased considerably, this should prevent it concentrating too heavily on its management-support role. Let us think then for a moment about its wider membership.

First a general point. Certain professions and institutions have traditionally been heavily 'party-saturated', that is a large proportion of their members belongs to the party. The most highly saturated groups seem to be (a) ministers, members of Soviet executive committees, heads of government departments at town level and above, enterprise directors and collective-farm chairmen – of whom virtually all will be party members (b) judges, army officers, and possibly the police where approximately 95 per cent of the profession are party members, followed by (c) lesser government officials, other managerial personnel, and supervisory staff in industry or agriculture, engineers, teachers, doctors, trade-union and Komsomol officials – among whom party membership may range from 50 per cent to 20 per cent.[4] One might want to distinguish between teachers in higher education where the incidence of party membership is very high and primary-school teachers where it is much lower; but primary-school *head* teachers are likely to be a highly party-saturated group. It is probably true that within each broad occupational field – industry, education, the army – the degree of party saturation increases as one moved up the skill and administrative hierarchy.

Table XIX, based on a sample, gives an indication of this general pattern while showing that it does not necessarily follow for all grades.

Table XIX Party Membership in Machine-Construction, Leningrad, 1965

Occupational group	% Party members
Unskilled manual	3·7
Semi-skilled clerical	7·8
Semi-skilled manual	12·2
Skilled manual	16·2
Highly skilled, craftsmen	23·4
Lower administrative	19·6
Specialists	19·8
Management, supervisory (excl. directors, shop and dept heads)	54·4

Source: O. I. Shkaratan, *Problemy sotsialnoi struktury rabochego klassa SSSR*, Moscow, 1970, p. 406.

Khrushchev's recruiting drives – to bring in more of everybody – plus this pattern of party membership have had the following consequences. First, in certain institutions or sub-sections of institutions – for example, the ministries or factory administration – *most* of the employees are party members. This makes it difficult for the party to be seen as a separate organization from the parent body. Indeed, in 1966 at a conference organized to discuss the work of party committees in the newly established ministries, the image of the party organization as the vanguard or nucleus was queried, because its membership coincided with that of the ministry itself.[5] If all the members of the factory administration are party members, do they need to have one meeting to discuss current problems in their capacity as administrators, then repeat the meeting as the party organization? As we can see the very concept of the party as a separate organization, of party membership meaning something, becomes doubtful in these circumstances. The party organization simply reflects the groups, interests, and attitudes contained within the parent institution. In the cases quoted above it *is* the parent institution and will act no better and no worse than the institution itself as an executor of orders. In the enterprise as a whole or in the collective farm it embraces employees of all occupational groups, albeit relatively more of the highly skilled and managerial. Compared with the party organization of the Stalin period it is more representative in the sense that it includes more both absolutely and relatively of the blue-collar labour force but simultaneously the administrative grades have become even more heavily party saturated. Here then the party organization has become bigger, with a wider range of membership.

What consequences might such a recruitment policy have on attitudes within the party? Although the question of why individuals join an organization is always difficult to answer (or rather it is difficult to know how to interpret the answers given), we can suggest the kinds of reasons for joining that might be encouraged by such a policy. It is worth reminding the reader that, since the earliest days of Soviet power, people's reasons for joining the party have been sharply different and have changed with circumstances. To join the party at the time of the civil war when a party card was 'a passport to Denikin's gallows' entailed a rather different commitment from that during the mass enrolment of administrative personnel in the thirties – when not to join might have offered an excuse for denunciation in the Purge. Yet even during the civil war there were continual complaints about white-collar careerists sneaking into the party, and in the thirties there were those who thought of party membership as a selfless commitment to creating a new society.

The present different levels of recruitment from different occupational groups must affect attitudes towards membership within the groups. For someone with higher or specialist education –

especially if he is in the legal profession, education, industrial or agricultural administration – joining the party is often the norm. It requires no particular individual effort or commitment; it becomes part of the occupation itself. Party obligations – social work, committees, attendance at meetings – will be tolerated as part of the job and, in return, the party member is privy to more information on domestic and international affairs than the ordinary citizen. Within this general framework there is room for the individual at one extreme who is convinced of the party's historic mission and the infallibility of the leadership, the individual who feels that the party (although corrupt at present) is the only political organization through which change can be effected and, at another extreme, the cynic who joins simply in order to follow a particular career. With such high levels of recruitment among this stratum and the almost automatic association of certain professions with party membership one would expect to find the party reflecting the range of opinions of the stratum itself. In this sense it is non-selective.

It is rather different for workers and peasants. Here much more of a conscious effort must accompany the decision to join the party, but even here, as we saw, skill and party membership are related. It may be that, as workers move up the skill hierarchy, they look upon joining the party as part of a skilled worker's job and responsibilities – again an adjunct to a job rather than something independent. It may be that, particularly among the less skilled, the party attracts those natural 'activists' – people who like social obligations, committee work, organizing others. And of course party membership, along with its obligations, does carry both the privilege of belonging to a select group, privy to more information, and the possibility of moving up through party or trade-union channels to more responsible work – although, given the increased educational opportunities, the party no longer acts as a channel for upward mobility for the less advantaged in the way that it did in the twenties and thirties. More generally one would expect to find the white-collar member accepting his place in the party as right and normal – something befitting a better-educated, more responsible member of society – whereas the worker and peasant members, particularly the less well skilled, would be more aware of their special status, of themselves as a minority within their class, and be more anxious to distinguish themselves from their peers by their behaviour. Thus, quite apart from any other differences, white-collar and blue-collar worker will look on the party rather differently: for the former it is 'his' organization, for the latter it is part of a new world.

Let us now think back to Khrushchev's aims – at local level the party organizations were actively to pursue the leadership's policies, goading and spurring on their parent institutions, and simultaneously encouraging initiative and enthusiasm at the grass roots. However, as we can now see, the party organizations are unsuited for or incapable of carrying out either task and the attempt to do both only makes matters worse. In the higher ranks of the government administration where decision-making matters – at ministerial level for example – the expansion of party membership produces party organizations indistinguishable from the institutions themselves. As a distinct executive organization the party at this level no longer exists in any meaningful sense. In enterprises, farms, and institutions, with limited scope for manoeuvre and faced with conflicting directives from above, the party secretary or committee can do little but take the existing incentive system, the one that governs the activity of the enterprise anyway, as its guide. In line with its controlling executive function, the composition of the committee is weighted in favour of those who direct the productive or other process. Although the recruitment campaigns have brought in a larger and more varied membership – to provide a wider basis for support – this has not changed either the committee's functions or its relationship with its membership. Despite the talk in the early post-Stalin years of the need for criticism and discussion, for 'democracy' at the grass roots and an end to interference by the higher organizations – all necessary if the party was to become active and attract support – little actually happened. It is not difficult to see why. Had such activities really been encouraged, they would have threatened both the party as an executive machine and the whole system of centralized control from above.

Discussion and criticism in a situation where a wide range of conflicting opinions were held by an increasingly large membership, where conflict and disagreement long since engendered and then suppressed by Stalinist policies were emerging in the wake of new policies, would have revealed a party split a hundred ways on every issue. The larger Khrushchev made the party, the less harmonious an organization it became. The more 'democratic', the clearer the conflicts would have been. Had discussion been allowed at the grass roots, the restrictions imposed by the planning system and the inability of the party committee to effect changes would have come into question; wider powers for the party committee would have necessitated changes in the relationship between enterprises or institutions and their superiors. 'Democratic' voting in a situation where those elected cannot satisfy their electors will give no satisfaction to elected or electors; an appointed committee arouses far fewer expectations. And, where the electors are divided, 'democratic' voting will result in a committee unable to agree. In all these ways and more a return to 'Leninist democracy' (in the words of its advocates) was dangerous and impracticable from the leadership's point of view. To maintain its control and to retain an executive which would implement orders, the leadership had to continue with detailed supervision from above, it had to restrict the scope for activity and freedom of discussion within the lower echelons. But in turn this means that at the primary level – and for the majority of both the membership and the non-party population the party at primary and district level *is* the party – the organization is little more than a cog in a machine operated from above. It is hard to inspire enthusiasm in people who are not allowed to do anything. The obkom, which is the lowest tier allowed any real degree of decision-making – is too far removed and, with the creation of the new bottom tier, becomes an even more distant body. It is a large jump from primary to obkom but we shall now make it.

The Obkom

The obkom is the authority of the region. It has at least one department responsible for industry, checking that enterprises are meeting targets, attempting to get additional resources from the centre, and sorting out rival claims between enterprises. It is directly responsible for the region's grain and other agricultural products, intervening where necessary in farm affairs. It has departments responsible for overseeing the regional press, for vetting all cultural activities and education curricula. Officials in charge of the lower party organizations will sift information sent up by the district committees; take up complaints and criticize shortcomings. And the personnel department will be responsible for the *nomenklatura*, or appointment and vetting of personnel.

Who then sits on such a prestigious body? 'Workers and collective-farm workers account for 40 per cent of the members and candidate members of the raikomy and gorkomy, and almost 30 per cent of the obkom and central committees of the republican parties. Practically all the bureaux of the gorkomy and raikomy have workers or collective-farm workers among their members.'[6] As we see the 'worker delegation' persists as one travels up the hierarchy but becomes relatively smaller. At obkom level membership is dominated by two main groups: full-time party workers (or *apparatchiki*) and officials from important institutions. By way of example Moscow obkom in 1971 was made up as follows:

Table XX

	Moscow Obkom 1971	
	Members	Candidate members
Workers	20	11
State-farm workers	5	6
Collective-farm workers	1	3
Collective-farm chairmen	3	—
Directors of industrial enterprises, transport, etc.	11	3
Directors of State farms	2	3
ITR	—	2
Agricultural specialists	—	1
Soviet officials	19	9
Employees in science, culture, education, and health	8	6
Party officials	50	13
Other	8	4
Total	127	61

Source: *Moskovskaya gorodskaya*, pp. 173–4.

The 'party officials' contingent will contain those who work in the obkom apparatus, in the raikom, and in primary organizations. The 'other' category will include representatives from the military (the commandant of the region), the secret police, and the secretary of the Komsomol; and the Soviet and industrial representatives will include leading men – the *chairman* of the regional Soviet committee, important enterprise directors. A smaller inner group of these leading officials, with party workers making up the majority, will hold the bureau places. Thus at this level we have a committee composed of the 'important' people of the region, plus some from below, plus a 'rank-and-file' element, and a bureau which brings together those who matter most. In the committee we can see the way in which different units in the party structure are linked vertically one with another, and the way in which the party is linked horizontally with other institutions. It embodies the different institutions of the region. And simultaneously of course party officials will be elected onto Soviet committees, as will enterprise directors and military officials. At a given moment in time the different 'elected' bodies overlap in terms of personnel, and over time officials may move from one institution to another. The chairman of the Soviet executive committee or an enterprise director may move into the party apparatus; a party official may become the chairman of a Soviet.

By way of an example of the degree of 'integration' we can look at the 'duties' noted in the diary of a leading Leningrad enterprise director. As a young man in the twenties he was a worker in Moscow; in the early thirties he attended a technical institute and thence moved to the Leningrad factory; after the war he had the job of enterprise party secretary for two years; he moved away to become chairman of the Soviet executive committee, and then in 1955 came back as director.[7]

1968 One month's engagements:

Date		
8	9 am	Economics course in the Polytechnic Institute
10	2 pm	Meeting of the party committee
11	11 am	City conference on specialization

12	10 am	Meeting of commission to prepare for forthcoming meeting of the city party committee
	12 am	Conference with deputy-minister
13	9 am	Trade union election conference in the factory
15	4 pm	Meeting in the district party committee
16	10 am	,, ,, ,, city ,, ,,
18	5.30 pm	,, with a group of Soviet deputies
19	9 am	Study circle for members of the district party committee
20	3 pm	Meeting of party *aktiv* of the factory
23	10 am	,, ,, *aktiv* of all enterprises in the trust
24	10 am	,, with the head of the trust
	2 pm	,, of the factory party committee
25	2 pm	,, ,, ,, Soviet executive committee
29	3 pm	,, ,, *aktiv* of the factory
30	5.15 pm	Party meeting of the production section of the factory administration

At obkom level then the leaders in the region come together, most of them important administrators in charge of institutions or enterprises, and as such they will defend the interests of 'their' institutions. This, one should imagine, will lead to disagreement rather than unity. Soviet officials will not see eye to eye with enterprise directors on the subject of pollution or where new housing should be situated; enterprise directors and farm chairmen will have different attitudes towards the use of industrial labour to bring in the harvest; and there will be strong disagreements over priorities for available funds or appeals to the centre for funds. All that really unites them is a common front against the central leadership – that is the body from whom resources must be sought, failures hidden, and interference resisted – but then this hardly fits with the 'role' of the obkom as a crucial link in the centre's executive machine.

The obkom, however, only meets three or four times a year and perhaps is more of a discussion body than a decision-maker. It is the full-time party officials who are intended to provide the unbreakable thread in the skein that runs from the central political leadership down to the grass roots. Given the system of appointment from above and apparatus strength on the committees and bureaux – particularly on the bureaux which, through the departments, run party affairs – it is clear that the potential authority of the apparatus is greater than that of any other institution.

The Party Apparatus

We do not know how large the apparatus is – estimates range from 100,000 to 250,000 – nor do we know its size at any particular level in the hierarchy. In early years approximate figures were published; nowadays mention is made of cuts in its membership but no absolute figures are given. In 1922 it was estimated at about 15,000 or 4 per cent of total party membership; in the thirties it grew in both absolute and relative terms, then in the fifties it was cut down. Certainly as a proportion of total party membership, given the size of the present party, it must be as small as it ever has been. It includes all those who work full-time for the party: secretaries (from Brezhnev down to the full-time secretary of a primary organization), instructors and officials in the secretariats at all levels, editors of party publications, teachers at party institutes and schools, party organizers in the armed forces, etc. For most of its members a raikom secretaryship or a post in an obkom department is the limit of their career. From there some will move into Soviet posts or into party work in other institutions. A very few will attain an obkom secretaryship. At this level officials in charge of departments will look for new recruits from among party workers of subordinate organizations – regional secretaries and instructors, energetic secretaries of primary organizations or Komsomol organizers, and those administrators or specialists (technical experts, industrial directors, journalists, and teachers) whose skills and talent would benefit the apparatus. Thus some work their way up the apparatus, some go out and come back in at a higher level, some come in for the first time at raion or oblast level. It is probably the case that above and perhaps even at oblast level jobs are filled by those who have had at least some past experience of party work. This may not be right – the central Secretariat may take on bright young men to begin their party career at the centre – but certainly the responsible jobs at republican and central level are unlikely to be filled by specialists with no previous experience within the apparatus.

The several thousand secretaries who from raikom to republican level run the secretariats and organize the affairs of the bureaux or party committees are, by definition, white-collar personnel. Their educational qualifications are high – approximately 98 per cent had higher education in 1973 and 60 per cent of them were engineers, technicians, agronomists, or economists by training. However, more than 80 per cent of the secretaries of the obkomy and republican parties began their careers as workers or peasants. The people in these positions and in responsible posts in the central Secretariat tend to be of that age group which benefited from the social mobility of the thirties and forties – their combination of qualities as workers and political loyalty won them places in technical institutes from which they returned to take up party work or went into industry and then the party. For the older members the great revolution of the thirties was the period of their youth, for the younger – the war. As one moves down the hierarchy, the age group is younger and, one suspects, started off rather differently. Among the forty-year-old secretaries of the raikomy and gorkomy one would expect to find fewer who began their careers as workers, more who received a higher education on finishing school, started specialist or administrative jobs, and then moved to party work. Indeed Khrushchev stressed the importance of bringing specialists into the apparatus – recently qualified engineers, directors, agricultural experts – and this is probably reflected in the lower levels. It is noticeable that the occasional high flyer who has made the upper ranks of the apparatus at an early age is of this type.

Although the term 'the party apparatus' refers only to those who, at a given point in time, are working full time for the party, the term *apparatchik* or 'party worker' sometimes has a wider meaning in everyday usage. As we noted above, individuals may move out of the apparatus to take up a job in Soviet administration, in education, in the trade unions. Some of these move back, others – who have reached the limit of their career in the apparatus and are wanted out to make room for younger talent – remain in non-party employment. Thus, at any point in time, there are 'old' (and not necessarily in age) party workers in other institutions who have an apparatus background.

Some writers refer to 'apparat attitudes' as though there existed a distinct and homogeneous set of attitudes among party officials. Sometimes these are specified as 'conservative' or 'ideological' to be contrasted with the 'rational', 'technical' approach of the specialists. Now it could be that party officials do react in a particular way to policy proposals or events, but, if this is so, it cannot be because of their backgrounds. As we have seen, it will not do to talk of the existing apparat as though its members had one particular type of background and, furthermore, the types of background and career pattern found within the apparat are also found without it. Is it the case then that the apparatus is an organization with sufficiently strong traditions and a stable enough role to mould its members in its own image (in the way that an army or some civil service departments do) and if so what *is* the image, or would we expect to find conflicting elements within it?

This is not an easy question to answer, but we can go some way towards it. We can think of the apparatus of the early thirties as a body of confident, unchallengeable administrators: they were the authority in the land, their word was law. The purges destroyed the individuals themselves and this type of authority. The new *apparatchiki* were men of little experience who suddenly found themselves occupying positions in a dangerous hierarchy, one subject to police surveillance and to whims from above. It was a hierarchy down which orders were passed, orders which had to be obeyed blindly and passed on down to subordinates, regardless of how sensible or appropriate they were. There was no place for initiative or independent judgement. When Khrushchev came to power there were changes. He demanded that the apparatus, that officials at all levels, use their own judgement and show initiative; that they encourage new phenomena and direct the energies of the population (so long stifled under Stalin) into new and creative paths; that they no longer bully but use persuasion. At regional level the party secretaries acquired a new importance with the creation of the *sovnarkhozy*. In 1962, with the division of the committees into agricultural and industrial units, Khrushchev was advocating the appointment of men with the appropriate expertise as secretaries. New recruits to the apparatus should be men with technical knowledge who could understand and advise on production problems. And, Khrushchev argued, a good party worker was not one who spent his time arranging meetings and delivering ideological homilies but one who could sort out production difficulties or see that technological innovations were introduced.

But Khrushchev himself was inconsistent. An obkom secretary in the south who had called short-sleeved dresses indecent was upbraided by Khrushchev for his Stalinist attitude of objecting to anything new. A collective-farm chairman who had refused to plant maize because he knew it would not grow was congratulated: a subordinate should not carry out instructions from above slavishly. But, while inveighing against such 'Stalinist' behaviour patterns, Khrushchev himself remained a prisoner to them. If *he* decided maize was the crop of the future or that Lysenko's theories of genetics were correct, he expected others to agree without question. For every collective-farm chairman he upbraided for carrying out orders which produced appalling results, there were ten who won praise or promotion although they had acted no less stupidly. He might talk of experimentation in the arts and of leaving the artists to settle their own disputes, yet, when angered by the exhibition of abstract art, he had the evening papers calling for a re-organization of the cultural unions and, when shown Fellini's film $8\frac{1}{2}$, he insisted that the Moscow Film Festival jury award the prize to anyone but Fellini. He did not want slavish officials, continuing to act in a Stalinist manner, but – on the other hand – he did expect them to realize he was right on topics he cared about. He made no attempt to change the *nomenklatura* system or the rules on lower party bodies obeying their superiors – after all it was these that gave whoever headed the Secretariat a good measure of control over personnel (thus safeguarding his position) and an apparatus geared to carrying out the central government's policies with a minimum of opposition. Neither is there any evidence that Khrushchev attempted to dislodge the upper stratum of officials who, trained in the Stalinist environment, were accustomed to a system of administration under which orders from above were to be blindly carried out and subordinates were to accept them without question. He merely asked them to behave differently and gave them bewildering instructions.

As might be imagined, this produced strain. It is difficult to know how much. The only direct evidence is the somewhat anxious letters to the party journals from officials who felt that the new specialist recruits did not understand the vital task of the party worker as an overall administrator, or from those who questioned the extent of the party's involvement in technological or specialist problems. The new leadership – probably both because it felt that division of the party committees was not the way to help solve the country's economic problems and because of discontent within the apparatus – brought back the original structure. Brezhnev stopped the public exhortations to officials to get out of their offices and into the plants and farms and began again to emphasize the importance of proper ideological training, but there is no evidence that he disagreed with Khrushchev on the need to bring technical and other specialists into the apparatus. It seems plausible to suggest that many of the old Stalinist *apparatchiki* did find their tasks bewildering and they must have felt at least slightly threatened by the new young men who had recently completed their higher education and were coming in at lower levels.

Certainly in terms of its composition the apparatus is not homogeneous or unique. Nor is there any evidence that we can attribute a particular policy line to the apparatus – either in the making or the implementing of it. It is probably more correct to talk of Stalinists and others or of 'conservatives' and 'reformers' within the apparatus and to recognize that these distinctions can be applied to a wide range of officials and specialists in other institutions. It was not only party officials but ministers, directors, collective-farm chairmen, and intellectuals who were used to obeying orders from above and bullying their subordinates. The Khrushchev reforms – in whatever field – tended to divide all, regardless of institution, into conservatives and reformers. The kinds of reform that were proposed, passed, or rejected were not ones that produced and made explicit some kind of 'apparat interest'; for that to have been the case the reforms would have had to have been much more radical and, in those circumstances, the apparat would undoubtedly have found other institutional support.

The Party's Future

Khrushchev used to waver between describing the party as the vanguard of the working class and referring to it as the party of everyone. At times he would stress the increased worker and peasant recruitment as evidence of its working-class nature, at others he would suggest that, because the new Soviet intelligentsia were all the sons and daughters of workers and peasants, the class composition of the party was irrelevant to the claim. The latter argument can, of course, be used to justify any social composition of the party: it does not matter if the intelligentsia do dominate numerically because their 'original' social background plus the absence of class conflict in Soviet society makes them as working-class oriented as anybody else. Brezhnev argues rather differently. The party represents a class, and social composition is important. The fact that worker and peasant membership combined makes up more than 50 per cent of the total is an indication of the leading role of the working class in Soviet society. 'Its revolutionary spirit, discipline, organizational ability, and collectivism places it in a dominant position in the system of socialist social relationships.'[8] In some unspecified way the working-class nature of the party, as reflected in its composition, ensures a democratic approach to social problems and the furtherance of the 'best' interests of society.

If the Khrushchev argument is not very clear, the Brezhnev approach lacks conviction. After all there have been considerable periods when the working class has *not* held the dominant position in the party and yet Brezhnev would not concede that during these periods the party did not represent the interests of the working class, was not imbued with working-class qualities and values. The most he might concede (and even this is doubtful) is that the party did better when it was more working class – but this is a difficult position to defend. One wonders why Brezhnev should consider it right or necessary to produce this kind of argument.

One simple answer is that he does it, unthinkingly, because it is part of the accepted creed. But both Stalin and Khrushchev produced variations on the original idea that the party was the vanguard of the working class. Why should Brezhnev have felt it necessary to stress this (rather than 'the party representing all' angle) and to link it with social composition? Leaders will interpret, change the emphasis in a set of inherited beliefs, in accordance with their own needs and the circumstances in which they find themselves. Hence to answer the question we must ask what it was that Khruschev and then Brezhnev were trying to do with the party. Khrushchev inherited a heavily white-collar party, one which was thin on the ground in industry and very thin in the countryside; a party which no longer functioned as the nervous system of Soviet society but instead crept along as merely another institution carrying out Stalin's wishes. Khrushchev wanted to bring in new people – particularly from the grass roots in industry and agriculture – both in order to make the party more of a 'national' institution and to make it a more accessible institution with 'ordinary' people in it. Simultaneously he was concerned to devise a system to make the economy more efficient, to 'modernize' the still backward sectors of Soviet life and, for this, he thought it necessary to 'modernize' the party – to bring in specialists and to give a more competent organization greater control over the welter of bureaucratic institutions that too often stifled any attempts at change. Thus on the one hand he was attempting to broaden the party's base; on the other he felt it desirable to rely even more heavily than Stalin on the specialists because they were the people who, in his view, held the key to the future. Hence his shifts between stressing the importance of working-class recruitment and his denial of the importance of present class status.

Some western commentators have argued that the high recruitment figures for white-collar personnel are explained by the leadership's desire to keep this section of society in particular under party control. In order to maintain existing levels of party saturation among the expanding intelligentsia, it has been obliged to recruit heavily; but to limit recruitment to this would create an extremely lop-sided party – a white-collar preserve – hence the increase in worker recruitment to preserve the balance.[9] This may contain an element of truth but not more. The leadership has after all been raising the level of party membership within the intelligentsia and stressing the importance of education and technical expertise within the apparatus. It does seem to see white-collar attributes as of importance to the party itself. Brezhnev's recent emphasis on increasing working-class membership may in part be an attempt to play down the specialist leadership of the party and to preserve the balance, but one suspects there is more to it than this. It was the specialists and intellectuals who spear-headed the movement for change in Czechoslovakia in 1968, and it was the workers in Poland in 1970 who objected to the policies of a leadership that had lost touch with workers' demands. The Soviet leadership has no intention of allowing either the Czecho-slovak or Polish events to happen in the USSR. One way of making it clear that it has no sympathy with fancy intellectual ideas of the 'socialism with a human face' variety is to stress its adherence to established traditions, symbolized in expressions of the kind 'the party is the vanguard of the working class', and to emphasize the importance of class attributes. Simultaneously it is anxious to build up party groups among the workers in order to establish a network to provide information to the workers or about worker attitudes.

But this 'traditionalist' approach to the party – accompanied by a renewed emphasis on the importance of 'ideology' as the cement that binds the party together – fits badly with the reality of a party that embraces such a large and varied slice of the population. The Brezhnev-Kosygin leadership has continued Khrushchev's recruitment policies – which stemmed from a cer-tain conception of the party and its role in society – while not necessarily sharing his concepts. Lately recruitment has slowed down and in 1973 there was an exchange of party cards (that is a review of all members). The reasons for the exchange were never made really clear – whether it was intended to weed out certain elements, and if so which; whether it was to herald a new recruit-ment policy. It may be that the leadership itself was divided and this explains the absence of a clear line, but it is tempting to suggest that the leadership itself is uncertain of the future of the party. An exchange of party cards is a respected party tradition and a useful time-consuming operation for the lower bodies to be engaged in while the leadership thinks. The party has doubled in size since 1956. It is now a huge mass organization of fourteen million with a well-developed network of party units and with nearly one in every three specialists a party member. If present trends are continued, when are they to stop and why? Is the existing organizational framework appropriate for such an enormous party? It does not seem to function well either as executive machine or popular organization, but what is the alternative?

11 An Assessment

How should we, in conclusion, characterize and hence 'explain' the Soviet political system today? Is it an authoritarian relic, incapable of coping with the problems of an advanced industrial society or have its communist leaders successfully produced a new system of government that can solve all social ills? Should we see it as the desperate attempt of a new ruling class to perpetuate itself or has the revolution produced a new type of political elite? The analysis so far, at times explicitly, at others implicitly, has been concerned with these questions. In this final chapter we address ourselves to them directly, expanding the ideas a little and referring back to the preceding account in arguing for or against a particular interpretation. Hopefully the reader could do this for himself and write his own last chapter. In any event he can at least see where he disagrees with our assessment.

Soviet Arguments

It is common for western writers of very different political persuasions to describe the rulers of the Soviet Union as a political elite or as members of a new white-collar elite or ruling class. Soviet theorists who talk of power resting with the working people whose best representatives in the CPSU lead and guide social and political activities of course deny such claims. Let us start by looking a little more closely at their objections to western arguments and hence, simultaneously, at their own claims.

The Soviet argument runs as follows: although it is true that the leading administrative, technical, and political posts in society are occupied by members of the intelligentsia, it is not correct to talk of rule either by the intelligentsia or by a new white-collar elite or class because

(a) the intelligentsia as a social stratum has no peculiar interests of its own; in both capitalist and socialist society, it is a 'floating stratum' whose members serve the interests of one or other of the basic classes and, under a system of social ownership where there are no antagonistic classes, it serves the common interests of the working people;

(b) the administrators and officials are by origin working class;

(c) they carry out their tasks under the aegis of the Communist party and, furthermore, they are subject to control from below by the working masses who participate in Soviet and social organizations.[1]

The most important argument is that, under a system of social ownership, there can be no basic conflict of interests: hence the idea of a class or elite (which entails the idea of it safeguarding its own privileged position) ruling in its own interests makes no sense. Society is seen as a harmonious whole where no conflicting, irreconcilable interests exist and where the main agent of change is the Communist party which interprets social developments and rules in the interests of all, guiding society forward to communism. Despite the mistakes of the Stalin period, the party remains the true descendant of the original Leninist party, because it kept the spirit of Marxism-Leninism alive.

One might have thought that the denunciation of Stalin would have undermined this conceptual view even within the USSR. It did for some individuals but, for a number of reasons, the political leadership sought and has managed to preserve the orthodoxy. Church dignitaries may dethrone a pope without questioning the value, heritage, and importance of the church, and those who dethroned Stalin held responsible positions within the 'church'. The party leadership, ideologues, and lesser officials owed their political and social position to the existence of the party: they were the bishops and cardinals who traced their authority back through 'generations' to the early apostles. For them to question either the continuity of the faith or whether the behaviour of the church had at any time departed so far from its original ideals and practice that it ceased to remain the same organization would have been to question their right to rule and the present political organization of society. The Catholic church, which has survived for centuries and feels its position secure, can permit some critical re-interpretation of the church's activities in far distant periods (although it is surprising how unwillingly even this is allowed); the CPSU is still a very new organization and one which in 1956 found itself under attack from both friends and enemies.

Since the end of the twenties any serious discussion of social stratification, class relationships, or conflict under a system of social ownership has had no official forum in the Soviet Union. The political leadership is unwilling to allow economists or sociologists to collect and publish data on, for example, income distribution, social mobility, or social attitudes, but it is too simple to suggest that this is prompted solely by a concern that such analysis might raise awkward questions. Of course it might. Any serious discussion of inequality, privilege, discrimination, or any other source of social conflict is dangerous because it leads almost inevitably to the question 'who is getting what and why?' and hence to comparisons of the economic, social, and political position of different social groups. This is a Pandora's box best left closed. Some groups in society – notably the new adminis-trators, decision-makers, highly skilled specialists, and artists – do receive a disproportionate share of society's goods and ameni-ties. Certain regions and cities fare better than others. And what of the distribution of resources between the different republics? In what sense are the policies responsible for this in 'the interests of all'? This in turn cannot but lead to the question of whose interests the leadership and the communist party are furthering, and whether in fact the introduction of social ownership has removed all irreconcilable conflicts of interest.

But we must remember that the political leadership has been reared on the idea that the major source of social conflict, indeed the only one that really matters, is private ownership of the means of production. This encourages the view that where social con-flict still exists in the Soviet Union it is either a remnant of the past (nationalism, for example) or it is a temporary phenomenon, the result of hard conditions or 'backwardness', things that will disappear with time. And there is also a tradition of keeping awkward problems or unpleasant facts – be they poverty in the countryside, crime statistics, or air crashes – out of public discussion, on the grounds that no good comes from making all information public and, indeed, if publication might have harmful consequences, it should certainly not be permitted.

There are then cultural as well as political reasons for the preservation of certain fundamental tenets of Stalinist orthodoxy. But, were there political reasons alone, we would not need to conclude, nor should we, that the leadership is cynical about its beliefs. It is very common for people to accept as right and proper those views which justify to themselves their own existence. To return to the earlier analogy, the bishop or cardinal does not usually question his right to a palace or to pronounce on what is good and evil; he is aware of the vast gulf between his material and social position and that of some of the tenants of property owned by the church, he is aware of the atrocities that have been committed in the name of Christianity, but none of this undermines his belief in the importance of the church (and his place within it) and its duty towards mankind. We accept that *he* need be neither insincere nor a cynic, and neither need the party leadership.

The idea of social harmony, of the absence of conflicting interests, is essential to the theoretical justification of the leadership's position. The party and hence the leadership rules not because it has received a majority vote from the public at large, or a mandate from a particular section, but by virtue of its ability to produce the 'best' policies, to find solutions that are in the interests of all. It is true that at times the leadership talks of having a mandate, but the 'real' justification for its existence is its ability to rule in everyone's interests. But, if it is to do this, the interests of the different social groups must be reconcilable one with another. However, there are problems with this type of legitimation, some more theoretical, others more practical.

If it is assumed that there are no conflicting interests, it follows (logically) that the leadership always rules in the interests of all – because it is not clear who else's interests it could be pursuing. But we find Khrushchev charging Stalin with having made mistakes and he in turn was accused of 'hare-brained schemes'. The leadership then is fallible and can produce policies that are not in everyone's interest. How then could we tell whether the leadership was ruling in everybody's interest? Unfortunately the concept of 'interests' is so vague that there is no way in which we could.

First there is the problem of deciding let alone agreeing on what people's interests are. In reply to the argument that a certain action or decision is against a particular group or community's interests, it may be countered that the action does accord with their 'real, long-term interests'. If pushed, the Soviet theorist will argue that interests should be understood in this sense – reaching communism is in everyone's real interest and this is what motivates the political rulers. But that is a useless criterion for judging individual policies. Of course this is not a problem peculiar to Soviet theory. How would one 'prove' that a political elite was acting in its own interests and against those of the rest of society? A separate but related problem is that of what might be meant by 'the social interest' or, as it is commonly referred to in Britain, 'the national interest'. Most governments like to argue from time to time that their policies are in everybody's interest, but there is no easy or obvious way of deciding what this means – if it means anything at all. How can one compare and evaluate different types of interest? Attempts either to measure or to compare the performance of different political systems in terms of their serving the interests of their respective societies founder very quickly.

This does not mean we should not attempt to establish whose present and obvious interests are being served by a particular political order. We can and do talk in an intelligible way of policies working in favour of or against certain groups. Indeed it would be impossible to understand or participate in political activity without employing the notion of 'interests'. But it is a notion that can mislead very easily, particularly if it is awarded a precision it does not possess. The point here is that in Soviet theory the nebulous concept of 'the harmonious interests of all' provides the justification for the political authority's existence and the idea of a conflict of interests is ruled out.

As we saw in the last two chapters there are plenty of instances when institutions or groups feel that their interests are being threatened by the preferential treatment awarded to others, instances when it is clear to the protagonists that their interests cannot be furthered simultaneously. It is now possible to suggest, cautiously, that different social and occupational groups may see things differently, may wish to improve their position relative to others, may – to some slight extent – have conflicting interests. But this type of suggestion does not get very far. We shall come back to the question of sources of conflict later; suffice it here to point out that there is no Soviet theory on the nature of conflict under social ownership, only references to its absence.

The second strand in the Soviet argument relates to the working-class origin of the decision-makers. But, if one accepts that there are no conflicting interests in society, then the class origin or immediate background of the rulers is irrelevant. Any policy-making group, by pursuing its own interests, will further those of everyone else. However the idea that class origin does matter, even under socialism, dies hard and there are very good reasons why the official theorists should emphasize the working-class origin of today's administrative elite. Ever since the revolution the leadership has stressed that in the USSR 'equality of opportunity' is far more real than in the capitalist west. Whereas under capitalism, it is argued, the educational system tends to perpetuate class divisions; owners of capital pass their wealth and its privileges on to their sons and daughters; politicians, government officials, the officer corps, and professional groups are recruited disproportionately from children of non-manual occupational groups – under socialism there is equal opportunity for all to aspire to these positions and it is the sons and daughters of workers and peasants who, in the Soviet Union, occupy them. And indeed the twenties, thirties, and forties were a time of rapid social mobility. Those young men of the thirties who survived the Stalin period and since his death have occupied the commanding posts in society come predominantly from poor backgrounds. To them this feature of Soviet society is very important.

This, plus the abolition of private ownership of the means of production, is enough to make them impatient with suggestions that there is a new ruling 'class' in the Soviet Union. One of the characteristics of a ruling class – as spelt out by Marx – is its tendency to perpetuate itself, to pass its wealth and privileges on to its children. Ownership confers this privilege or, to put it another way, the concept of ownership contains the notion of the right of disposal. An 'owner' as distinct from a tenant has certain rights of selling or giving away. The inheritance of wealth and property is accepted by Marxists as one of the features of a class society, one of the means by which class divisions are preserved. Obviously then it becomes difficult to talk in class terms of a society where social mobility is such that the offspring of the poorest in society make up the next generation of rulers, only to be displaced in turn by another wave of 'outsiders'. To those who have come from the 'oppressed classes' and now occupy the command posts it is self-evident that they are not a 'ruling class' as some of their critics have alleged.

But who are we talking about when we refer to 'the rulers' or those who occupy the command posts? Any attempt to establish whether it is appropriate to think of a ruling class or of elite rule, indeed any attempt to analyse the political system, must spell out who *are* the powerful in society. In Marxist analysis (and indeed not only Marxist) the powerful may not themselves hold the reins of government but may stand behind and above the politicians and influence their actions. In the Soviet case, given the fusion of economic and political, of all forms of power in the hands of the State authorities, no such division exists. We can point fairly easily to the locus of power. As argued earlier, there is a reasonably clear division between the rulers – those who make the rules that guide or restrain social activities and control the means of coercion – and the ruled, and the former are a relatively small group. It consists of those who from regional level and above sit on the committees, praesidia, or bureaux and those who head the ministries, State committees, and Secretariat departments and sections. It is one which includes party officials, industrial administrators, diplomats, journalists, generals, secret-police men, trade-union officials, artists, and the occasional worker or peasant.

Let us for the moment refer to this as the ruling group. In terms of its composition and scope as a decision-maker it is a catholic body embracing the major institutional interests, a group of decision-makers who, acting collectively although not necessarily harmoniously, make the major social, political, and economic decisions. Hence it will not do to talk of the ruling group bargaining or competing with 'the military leaders' or 'the industrial planners'. The bargaining that takes place between the upper echelons of the military, Secretariat officials, and industrial planners occurs *within* the ruling group. And, as we have said, the concentration of power in the Soviet Union produces a ruling group that is simultaneously the political authority. We are used, in the west, to talk of the political authorities as something separate from the religious or military leaders, the industrial or trade-union leadership. This way of looking at social arrangements may become less and less meaningful as the State takes over responsibility for more activities. Indeed it makes a great deal less sense now than it did fifty years ago, and in the Soviet context it is actually misleading. If we are talking of the political authorities in the Soviet Union, we are talking of a small, closely knit group that includes the leaders of different institutions. Hence it will not do to talk of the party apparatus as the political authority: its leaders are part of it but its lower officials are not. Similarly the party as a whole cannot be a candidate – its lower echelons, the mass membership, is excluded from participation in decision-making in any real sense.

To what extent though can we call this ruling group, this political authority, part of a ruling *class* or a political *elite*? It is certainly true that Soviet society is stratified in terms of income, status, and privilege and it is the case that the ruling group is heavily white collar and well educated, drawn predominantly from the most privileged strata in society. But, as we noted above, its members would claim that they came from the underprivileged and that in the Soviet Union the opportunity to rise is there for all. Clearly the present rates of social mobility are relevant here. Although legally all that the present incumbents can pass on to their children is their personal wealth – a house, car, savings – can they also pass on their right of disposal of society's goods and services by ensuring that their children occupy the future command posts? Are the present twenty and thirty year olds, who receive a higher education in the more prestigious universities and institutes and take the best jobs, the sons and daughters of workers and peasants or are they the offspring of today's rulers?

Soviet sociologists have tended to concentrate on career aspirations of school children rather than on the backgrounds of a new generation of administrators, but we can at least say the following. In the competition for higher education the sons and daughters of the better educated fare better than those of workers and peasants. Their career horizons are wider (and their ability to fulfil them is better) than those of children from working-class backgrounds. At the very least it is difficult not to think of a broad stratum of those with higher education perpetuating itself. The children of this group will rarely re-join the ranks of workers and peasants.[2] But this still tells us very little. It could be that the children of today's ruling group move into high-status, privileged jobs – in the artistic, academic, scientific world – but that the reins of government are taken over by the offspring of low-ranking officials, academics, or by the aspiring entrant from the ranks of the working class. The overall slowing down of social mobility could take the form of the crystallization of the top stratum even within the better educated, or of a division between those with higher education and the rest but considerable movement within each of these categories, or the maintenance of some social mobility in particular spheres. We do not know. We can say that equality of opportunity is not as real as it was. This is hardly surprising. On the one hand the aspiration and ability to rise to high office in one capacity or another regardless of background, sex, race, etc., has been stressed as one, if not the supreme, virtue of socialism. On the other hand unequal rewards and a hierarchical ordering of society have been defended as right and proper. Although it is perfectly consistent to advocate all simultaneously, the result will be a stratified society in which special safeguards will be necessary if mobility is to be maintained once a new educated intelligentsia has been created. One does not need a class analysis to explain the reluctance of social groups to see their children deprived of a privileged position. This will occur wherever rewards are unequal and tied to educational qualifications. The less meaningful 'equality of opportunity' becomes, the more difficult it is to espouse – and the more dangerous. Thus one would expect both discontent as social mobility decreases and some re-definition of the concept itself.[3] But, to predict where discontent will be greatest, we would have to know more about the different patterns of mobility itself. And, to talk of the perpetuation of a ruling class in Marxist terms, we should have to show that the major dividing line is not between the better educated and the rest but between those who 'own' or 'control' the means of production and the remainder.

But what of the third strand in the Soviet argument, that which denies the existence of a new ruling elite of well-educated administrators because of the party's superior position and because of control from below by the working masses? This is thin indeed. First, empirically, it is not the case that the Soviets and social organizations at the grass roots control the activities of the decision-makers at regional level and above. There is little scope for participation in taking decisions, given the hierarchical system of orders coming from above and the small degree of responsibility allowed the rank-and-file organizations. This then leaves the party to check and control the well-educated administrators and decision-makers at all levels. But, as we have argued earlier, they themselves are in the party, sit on the committees, move in and out of party posts. *Quis custodiet ipsos custodes?* It is true that the party has a large percentage of workers and peasants among its membership, but they no more control decision-making within the party than do the masses of the population control decision-makers or society at large. But again, theoretically, this kind of 'control from below' argument seems to run counter to the claim that all have the same interests anyway. If this is so and if, as it is claimed, education and training improve the quality of decision-making and administration, then it is not clear why there should be any need for control from below, from those who are less educated and hence, presumably, less capable of finding the best solutions. The emphasis on the value of an 'honest proletarian consciousness' fits uneasily with the idea that the able should acquire higher education and move into specialist positions.

A New Ruling Class?

The Soviet arguments do not convince that decision-making does not rest in the hands of relatively few who form part of a larger privileged stratum in society. But they do raise some of the problems associated with the 'new class' analyses. If one defines the ruling class narrowly – in terms of those who control the means of production and dispose of goods and services – then one has to refer to the central and regional political officials, our ruling group.[4] This implies a society composed of a tiny ruling class, a very large white-collar stratum ranging from poor and well-paid officials and school teachers to wealthy enterprise directors and artists, an industrial working class, and a peasantry. Although this tiny 'ruling class' does stand in a unique relationship to the means of production, there is the problem of showing that it perpetuates itself or indeed behaves like a class in other respects. Hence others have proposed different candidates and would see this ruling group as merely a part of a broader class.[5]

The intelligentsia, defined as the educated, white-collar stratum, cannot be a candidate in Marxist terms. But, even if we dropped any attempt to define 'class' in a Marxist sense, it is difficult to identify the interests of the ruling group and the intelligentsia as the same – and this is largely because the latter is such a broad social category including so many disparate elements. The relationships of the different sections of the intelligentsia to the ruling group vary considerably – for some there are material privileges and scope for work, for others only one of these; some suffer both a falling standard of living and restrictions on their activities.[6] A rather different candidate is 'the bureaucracy', taken to mean a much larger slice of officialdom, presumably *all* government, party, and social organization officials, presumably too the directors of industrial enterprises and farm chairmen. These are taken to be the 'controllers' of production, the functionaries of the State who prevent the working class from exerting political and economic control. The trouble with this is that it is difficult to see the sense in which this 'bureaucracy' does stand in a specific relationship to the means of production – that the relationship of the industrial minister, official of the local Soviet, and enterprise director have anything in common one with another – or the sense in which the majority can be said to 'control' the means of production. If one uses the 'relationship to the means of production' criterion, it is difficult to distinguish anything more than the very small ruling circles. If one drops that criterion and simply uses 'bureaucracy' in its usual sense of administrative officials paid by the State, one ends up with an enormous category ranging from accountants in enterprises and head teachers to secretariat and ministerial officials. But any definition that produces a category which includes the privileged leading personnel and the lower ranks of the administrative or industrial apparatus runs into the problem of specifying the common aim of such a 'class'. Even if one agrees that 'the accumulation of capital and wealth' spurs on the rulers, those who make the decisions, it is difficult to see how this can be said of the lower ranks and how the leadership's pursuit of these aims serves their interests. Materially they fare worse than several other privileged groups, and in status terms; they are harried from above and probably enjoy less secure employment prospects than any other group in society.

Of course, if one starts by assuming that a ruling class exists, then one will find it – just as the interest-group theorist inevitably finds his interest groups. But the unsatisfactory nature of the finds should suggest that perhaps here is a social phenomenon that does not lend itself to a traditional class analysis. There is a small ruling group whose members are part of the more privileged sections of society, but one which it is difficult to identify with or see as ruling on behalf of a larger social group or class. There is no broader social group whose interests are homogeneous and can be identified with those of the ruling group. Neither will it do simply to identify the ruling group with 'the privileged' because it is clear that only in certain limited respects does the ruling group pursue the interests of such groups as scientists, artists, or even enterprise directors.

But, if this is so, if we are faced with a ruling group that does not represent a class or a social stratum, we have to decide how we can best explain the political relationships that exist. If we are happy with neither the Soviet claim that the political leadership is guiding society gently but firmly forwards to communism by following Marxist-Leninist precepts nor with the suggestion that, on the contrary, the rulers are caught in a class conflict that spurs the system forwards, then we must offer something else.

Maintenance of the Present System

We can refer to the ruling group as a political elite if we wish to emphasize its existence as a small, self-selecting group of privileged men who make decisions which affect the vast majority of the population and who seek to maintain this situation. But this in itself tells us little. We now have to decide what enables the rulers to maintain their position and what it is that provides the system with its momentum.

Let us first think of the political structures themselves. There is a set of hierarchic institutions coordinated and controlled at the top. Posts are filled from above, discussion and criticism is restricted by the political leadership, which is ready and willing to use coercion against even mild forms of opposition. This is a situation in which it is extremely difficult to produce alternative strategies, be they 'reformist' or more radical, let alone create any organizational support. It is not so much that 'dissident' theories are weak or naive and their supporters few and fragmented but that the political structures militate against the formation of coherent blocs even within the party. The 'neo-Stalinists' cannot sit down and produce a platform for serious discussion any more than the 'social democrats' can. It is a situation which lends itself to sporadic splinter activity and little else and this works to the advantage of the ruling group.[7]

Rather differently the hierarchic nature of the system localizes conflict within the political structures themselves by concentrating the attention of each level on the one immediately above and below itself. This is important, because in a system where economic and political power are fused – and where the leadership makes itself 'responsible' for social progress – it is more difficult for the political authorities to divorce themselves from the sources of discontent. For example, 'unfair' wage differentials or price rises cannot be blamed on 'the market'. (Of course this works both ways: the political authorities can and will take credit for all the 'good' things.) Hence the political leaders will try to divest themselves of responsibility by making subordinates the targets. In turn this means that the rights of the primary organizations – be they trade-union committees, primary party organizations, local Soviets – must be kept very limited. If they were given a proper part in running production or the affairs of the town, it would soon become apparent that the source of their ills is the centre after all, rather than there being a benevolent ruler badly served by his subordinates.

If the political structures make coherent opposition very difficult and tend to localize conflict within society, the political and economic mechanism as a whole produces a fragmentation of social groups and institutions which, in its turn, weakens any potential opposition. And simultaneously the political elite's ability to produce at least some of the goods – notably increases in the standard of living, opportunities for individual social advancement, *and* the maintenance of privileged positions, peace, and international success – in a situation where no coherent alternative is available for consideration generates support as well as frustration.

We have then a situation which seems eminently suited to the maintenance of the political *status quo*. This assumes that the ruling group will not spontaneously and willingly divest itself of its power, authority, and privileges; it assumes that ruling groups only do such things in response to pressure. And this is a fair enough assumption. But is this really an unchanging situation and, if not, what are the sources of change? How do we after all explain the ruling group's actions since Stalin and what of the future?

In any society political change results from conflict. Although by itself this remains an empty statement, it can be useful if it directs our attention to the sources of conflict in a society and hence the potential pressure points of change. We have referred, at various places in the narrative, to different forms of conflict within the Soviet system. Now let us see whether we can locate particular types that make for change.

Sources of Conflict and Change

Under the Soviet system private ownership has been replaced by social ownership; control over the use of resources is concentrated at the centre and highly concentrated at that. We have the administrative allocation of resources, rather than a market mechanism, but money remains and the individual, in terms of his daily activities, uses his 'money' to choose between different commodities in the same way that his counterpart in the west does. This has led to the argument that hence in a Soviet-type system there exist two different 'power structures' simultaneously and conflict between them.[8] The first stems from party rule, the type of party authority that rests on its claim to lead society to a better future, and hence justifies political control over the distribution of resources. This produces a power structure that can be termed 'officialdom' – officials control resources. But simultaneously the use of money as a means of allocating resources (e.g. wage differentials) and determining consumption patterns introduces a different plane of inequality, a different structure of power and opportunity, one that does not coincide with 'officialdom' and can be called a 'class' structure. The argument, although interesting, needs elaborating before much can be inferred from it. But what it does rightly point to is the strange mixture of social relationships in Soviet society, and it focuses on property relationships as important.

Let us think back to what produced the present. The revolution abolished the old system of private ownership and with it the old ruling class and those social phenomena associated with it – its privileges, self-perpetuating wealth, the association of office with family, and its aristocratic 'culture'. The basis for class conflict, that is between the owners and the labouring classes, had gone. But this was a situation which left unsolved the conflict between worker and peasant, it was one which allowed conflict *within* the peasantry to develop, and which released the conflict between different national groups. If class conflict is particularly sharp, it may well dominate, suppress even, other forms of social conflict: the worker or peasant sees the owner or landlord as the enemy while the worker–peasant relationship or that between nationalities is pushed to one side. But once the owner is removed, in a situation of adversity, other social conflicts emerge as important and can flourish. With the abolition of private ownership, the *form* that social ownership assumes is going to be the crucial factor (in conjunction with existing social relationships) that determines future social relationships and hence the nature of conflict within the society. Bolshevik rule both released and produced new patterns of conflict, as we saw in an earlier chapter. But it was with the Stalinist revolution – with the introduction of the centralized administrative allocation of resources and tight political control to achieve rapid industrialization – that social ownership assumed a certain form of State ownership which in turn determined future developments. Some of the earlier conflicts were forcibly eradicated. The peasantry, for example, were squeezed into one social mould of, in effect, State employees and the State broke the connection between town and country.

Of course a crucial question is why social ownership assumes the form it does, why in our case the Stalinist State arose. That we have already discussed. Here we simply remind the reader that it was not somehow an 'inevitable' consequence either of the political structure of the Bolshevik party or of existing social relationships and the world situation. Both these made the outcome possible, but that was all. Here we are more interested in the consequences. What happened was that with the decisions that made up the Stalinist revolution the State rose *above* society. The fusion of economic and political power did, at least temporarily, allow its wielders to rise above the social environment. This was a situation in which it was *not* possible to talk of the State being the tool of a ruling class, and class conflict was certainly not the dynamo of the system. Instead it was a situation in which a political leadership was able to grab power, and it was precisely because it was not the creature of an existing class that it was able to act in such a voluntaristic way and so drastically affect social relationships by political means.

More practically this meant that the decision to go for rapid industrialization, to collectivize the peasantry, and to effect this by Stalinist means was responsible for the type of social relationships that ensued and hence the conflicts that have arisen since.

The use of coercion, of persuasion, and marked differences in rewards, the nature of the planning and incentive system not only created an impoverished peasantry and working class deprived of any control over production, facing a privileged stratum of new administrators and specialists (difficult enough to reconcile with earlier aims) but also generated conflicts between institutions and between sectors, within the different hierarchies and within the party itself. The political leadership had no social basis for support and was fast undermining its original political basis, the party. This was a dangerous situation. As we saw, the political leadership responded by instituting a more rigidly centralized system of control, suppressing political activity, and using coercive measures against any actual or imagined opposition.

If the State has no social basis of support, if the rulers do not have the backing of the dominant class (if one is a Marxist) or of a sufficiently strong cross-section of social groups (if one is not), then it will have to maintain its position by force. (The obverse does not follow: a ruling class may use coercion to maintain itself but its power may rest primarily on other means.) The young Stalinist State certainly rested on coercion, but simultaneously it began to throw up new potential supporters: *apparatchiki* and ministerial officials who gained positions of importance, the upper ranks of the military and secret police, young men of talent who could acquire an education and work in scientific or engineering fields, artists and writers who received privileges and apartments. These were the product of Stalinist policies. But they were an inadequate basis for support. As we have argued the Stalinist system created conflicts between groups, and between privileged groups at that, conflicts over power, status, and rewards; it produced competing groups, some of whose interests sometimes coincided but never sufficiently to produce a constellation strong enough to form a united bloc and support the political authorities as their offspring. In turn the use of coercion by the leadership to maintain its position, the refusal to recognize, let alone institutionalize conflict or discontent, discussion or opposition, both lost its potential support and hindered the consolidation of any into larger units.

Although in a specific historic situation the State can take on a new form and rise temporarily above its social environment, this cannot last for long. The social relationships created as a result either provide a basis for the State or, if hostile to it, must be contained if the rulers are to survive. In either case State and society are again intertwined. We have argued that in the Soviet case the new social relationships threatened the State and, in turn, the political structures 'responded'. In doing so both the nature of the State and the relationships it fostered were affected.

The post-Stalin leadership tried to create a social basis for support by substituting placation for coercion. Thus we find Khrushchev directing his energies towards putting right what he saw (and rightly) as some of the major grievances: ending mass terror, improving living standards, easing harsh working conditions in the factories, greater intellectual freedom for the specialists and intellectuals, more rights for the republican authorities. If the ruling group is to enjoy the support of any substantial section of society (except perhaps the secret police), it has to move in at least some of these directions. And if it is to maintain its Great Power position or its leadership in the socialist world, it cannot afford to resort to counter-productive terror again. The ruling group then must attempt to establish a firmer basis for support.[9] But, and here is the rub, its attempts to do this aggravate the conflicts and produce new ones.

The Khrushchev attempts to satisfy the demands of what are competing interests inevitably accentuated the rivalry between them. As the standard of living improves, differences in consumption patterns between the privileged and the rest become more obvious. Cars and cooperative flats are now available for the better off. It is therefore perhaps not surprising that a reduction in differentials accompanied the wage increases, but differences remain very marked. Moreover the lower paid still have a very low standard of living while the better off fail to find the quality and variety of goods they want. Neither side is satisfied and inequality becomes more apparent. To what extent the improvements in harsh working conditions and wages have generated working-class support, it is very difficult to tell. But improvement has been slow and uneven and there are other factors to take into account. Redundancy has emerged as a problem, and local unemployment. One can go on to hazard a guess that the slow-down in social mobility is beginning to produce a second- and third-generation urban working class which is unlikely to be satis-fied with a slow improvement in its material position – and one over which it has so little control.[10] On the other hand gains for the workers have meant losses for management: both financially and in terms of its rights.

Greater intellectual freedom for the specialists and artists re-sulted, not in an upsurge of united support for the rulers, but in open splits within the intelligentsia, an increasing frustration within sections of the technical and scientific community with the form of political decision-making, and led to open opposition from some of the artists and writers. The increase in republican rights led to demands for more resources from the new, educated elites of the once 'backward' republics which still lag behind their wealthier neighbours, who, in turn, argue that they are being robbed. As more discussion is allowed, more groups stake their claims, only to find they conflict with others.

Thus the ruling group is caught in a trap. Its search for support produces conflict, because to meet the demands or satisfy the grievances of one group or section of the community is to pro-voke opposition from another. To contain the conflict it must use the existing political structures to suppress or deny the as-pirations of the different groups. This in turn both fosters new grievances and prevents the coalescence of different groups into a bloc strong enough to provide a basis of support on its own. The political structures may make opposition difficult but they simultaneously deny the ruling group a social base. We shall look at the implications of this for the future in a moment, but first let us pause to consider something else.

An 'Outdated' Political System?

Is this the same as saying that the political system is now some-how out-of-joint with the present social and economic system, as some western authors and Soviet dissidents have argued?[11] In one obvious sense we are *not* saying that, because we suggested that an important reason for the repressive authoritarian system of the thirties and forties was that the social conflicts produced by industrialization and collectivization were such that they could only be held in check by that type of political control. Hence, if the suggestion is that the political relationships do not somehow 'accord' with the social relationships of today, the same would have to be recognized to have been true of an earlier period. But of course what is not clear in such a suggestion is what is meant by political relationships being 'out-of-joint'. The argument seems to be as follows: as a result of 'industrialization' Soviet society is now a complex, socially differentiated society with a level of industrial development to which centralized decision-making and one-party control is no longer 'appropriate'. Let us interpret 'appropriate' (in the most charitable fashion possible) to mean: whereas the economy of the thirties could develop within the confines of tight political control, now that it is more complex it cannot. The assumptions here seem to be: the problem of industrializing a primarily agricultural country is relatively simple (and 'Marxist-Leninist ideology' and authoritarian rule can cope with it quite well); the problem of running an industrialized society is much more difficult because of its complexity and it can only be solved by decentralization, autonomy for different groups, democratic discussion and management. But these assumptions are false.

Industrialization is not at all simple. It can be *made* simple by adopting simple aims (steel at all costs) and ignoring any others – but that is a conscious choice. The economy can become simple or complex at any point in time depending on what it is that the actors are trying to achieve. To those struggling to propose alternative strategies in the twenties the economy looked extremely complex: it was Stalin who 'simplified' it. (Rather differently one should be suspicious of vague references to 'increased social differentiation' within society. The social structure has certainly changed, but in what sense has it become more 'differentiated'?)[12] In one sense and one sense only does the presence of a developed industrial base complicate matters. If the point has been reached when surplus steel is being used to make hats, artificial flowers, and baby toys, a commitment to the simple aim of steel production becomes less and less likely. But, long before this point was reached, the Soviet leadership were questioning the original priorities. And there was nothing in the nature of the economy in the twenties that precluded their thinking in terms of consumer demand, relative costs, or balanced growth even then.

However, they did not, and the type of planning system and political control from above accentuated the emphasis on simple targets and unbalanced growth. Such a system, as we have seen, does not respond particularly well to the endeavour to switch the pattern of resource allocation, to improve consumer welfare by increasing the variety and quality of goods – although we should remember that the increase in consumer welfare since the mid-fifties has been very substantial. But is this what is meant by the argument that the political arrangements are hampering further development? What might we mean by 'further development'? It is true that the overall growth rate has slowed down but, as we saw in an earlier chapter, there is no agreement that this is anything to do with the political arrangements; furthermore it is very respectable by western standards. It is true that the increase in productivity has slowed down (again the reasons for this are not self-evident) and, given that productivity on average is lower than in the US, this makes the aim of catching up with the United States or even maintaining the present ratio a more difficult task. It is true that there is enormous 'waste', the inefficient use of labour and resources, but then there always has been. The costs in the Soviet economic mechanism have been rather different from those in a market economy.

It might well be that the introduction of a market mechanism would 'correct' some of the faults of the Soviet economic mechanism (although how one would evaluate the advantages compared with the disadvantages is not at all clear), but that is not really what the advocates of political reform have in mind. As is well known the market can flourish under a dictatorship just as well as under democracy. Their suggestion seems to be that the absence of free interplay between groups, of democratic elections, opposition, criticism, and specialist autonomy is what is responsible for the present failings. But why changes of this kind should produce 'remedies' is not spelt out: the most likely result would be a collapse of the economic system in a situation of unorganized and aimless social conflict.

The Future

However, we are not going to see the introduction either of the market or of a liberal or socialist democracy in the near or even the foreseeable future. Either would mean dismantling the present structures which maintain the ruling group, and that can only come as the result of pressure upon them. The pressure that does exist is not of that kind. In its attempts to redress grievances, to lessen discontent, the ruling group inevitably accentuates it, fans it into new channels, and then responds by hardening the line against opposition or signs of discontent. The result is to produce new and more extreme forms of opposition or simply apathy and disillusionment. For example, nationalist feelings or demands are suppressed by the centre, which in turn 'justifies' and encourages nationalistic aspirations; the attack on critical writing and the trials sponsor Samizdat and the dissidents. But, as we argued earlier, it is only where discontent can be focused on one easily recognizable issue by a small group that it takes on an organized form. Both the political organization of society and its fractionalized nature work against more coherent forms of opposition. We can expect more dissidents, even fewer ballet dancers left at the Kirov, demonstrations of nationalist feelings, and some unorganized industrial protests, but these will not make the present rulers tremble or even think of reform.

It will need much more than that to produce any real changes. Can we then suggest the circumstances under which discontent might be translated into concerted action? Because it remains by and large unformulated, the nature and strength of discontent are very difficult to assess. However, one factor which clearly affects it is the standard of living. If the slowdown in the rate of growth and productivity makes it increasingly difficult to maintain improvements, we can expect discontent to rise. (The relative isolation of the Soviet economy from the influence of world markets has meant that the recent world inflation has had little impact, if any, but rapid escalation of military expenditure could have a serious impact on the domestic economy.) As we already mentioned, the advantages of being well paid become more obvious as more consumer goods are available but, more important, if present increases cannot be maintained, how is the smaller 'cake' to be distributed? Who is going to benefit – the poorly-paid or the more privileged sectors? Expectations are greater today, after the promises and practice of the past twenty years, and may not be easily damped down. If the political authorities can neither produce substantial improvements in the standard of living nor maintain a system of social mobility that benefits the less advantaged, then it is difficult to see how it can hope for any support from the workers and peasants. Much then depends on economic performance. If there is something for everyone, the leadership can assuage a major source of discontent and can more easily defend its claim to represent the interests of all. If it becomes increasingly difficult to improve everyone's standard of living, even if only a little, a choice has to be made as to who is to benefit.

The choice has to be made – by the rulers, not by the 'market' – and the claim to be furthering everyone's interest becomes thinner and thinner. We can think of the Khrushchev period as one in which ruling group and others could live with the idea that life was going to get better for everyone. Now appetites have been whetted and growth rates are down. In this situation both rulers and ruled can see more clearly that there are opposing interests and that decisions to benefit some will damage others. But yet, and this is the irony of the·situation, the ruling group has no clear idea of the way to move. Here is a planned economy, a system in which economic and political power is concentrated in the hands of the rulers – the power is there to control the distribution of wealth, to mete out social justice – and the rulers do not know what to do with it. They have no criteria by which to evaluate the desirability of acting in favour of some and against others, because they do not rest on the support of a specific social interest. Hence the ruling group hesitates, tries to avoid making choices, and continues where possible with existing policies. Of course, in such a situation, existing privileges and inequalities remain and in this sense one can say that the rulers are favouring the privileged groups. But the privileged are divided between technocrats, artists, generals, political officials, and scientists, between neo-Stalinists Christian socialists, market supporters, nationalists, and social democrats. They cannot be thought of as a group which unites in favour of the present political arrangements or provides the rulers with guide-lines for action.

It is not surprising that in this situation a hard-line, more conservative, even neo-Stalinist faction gains strength within the ruling circles (and not only within them). The ameliorative policies of Khrushchev only revealed more clearly the social gulfs and conflict within society; reforms merely produced new divisions within the party, clashes between institutions, and open conflict within sections of the intelligentsia. The present leadership has consequently drawn back, hesitating. There seems to be much less room for manoeuvre, nowhere to move to. Attempts to meet grievances produce demands which cannot be accommodated within the confines of the existing political system; yet all that sustains the ruling group are the existing political arrangements and, if they go, it goes too. Hence we find the leadership falling back on its role as guardians of the country against external enemies. At present the Chinese are the enemy – and a useful one. It is much easier to arouse nationalist feelings and fears of the Chinese than, for example, anti-American sentiments. And we find a new claim made for socialist democracy:

The undisputed superiority of socialist democracy, which is inspired and directed by the Communist party, consists of the fact that it guarantees social progress in conditions of *political stability, unshakeability*, and is based on the close union and unity of all classes and strata of the population, of all nations and natio: alities.[13]

In this situation – and we are not of course suggesting that rulers or their subordinates think in these terms or would accept this type of explanation – the pre-Khrushchev period appears in a favourable light. The rule of terror is conveniently forgotten. Firm direction, control, strong leadership, none of this intellectual whining and absurd nationalist complaining. The attitude reflects the impasse in which the ruling group finds itself – having nothing new to offer, it harks back to its image of the past. We are then unlikely to see the replacement of the present leadership by a more reforming group. Instead we shall see either the continuation of the present cautious, conservative line or – and this would seem the more likely if the economy begins to falter – the emergence of a more repressive, hard-line leadership, emphasizing central control and direction, and perhaps using Russian nationalism in the attempt to gain support. Neither of these (nor indeed a more reform-minded leadership) can prevent social discontent and conflict becoming more acute, but either could last quite some time. Neither military nor the secret police would challenge these alternatives. The nationalist movements are potentially more disruptive but are weakened by their mutual antagonism, and a policy of conciliation and repression should prevent their posing a real threat to central authority – certainly for the foreseeable future. The intelligentsia, as we have argued, are a large divided stratum, some of whom are privileged, some not; some of whom support the present arrangements, others who disagree violently over what is wrong and how to remedy it; and few indeed who can imagine any kind of action. This leaves the workers and peasants. If social discontent rises sharply, then it will be translated into action. But what kind of action? Apathy, shoddy work, heavy drinking, petty crime, nationalism, or spontaneous industrial action? Concerted political action, for all the reasons we have mentioned, is a long way off. But maybe we shall see some unprecedented action, and I mean unprecedented. The society that has evolved within the unique political and economic framework of the past seventy years will prompt new patterns of social and political behaviour and they in turn will require and, it is to be hoped, provoke new theoretical and practical solutions.

Calendar of Major Events 1861–1976

This is intended simply as a quick reference-guide for the reader who, at some point in the text, needs to remind himself of events and their dates.

1861	Edict of Emancipation.	
1889	Founding of Socialist-Revolutionary Party.	
1903	The Russian Social Democratic Labour Party splits into the Bolsheviks and the Mensheviks.	
1905	Near revolution; the Tsar grants a Duma.	
1914	First World War breaks out.	
1917	February:	Revolution – the Provisional Government.
	April:	Lenin Returns.
	October:	The Bolshevik Revolution.
1918	January:	Dissolution of the Constituent Assembly.
	March:	Treaty of Brest-Litovsk.
	July:	A new Constitution.
1918–20	Civil War; War Communism.	
1921	March:	Kronstadt rebellion.
		Introduction of NEP; resolution forbidding factions at Tenth Party Congress.
1924	January:	Death of Lenin.
1925	Defeat of Trotsky and the left in the leadership and policy struggle.	
1927	Defeat of Kamenev and Zinoviev.	
	December:	Decision to move ahead with industrialization at Fifteenth Party Congress.

1929   Defeat of Bukharin and the right.
        Forced requisitioning of grain.

1930   Five-year plan speeded up.
        November: Wholesale collectivization.

1934   Seventeenth Party Congress: The Congress of Victors.
        December: Assassination of Kirov.

1936   New USSR Constitution.

1936–8 The Great Purge.

1939   Eighteenth Party Congress.

1941   Germany invades USSR.

1952   Nineteenth Party Congress.

1953   March: Death of Stalin.
        Collective leadership of Malenkov, Molotov, Beria,
            Kaganovich, Khrushchev, etc.
        July: Removal of Beria.

1954   Virgin Lands Campaign.

1955   Malenkov loses Chairmanship of Council of Ministers.

1956   April: Khrushchev's secret speech to Twentieth
                       Party Congress.

1957   May: Sovnarkhoz reform.
        June: Khrushchev defeats anti-party group.

1961   Twenty-second Party Congress: renewal of
            de-Stalinization.
        Publication of *One Day in the Life of Ivan Denisovich*.

1963   Growth rates down; poor harvest.

1964   October: Ouster of Khrushchev.
                   Collective leadership of Brezhnev,
                       Kosygin, and Podgorny.

1965   Economic Reform.
        Arrest of Daniel and Sinyavsky.

1966   Twenty-third Party Congress.

1968   Invasion of Czechoslovakia.

1969   Disappointing results of Economic Reform.
1971   Twenty-fourth Party Congress.
1972   Weapons and Trade Agreements with US.
       Tougher measures against dissidents.
1976   Twenty-fifth Party Congress.

Glossary of Russian Terms

Aktiv	A group of party 'activists' who take on special responsibilities.
Apparatchik	A member of the party apparatus.
Glavlit	The Censorship Agency.
Gorkom	City party committee.
ITR	Administrative-technical personnel.
Kolkhoz	Collective farm.
Kolkhoznik	A member of a collective farm.
Komsomol	The party youth organization.
Nomenklatura	The system of appointing and vetting personnel by party bodies.
Obkom	Regional party committee.
Oblast	Region.
Raikom	District party committee.
Raion	District.
Samizdat	Unofficial 'underground' literature.
Sovkhoz	State farm.
Sovnarkhoz	Regional economic council.

References

* Where simply the author's name is given in a reference, the title of the book is to be found in the Bibliography for the appropriate chapter.

Introduction
1. The Soviet republic and then the Soviet Union were the names given to the new multi-national State which, to all intents and purposes, replaced the old Russian empire. The Russian republic or the Russians themselves are only part of the whole; hence 'Russian' and 'Soviet' are not synonymous.

1 Autocracy
1. Article I of the Fundamental Laws of the Empire, quoted by Kochan, p. 60.
2. Yarmolinsky, A. (ed.), *The Memoirs of Count Witte*, Heineman, 1921, p. 213.
3. Quoted by Robinson, p. 162.
4. *ibid.* p. 194.
5. Preface to *The Communist Manifesto in Russian* (1882), trs. in Marx, K. and Engels, F., *The Russian Menace to Europe*, The Free Press, Glencoe, 1952.

2 Revolution
1. At the time of the revolution the Russians used a calendar which was thirteen days behind that used in the west. According to that calendar the revolutions occurred in February and October; by the new calendar they become the March and November revolutions. We use the old dates in this chapter.
2. Quoted by Kochan, p. 193.

3 Socialism and Democracy
1. A reference to Lenin's return to Russia via Germany in a sealed railway coach with the permission of the German government.
2. Quoted by Filene, p. 104.
3. The capital was moved from Petrograd (re-named Leningrad after Lenin's death in 1924) to Moscow in the spring of 1918.

4. For examples of the Bolshevik decrees, see Bunyan and Fisher, and the appendices to Chamberlin.
5. At the time peasants in the field (as opposed to those in the army) were sending delegates to separate congresses; after January 1918 a unitary system was adopted.
6. Lenin, *Selected Works*, vol. II, p. 331.

4 Industrialization and Collectivization

1. See Bibliography (Chapter 5) for references to the secret speech.
2. Olga Berggolts, a Soviet poet, in 1956, quoted by Swayze (Bibliography, Chapter 9), p. 143.
3. Almond and Powell (Bibliography, Chapter 6), p. 273.
4. See, for example, Schapiro (Chapter 7) and the 'totalitarian' authors mentioned in the Bibliography to Chapter 5.
5. Shoup, P., 'Comparing Communist Nations' in Fleron (Bibliography, Chapter 6), pp. 76–7.
6. See his speech 'On the grain front', re-published in his *Works*, vol. II, and in *Leninism* (Bibliography, Chapter 5).
7. Lenin, vol. II, p. 817; Stalin, vol. 13, pp. 40–41.

5 Stalinism

1. Mandelstam, N., *Vospominaniya*, New York, 1970, pp. 152–6, (trs. as *Hope Against Hope*, see Bibliography).
2. This Constitution, with minor changes, is still in existence today; it is available as an appendix in Lane (Bibliography, Chapter 8).
3. Serge, *Memoirs . . .*, pp. 80–81.
4. Solzhenitsyn, *Gulag . . .*, pp. 419–31.
5. For conflicting estimates of the extent of the Purge, see Conquest and Swianiewicz (bibliography), and Nove, A., in *Soviet Studies*, vol. XX, April 1969, pp. 537–8.
6. Cliff argues this.
7. See Arendt, Friedrich, and Brzezinski, or indeed almost any study by an American author published in the fifties.

6 New Approaches

1. For some of the key studies and their interpretation, see 'Politics in the West' section of the Bibliography.
2. See Almond and Powell; Apter.
3. Hazard is an example of this.
4. It is interesting that Dahl, in criticizing Mills's power elite analysis of the United States, assumes a single elite in the USSR.

5. Skilling was the leading pioneer of the group approach; Linden argued the 'policy-disagreement' case.

6. See, for example, Barghoorn.

7. Hough, J., 'The Party Apparatchiki' in Skilling and Griffiths; and his article in *Problems of Communism*, March–April 1972.

8. Barghoorn, Gehlen, and Brzezinski tend to talk in this way.

9. Medvedev, R., in *New Left Review*, 1974, no. 87–8, p. 73.

10. See Baumann; Brus.

7 The Khrushchev Alternative

1. This chapter is a revised version of an article published in *Critique*, no. 2, 1973.

2. At this time the Politburo was re-named Praesidium; in 1966 it again became the Politburo. We refer throughout the book to it as the Politburo to avoid confusing the reader and to distinguish the leading party body from, for example, the Praesidium of the Council of Ministers. 'Praesidium' in the Soviet context means a smaller inner body which acts on behalf of its larger parent when the latter is not sitting.

3. Initially Malenkov took both the Chairmanship of the Council of Ministers and the First Secretaryship of the party; within a matter of weeks he had given up (either voluntarily or under pressure) the latter.

4. This is what most western commentators assume to have happened; as in many instances of leadership infighting, there is no definitive evidence. See, for example, the accounts offered by Schapiro, L., *The Communist Party . . .*, and Conquest, R., *Power and Policy in the USSR*, Macmillan, 1961.

8 The Central Authorities

1. Solzhenitsyn mentions this in *The Gulag Archipelago*, p. 230.

2. See, for example, articles in Farrell.

3. Brzezinski, *Dilemmas . . .*, p. 8.

4. Lane, *Politics and Society . . .*, has the party rules as one of his appendices.

9 Policies and Policy-making

1. *Khrushchev Remembers*, pp. 146–7.

2. *Itogi vsesoyuznoi perepisi . . .*, vol. V, 1970, Table 4.

3. Clarke, R., *Soviet Economic Facts 1917–1970*, Macmillan, 1972, pp. 518–19.

4. Tatu (Bibliography), p. 397.
5. Perhaps the best known in the west are the short stories by Abramov and Solzhenitsyn.
6. The document is translated in *Critique*, no. 2, 1973.
7. Quoted by Swayze, p. 150.
8. This at least is the view held by some and would explain why certain of the contributors to *From Under the Rubble* (bibliography) have not been harassed.

10 Execution and Participation: the Party

1. Unless stated otherwise data on party membership are from 'KPSS v Tsifrakh', *Partiinaya zhizn*, no. 14, 1973, pp. 9–26.
2. Lewin, *Political Undercurrents . . .*, Chapter 11, offers an account which has much in common with the one given here.
3. *Partiinaya zhizn*, p. 25.
4. The term 'saturation' and the groupings are taken from Rigby, *Communist Party Membership . . .*, pp. 449–50.
5. 'Partiiny komitet ministrov', *Kommunist*, no. 16, 1966, pp. 50–58.
6. *Partiinaya zhizn*, p. 25.
7. Forisenkov, S., *Zametki khozyaistvennika*, Leningrad, 1969, p. 65.
8. Brezhnev, quoted in *Partiinaya zhizn*, p. 15.
9. Matthews, p. 225.

11 An Assessment

1. See, for example, Amelin, P., *Intelligentsia i sotsializm*, Leningrad, 1970.
2. See Matthews, Chapter 10 in particular, and Lane, D., *The End of Inequality? Stratification Under State Socialism*, Penguin, 1971, for summaries of the Soviet research on mobility.
3. For example, a shift from talking of 'equal opportunity for all' to stressing 'the greater opportunities that exist under socialism than under capitalism'.
4. This in fact is how Kuron, J., and Modzelewski, K., in 'An Open Letter to the Party', *New Politics*, vol. 5, nos. 2 and 3, define their new 'ruling class' in the case of Poland.
5. See works by Cliff; Djilas, already cited.
6. See Ticktin, H., 'Political Economy of the Soviet Intellectual', *Critique*, no. 2, 1973.
7. Medvedev, R., *On Socialist Democracy*, Chapters 3–6, is particularly relevant here.
8. Baumann, in Parkin, F. (ed.), *The Social Analysis of Class Structure*, Tavistock, 1974.

9. Remember the nervous reaction of the leadership when Stalin died and when Khrushchev was ousted – the insecurity and the new programmes aimed at creating popular support.
10. Baumann, Z., 'Systematic Crisis in Soviet-type Societies' in *Problems of Communism*, November–December, 1971, argues this with reference to Poland; and see Holubenko, 'The Soviet Working Class,' *Critique*, no. 4, 1975, pp. 5–26.
11. Gehlen and Barghoorn, op. cit.; Medvedev, in *New Left Review*, loc. cit.; and to some extent Sakharov, A., *Sakharov Speaks*, Collins, 1974.
12. Social differentiation within the peasantry, for example, may well have become less over the period.
13. *Pravda*, 9 June 1974, p. 2. Italics added.

Selected Bibliography

General

Carr, E. H., *A History of Soviet Russia*, 10 vols., Penguin, 1966–75.
Deutscher, I., *The Unfinished Revolution*, Oxford, 1967.
Nettl, P., *The Soviet Achievement*, Thames & Hudson, 1967.
Nove, A., *An Economic History of the USSR*, Penguin, 1972.

Chapter 1

Blackwell, W., *The Beginnings of Russian Industrialization*, Princeton UP, 1968.
Confino, M., 'On Intellectuals and Intellectual Traditions in 18th and 19th Century Russia', *Daedalus*, vol. 101, no. 2, 1972, pp. 117–50.
Falkus, M. E., *The Industrialization of Russia 1700–1914*, Macmillan, 1972.
Florinsky, M., *Russia: a History and an Interpretation*, vol. II, Macmillan, 1947.
   The End of the Russian Empire, (1931)* Collier Books, 1961.
Haimson, L., *The Russian Marxists and the Origins of Bolshevism*, Harvard & Beacon Press, 1966.
Keep, J. L., *The Rise of Social Democracy in Russia*, Oxford, 1963.
Kochan, L., *Russia in Revolution*, Paladin, 1970.
Lenin, V. I., *Selected Works*, two-vol. edition, Moscow, 1947.
Marx, K., Engels, F., *Selected Works*, 2 vols., Moscow, 1958.
Perrie, M., *The Agrarian Policy of the SR Party 1901–8*, Cambridge, in press.
Pipes, R., (ed.) *The Russian Intelligentsia*, Columbia UP, 1961.
Radkey, O., *The Agrarian Foes of Bolshevism*, Columbia UP, 1958.
Robinson, G., *Rural Russia under the Old Regime*, (1932) University of California Press, 1967.
Seton-Watson, H., *The Russian Empire 1801–1917*, Oxford, 1967.
Shanin, T., *The Awkward Class*, Oxford, 1972.
Trotsky, L., *1905*, (1922) Penguin, 1973.
   History of the Russian Revolution (1932) abr., Doubleday, 1959.

* Dates in brackets indicate original publication date.

Venturi, F., *Roots of Revolution*, Knopf, 1966.

Von Laue, T., 'Russian Peasants in the Factory, 1892–1964', *Journal of Economic History*, vol. XXI, 1961, pp. 61–80.

Wildman, A. K., *The Making of a Workers' Revolution: Russian Social Democracy 1891–1903*, Chicago, 1967.

Wilson, E., *To The Finland Station* (1942) Fontana, 1960.

Chapter 2

The following are but a few of the many books on the February and October revolutions, chosen to give the reader some idea of different interpretations.

The works by Carr, Kochan, Lenin, and Trotsky already cited.

Abramovitch, R., *The Soviet Revolution 1917–1939*, International UP, 1962.

Bunyan, J., Fisher, H., (eds.) *The Bolshevik Revolution 1917–1918* (documents), Stanford UP, 1961.

Chamberlin, W. H., *The Russian Revolution*, 2 vols., (1935), Universal Library Edition, New York, 1965.

Daniels, R. V., *Red October*, Secker & Warburg, 1967.

Liebman, M., *The Russian Revolution*, Vintage Books, 1972.

Lukacs, G., *Lenin* (1924), New Left Books, 1970.

Pipes, R., (ed.) *Revolutionary Russia*, Harvard UP, 1968.

Reed, J., *Ten Days that Shook the World*, (1920), Lawrence & Wishart, 1962.

Shub, D., *Lenin*, (1948), Penguin, 1966.

Shukman, H., *Lenin and the Russian Revolution*, Capricorn Books, 1968.

Sukhanov, N., *The Russian Revolution 1917*, (1922), 2 vols., abr. Oxford, 1955.

Chapter 3

Again Carr, Lenin, and Nove are important.

Avrich, P., *Kronstadt*, Princeton, 1970.

Bukharin, N., and Preobrazhensky, E., *The ABC of Communism*, (1919), Penguin, 1969.

Filene, P. G., *Americans and the Soviet Experiment 1917–1933*, Harvard UP, 1967.

Fitzpatrick, S., *The Commissariat of the Enlightenment*, Cambridge, 1970.

Footman, D., *Civil War in Russia*, Faber & Faber, 1961.

Lichtheim, G., *Marxism*, 2nd edition, Routledge & Kegan Paul, 1964.

Luxemburg, R., *The Russian Revolution*, (1922) University of Michigan, 1961.

Radkey, O., *The Sickle Under the Hammer*, Columbia UP, 1962.

Rigby, T. H., *Communist Party Membership in the USSR 1917–1967*, Princeton UP, 1968.

Shapiro, L., *The Origin of the Communist Autocracy*, Bell, 1955.

Serge, V., *Memoirs of a Revolutionary 1901–1941*, Oxford, 1963.

Trotsky, L., *The New Course 1923*, (1923), New Park Publications, 1972.

White, S., *Anglo–Soviet Relations 1917–1924*, unpublished Ph.D. thesis, Glasgow University, 1972.

Chapter 4

As before, Carr, Filene, Nove, and Serge.

Cohen, S., *Bukharin and the Bolshevik Revolution: A Political Biography*, Princeton UP, 1974.

Daniels, R., *The Conscience of the Revolution*, Harvard UP, 1960.

Deutscher, I., *Stalin*, 2nd edn., Oxford, 1967.
A Prophet Unarmed, Oxford, 1959.

Erlich, A., *The Soviet Industrialization Debate*, Oxford, 1960.
History of the CPSU: Short Course, Moscow, 1939.

Lewin, M., *Russian Peasants and Soviet Power*, Allen & Unwin, 1968.
Political Undercurrents in Soviet Economic Debates, Pluto Press, 1975.

Medvedev, R., *Let History Judge: The Origins and Consequences of Stalinism*, Macmillan, 1971.

Nove, A., *Was Stalin Really Necessary?*, Allen & Unwin, 1964, title chapter.

Preobrazhensky, E., *The New Economics*, (1926) Oxford, 1965.

Schapiro, L., *The Communist Party of the Soviet Union*, 2nd edition, University Paperback, 1970.

Schwarz, S., *Labor in the Soviet Union*, Praeger, 1952.

Stalin, J., *Works*, vols. XI, XII, Moscow, 1954.

Trotsky, L., *The Revolution Betrayed*, (1936) New Park Publications, 1967.

Von Laue, T., *Why Lenin? Why Stalin?*, Weidenfeld & Nicholson, 1964.

Chapter 5

Arendt, H., *The Origins of Totalitarianism*, Allen & Unwin, 1951.

Azrael, J., *Managerial Power and Soviet Politics*, Harvard UP, 1966.

Beck, F., and Godin, W., *Russian Purge*, Hurst & Blackett, 1951.

Brzezinski, Z., *Permanent Purge*, Oxford, 1956.

Cliff, T., *Stalinist Russia* (1955), revised as *Russia, A Marxist Analysis*, International Socialism, 1963.

Conquest, R., *The Great Terror*, Macmillan, 1968.

Djilas, M., *Conversations with Stalin*, Penguin, 1967.

Ehrenburg, I., *Men, Years and Life*, vol. IV, MacGibbon & Kee, 1963.

Fainsod, M., *Smolensk Under Soviet Rule*, Macmillan, 1959.
  How Russia is Ruled, Harvard UP, 1953.

Friedrich, C., and Brzezinski, Z., *Totalitarian Dictatorship and Autocracy*, Harvard UP, 1956.

Ginzburg, E., *Into the Whirlwind*, Penguin, 1968.

Harris, N., *Beliefs in Society*, New Thinkers Library, 1968.

Khrushchev, N., Speech to the Twentieth Party Congress, is to be found in: Wolfe, B., *Khrushchev and Stalin's Ghost*, Praeger, 1957; Gruliow, L., (ed.) *Current Soviet Policies – II*, Columbia UP, 1956; Nicolaevsky, B., *The Crimes of the Stalin Era*, New Leader, 1956

Mandelstam, N., *Hope Against Hope*, (Collins, 1971) Penguin, 1975.

Nicolaevsky, B., *Power and the Soviet Elite*, Pall Mall, 1966, Chapter I.

Serge, V., *The Case of Comrade Tulayev*, Penguin, 1968.

Solzhenitsyn, A., *The Gulag Archipelago*, Collins, 1974.
  One Day in the Life of Ivan Denisovich, Penguin, 1963.
  First Circle, Harper & Row, 1968.

Stalin, J., *Leninism*, Lawrence & Wishart, 1940.

Swianiewicz, S., *Forced Labour and Economic Development*, Oxford, 1965.

Chapter 6

Politics in the West

Almond, G., and Powell, B., *Comparative Politics: a Developmental Approach*, Little Brown, 1966.

Apter, D., *The Politics of Modernization*, Chicago UP, 1965.

Bachrach, P., *The Theory of Democratic Elitism*, University of London Press, 1969.

Berelson, B., *et al.*, *Voting*, Chicago UP, 1954.

Campbell, A., *et al.*, *The American Voter*, abr., Wiley, 1964.

Dahl, R., 'A Critique of the Ruling Elite Model', *American Political Science Review*, vol. LII, June 1958, pp. 463–9.

Eckstein, H., and Apter, D., (eds.) *Comparative Politics*, Free Press, 1963, Introduction.

Finer, S., *Anonymous Empire*, Pall Mall Press, 1958.

McKenzie, R., *British Political Parties*, Heinemann, 1955.

Mills, C. Wright, *The Power Elite*, Oxford, 1956.

Mosca, G., *The Ruling Class*, McGraw Hill, 1939.

Parkin, F., *Class Inequality and Political Order*, MacGibbon & Kee, 1971.

Truman, D., *The Governmental Process*, Knopf, 1951.

Approaches to Soviet Politics

Barghoorn, F., *Politics in the USSR*, 2nd edition, Little Brown, 1974.

Baumann, Z., 'Systemic Crisis in Soviet-Type Societies', *Problems of Communism*, November–December 1971.

'Officialdom and Class: Bases of Inequality in Socialist Society' in Parkin, F., ed. *The Social Analysis of Class Structure*, Tavistock, 1974.

Brown, A., *Soviet Politics and Political Science*, Macmillan, 1974.

Brus, W., *Socialist Ownership and Political Systems under Socialism*, Routledge, 1975.

Brzezinski, Z., and Huntingdon, S., *Political Power: USA/USSR*, Viking Press, 1965.

Brzezinski, Z., ed. *Dilemmas of Change in Soviet Politics*, Columbia UP, 1969.

Djilas, M., *The New Class*, Thames & Hudson, 1957.

Gehlen, M., *The Communist Party of the Soviet Union*, Indiana UP, 1969.

Hazard, J., *The Soviet System of Government*, 3rd edition, University of Chicago Press, 1964.

Hough, J., 'The Soviet System: Petrification or Pluralism', *Problems of Communism*, March–April 1972, pp. 25–45.

Inkeles, A., 'Models and Issues in the Analysis of Soviet Society' *Survey*, no. 60, July 1966, pp. 3–17.

Kautsky, J., 'Communism and the Comparative Study of Development', reprinted in Fleron F., ed. *Communist Studies and the Social Sciences*, Rand McNally, 1969.

Linden, C., *Khrushchev and the Soviet Leadership, 1957–1964*, John Hopkins Press, 1966.

Medvedev, R., 'What Lies Ahead for Us', *New Left Review*, nos. 87–8, 1974.

Meyer, A., 'Theories of Convergence' in Johnson, Chalmers, (ed.) *Change in Communist Systems*, Stanford UP, 1970.

Skilling, G., 'Interest Groups and Communist Politics', *World Politics*, vol. XVIII, April, 1966, pp. 435–51.

Skilling, G. and Griffiths, F., (eds.) *Interest Groups in Soviet Politics*, Princeton UP, 1971.

Slavic Review, vol. XXVI, March and June 1967, contains a discussion on different approaches; reprinted in Fleron, op. cit.

Waller, M., 'Marxist Criticisms of Soviet Democratic Centralism', unpublished paper, given at ECPR workshop, April 1975.

Chapter 7

The works of Brzezinski and Huntingdon, Fainsod, and Skilling and Griffiths already cited.

Khrushchev, N., *Khrushchev Remembers: The Last Testament*, (Deutsch, 1974) Penguin 1976.

Leonhard, W., *The Kremlin since Stalin*, Oxford, 1962.

Pethybridge, R., *A Key to Soviet Politics*, Allen & Unwin, 1962.

Schapiro, L., (ed.) *The USSR and the Future*, Praeger, 1963.

Tatu, M., *Power in the Kremlin*, Collins, 1969.

Tucker, R., *The Soviet Political Mind*, Praeger, 1963.

Chapter 8

Khrushchev and the books by Gehlen and Tatu are relevant.

Brown, A., and Kaser, M., (eds.) *The Soviet Union since the Fall of Khrushchev*, Macmillan, 1975.

Churchward, L., *Contemporary Soviet Government*, 2nd edition, Routledge & Kegan Paul, 1975.

Crankshaw, E., *Khrushchev*, Collins, 1966.

Farrell, R. B., (ed.) *Political Leadership in Eastern Europe and the Soviet Union*, Butterworths, 1970.

Lane, D., *Politics and Society in the USSR*, Weidenfeld, 1970.

Nove, A., 'The Uses and Abuses of Kremlinology' in *Was Stalin Really Necessary?*

Pyper, J., 'The Central Committee Apparatus of the Soviet Communist Party, 1964–73' unpublished M.A. dissertation, Essex University, 1974.

Rigby, H., 'The Soviet Leadership: Towards a Self-Stabilizing Oligarchy', *Soviet Studies*, vol. XXII, 1970, pp. 167–91.

Schapiro, L., *The Government and Politics of the Soviet Union*, 2nd edition, Hutchinson, 1975.

Chapter 9

Policy-making: General

Brown, A., 'Policy-Making in the Soviet Union', *Soviet Studies*, vol. XXIII, July 1971, pp. 120–48.

Dallin, A., and Larson T., (eds.) *Soviet Politics Since Khrushchev*, Englewood Cliffs, 1968.

Juviler, P., and Morton H., (eds.) *Soviet Policy-Making: Studies on Communism in Transition*, Pall Mall Press, 1967.
Khrushchev, *Khrushchev Remembers: The Last Testament*.
Linden, op. cit.
Skilling and Griffiths, op. cit.
Soviet Economic Prospects for the Seventies, Joint Economics Committee, US Congress, Washington, 1973.

Agriculture
Abramov, F., *The Dodgers*, Flegon Press, 1963.
Barrass, J., 'The Politics of Soviet Agriculture: Land Reclamation and the non-Chernozem Zone', unpublished M.A. dissertation, Essex University, 1974.
Hahn, W., *The Politics of Soviet Agriculture*, John Hopkins, 1972.
Millar, J., (ed.) *The Soviet Rural Community*, Urbana UP, 1971.
Nove, A., 'Soviet Agriculture under Brezhnev', *Slavic Review*, vol. 29, no. 3, 1970, pp. 379–410.
    'Agriculture' in Brown and Kaser, op. cit.
Ploss, S., *Conflict and Decision-Making in Soviet Russia: A Case Study of Agricultural Policy 1953–1963*, Princeton UP, 1965.
Schwartz, H., *The Soviet Economy since Stalin*, Gollancz, 1965.
Solzhenitsyn, A., *Matryona's House and Other Stories*, Penguin, 1973.
Strauss, E., *Soviet Agriculture in Perspective*, Allen & Unwin, 1969.

Industry
Berliner, J., *Factory and Manager in the USSR*, Harvard UP, 1957.
Brown, E., *Soviet Trade Unions and Labor Relations*, Harvard UP, 1966.
Campbell, R., *Soviet-type Economies*, Macmillan, 1974.
Ellman, M., *Economic Reform in the Soviet Union*, vol. XXXV, PEP, 1969.
Granick, D., *The Red Executive*, Macmillan, 1960.
Hardt, J., and Frankel, T., 'The Industrial Managers' in Skilling and Griffiths, op. cit.
Holubenko, M., 'The Soviet Working Class', *Critique*, no. 4, 1975, pp. 5–26.
Hough, J., *The Soviet Prefects*, Harvard UP, 1969.
Judy, R., 'The Economists', in Skilling and Griffiths, op. cit.
Nove, A., *Economic History* . . .
'Economic Policy and Economic Trends' in Dallin and Larson, op. cit.
Schwartz, op. cit.

Culture

Amalrik, A., 'Will the Soviet Union Survive Until 1984?' *Survey*, no. 73, 1969.

Conquest, R., *The Politics of Ideas in the USSR*, Bodley Head, 1967.

Cox, M., 'The Politics of the Dissenting Intellectual', *Critique*, no. 5, 1975.

Dewhirst, M., and Farrell, R., (eds.) *The Soviet Censorship*, Metuchen, 1973.

Ehrenburg, I., *The Thaw*, 1956.

Gibian, G., *Interval of Freedom 1954–57*, University of Minnesota, 1960.

Hayward, M., and Labedz, L., *On Trial*, Collins, 1967.

Johnson, P., *Khrushchev and the Arts*, Cambridge, Mass. 1965.

Labedz, L., (ed.) *Solzhenitsyn*, Allen Lane, 1970.

Medvedev, R., *On Socialist Democracy*, Routledge, 1975.

Pomerantsev, V., in *Novy mir*, no. 12, 1953, pp. 218–45.

Reddaway, P., (ed.) *Uncensored Russia*, Cape, 1972.
    in Brown and Kaser, op. cit.

Sakharov, A., *Sakharov Speaks*, Collins, 1974.

Saunders, G., (ed.) *Samizdat*, Monad Press, 1974.

Solzhenitsyn, A., *et al.*, *From Under the Rubble*, Collins, 1975.

Swayze, H., *The Political Control of Literature in the USSR, 1946–1959*, Harvard UP, 1962.

Chapter 10

By now the reader will have come across a number of books which deal with the party in more or less detail. All we shall do is to suggest three additions.

Hammer, D., *USSR: The Politics of Oligarchy*, The Dryden Press, 1974.

Matthews, M., *Class and Society in Soviet Russia*, Allen Lane, 1972.

Meyer, A., *The Soviet Political System*, Random House, 1965.

Index